Republican Leader

To
Jim Logsdon,
with best wishes

Mitch McConnell
Republican Leader
USS
4/5/10

Republican Leader

A Political Biography of Senator Mitch McConnell

John David Dyche

Wilmington, Delaware

Dyche, John David.

Republican leader : a political biography of Senator Mitch McConnell / John David Dyche.—1st ed.—Wilmington, Del. : ISI Books, c2009.

p. ; cm.
ISBN: 978-1-935191-59-9
Includes bibliographical references and index.

1. McConnell, Mitch. 2. United States. Congress. Senate—Biography. 3. United States—Politics and government—2001–4. Conservatives—United States—Biography. I. Title.

E840.8.M332 D93 2009   2008943222
328.73/092—dc22   0906

Published in the United States by:

ISI Books
Intercollegiate Studies Institute
3901 Centerville Road
Wilmington, Delaware 19807
www.isibooks.org

To My Family, with Love

Contents

1

"Washington's Most Important Republican"

A FTER THE 2008 ELECTIONS brought to power a Democratic president and large Democratic majorities in both houses of Congress,
conservative columnist George Will wrote that Mitch McConnell,
Kentucky's five-term U.S. senator and the Republican leader in that
body, was now "Washington's most important Republican and second-
most consequential elected official."[1]

Will's assertion was correct, but many Americans still know little
about this skilled and powerful politician.

This book is an attempt to remedy that situation by recounting the
political career of the man in whom conservatives have invested their
hopes of holding off the worst excesses of triumphant liberalism while
the Right attempts to regroup. The pragmatic McConnell may be an
unlikely source for ideological leadership, but his record of practically
uninterrupted political success suggests that conservatives can confidently count on him to lead a holding action in a time of crisis. His current mission may be defensive in strategy, but it will almost certainly
be aggressive, though often passively so, in tactics.

Many who are aware of McConnell know only two things about
him, both of which a mainly hostile mainstream media have turned into
stereotype. First, he has been the major opponent of campaign finance

reform. Second, as leader of the Senate's Republican minority since late 2006, he has used the filibuster and parliamentary procedure to become the "obstructer-in-chief" of Democratic legislative initiatives.

These things are, of course, true to a greater or lesser degree, but fall far short of doing the man justice. In his opposition to campaign finance reform, he is not the godfather of special-interest spending in politics, but possibly America's leading defender of the First Amendment among practicing politicians. He has, for example, cast the deciding vote against a constitutional amendment to ban flag-burning despite the fact that he represents a very conservative and conventionally patriotic constituency. And he opposed the so-called Millionaire's Amendment designed to "level the playing field" against wealthy candidates even as he faced a formidable one in his hard fought 2008 reelection campaign.

Likewise, in his "obstruction" of Democratic legislation, McConnell has not prevented passage for purely partisan reasons, but has blocked bad ideas in order to shape them into better, bipartisan legislation. He has consistently urged the Senate to work across the aisle to tackle the nation's biggest problems, including entitlement and immigration reform. "We're not sent there to avoid doing important things for America," he often says.

This deeply held belief arises from the fact that McConnell is, as Will accurately observed, "completely a man of the Senate . . . thoroughly marinated in the institution's subtle mores and complex rules." From boyhood it was his ambition to become not just a United States senator, but an influential one. Discipline, focus, and honesty are among the character traits that have carried him to that goal. One of McConnell's many guiding maxims has been, "You can't be a statesman until you get elected." It is his success at getting elected—a record five times in a state that for many years had almost twice as many registered Democrats as Republicans—that has allowed him to achieve his lifelong objective of becoming a statesman worthy of historic note.

McConnell has been taking principled stands on tough issues almost his entire life. Sometimes he has changed his mind or succumbed to cynical opportunism, but contrary to what his most passionate critics—and there are many of them—would have the public believe, his has not been the career of either a political mercenary or an inflexible conservative ideologue. He has evolved as his party has evolved, moving from being a moderate, maybe even a "Rockefeller Republican," to being a more conservative "Reagan Republican," before ending up in party leadership as a pragmatic, center-right, "Main Street Republican."

McConnell puts priority on getting, keeping, increasing, and using political power, but he does so to accomplish public ends, not to conform to doctrinal dictates or achieve personal self-aggrandizement. He recognizes that, as Harvard political theorist Harvey Mansfield has put it, "Politics means taking sides; it is partisan. . . . Politics always has political philosophy lying within it, waiting to emerge." Many will say that they are a conservative first and a Republican second, but for McConnell it is almost certainly the other way around.

McConnell's political life therefore represents a commitment to partisan politics as an indicator of where public opinion is, the best and most practical means of actually governing and getting things done, and, inevitably, the manifestation of applied political philosophy in either explicit or, more often, implicit form. Along the way he has courageously taken some politically unpopular positions and provided leadership on big issues that win him widespread admiration but earn him little political benefit back home.

Most McConnell profile pieces focus on the issues for which he is best known, such as campaign finance, earmarks, Iraq, and tobacco, but often overlook key characteristics, such as independence of mind, that have defined McConnell since he was young. For example, a grade-school photo from his childhood in the solidly Democratic South shows a smilingly defiant McConnell sporting an "I Like Ike" button.

As a campus politician at the University of Louisville, he introduced *über*-conservative Barry Goldwater at a speaking event, but did not back him for president because the Arizona senator opposed the Civil Rights Act of 1964. The young McConnell campaigned for a statewide anti-discrimination statute. He urged students at a 1964 "Freedom Rally" to march on the state capital with Martin Luther King Jr. and, more recently, worked with congressional Democrats to place a statue of civil rights hero Rosa Parks in the Capitol.

At the beginning of his career as an elected official, the chief executive of Jefferson County, he cleaned up and professionalized local government and began building what would become perhaps the most "pro-parks" political legacy in the Kentucky's history. Putting the good of the community ahead of his personal interests, he twice ignored political risk to work with Democrats for merger of the city and county governments.

In the Senate, McConnell earned bipartisan respect for his leadership role in the ethics investigation of Republican Bob Packwood, the Oregon senator who sexually harassed several women and obstructed an official inquiry. He introduced an expulsion resolution and pressed it until Packwood resigned.

Many of the Kentuckians who have repeatedly elected him remain unaware of McConnell's well-deserved international reputation on human rights. To China's consternation, he sponsored the Hong Kong Policy Act to protect that city's autonomy and freedom after the British relinquished it to Beijing's control. Nobel Peace Prize laureate Aung San Suu Kyi, activist-rocker Bono, and others have lauded him as America's foremost advocate for long-oppressed Burma. He has criticized administrations of both parties for focusing on Russia at the expense of freedom-seeking former Soviet republics.

McConnell has undoubtedly strayed from conservative orthodoxy in some areas. While he almost always favors spending less than the Democrats desire, he is not a fiscal hawk. Despite his fondness for earmarking funds to benefit his state, he has nonetheless amassed a respectable 89.81 lifetime rating from the American Conservative Union by being consistently strong on conservative fundamentals like abortion, gun rights, national security, and taxes.

There is another aspect of McConnell's career of which even those who are familiar with his senatorial accomplishments may be unaware. He is the architect who designed what is now a very solid Republican political structure in Kentucky. He conceived and implemented a strategy that has transformed the commonwealth, long dominated by Democrats, into a truly two-party state. He was, in the words of Louisville *Courier-Journal* political writer Al Cross, the "critical man" in making this change happen sooner, more completely, and more permanently than it otherwise would have.

He is also the foremost Republican in Kentucky history. When I suggested this in a newspaper column, some editors and readers, having little use for most Republicans, recoiled. How, they asked, dare anyone compare McConnell to his sainted mentor, John Sherman Cooper, or to John Marshall Harlan, who as a Supreme Court justice famously dissented from the "separate but equal" doctrine, or even Abraham Lincoln, the state's most historically significant native son?

Unlike McConnell, Cooper lost multiple statewide elections, failed in an attempt to lead the Senate GOP, and never did much to strengthen the party in his home state. Cooper's popularity stems primarily from his support for civil rights, his move from hawk to dove on the Vietnam War, his friendship with John F. Kennedy, and his genteel appearance and manner. While Harlan held a statewide office, his highest accomplishments were not as a Republican, but as a nonpartisan jurist. And while visionary, his opinion in *Plessy v. Ferguson* was, after all, only a dissent. Lincoln left Kentucky as a child, lost the state in his presidential elections, and may be the foremost Republican *from* Kentucky, but certainly not *of* it.

There are really only two Kentuckians whose political careers may exceed McConnell's and neither was a Republican. One is the incomparable Henry Clay, the Whig who was Speaker of the House, one of the greatest senators in history, and secretary of state. The other is Alben Barkley, who served as Senate majority leader from 1937 to 1947, Senate minority leader from 1947 to 1949, and vice president under Harry S. Truman from 1949 to 1953.

So who is this man who merits such comparisons? Where did he come from and what does his career mean? This book is an effort to answer these questions, but is an almost purely political portrait, limited to the public life and mind of its still active subject. It does not pretend to be the "definitive" biography. One of those will be well-deserved some day, but must await the conclusion of McConnell's service, when his papers will be available for study and people can speak with the candor and perspective that the passage of time, and of the subject from power, permits.

That said, some minimal personalization is in order. *National Review* once described McConnell, who turned sixty-seven in February 2009, as having "an owlish, tight-lipped public demeanor reminiscent of George Will." Gail Collins of the *New York Times* said he has "the natural charisma of an oyster." Opponents have ridiculed him as Howdy Doody or *MAD* magazine cover boy Alfred E. Neuman. There is a certain deceptive softness about his entire person, which may explain why adversaries have so often underestimated his determined, sometimes even steely personality.

When McConnell is not in Washington he derives an amused, almost perverse, pleasure from residing in a modest townhouse in the Highlands neighborhood of Louisville, the closest thing Kentucky offers to Berkeley or the gentrified precincts of Vermont. He does his own shopping, likes to watch movies at the city's only cinema offering anything approaching avant-garde fare, and enjoys a houseboat weekend with friends on one of Kentucky's beautiful lakes. He is an avid University of Louisville football fan (especially when the Cardinals are winning) and, in what is perhaps a carryover from politics, would just as soon revel in a rout of the opposition as see a close, competitive game.

He reads voraciously. His tastes run to biography, history, and politics. Works by David Halberstam, Paul Johnson, David McCullough, Edmund Morris, and Jay Winik appear on his recent reading list. Among columnists and magazine writers, Paul Gigot, George Will, and Fred Barnes are particular favorites, while Robert Novak is particularly not. A visitor to his home is likely to find the television tuned to Fox News.

Beyond that, McConnell is a textbook example of the species *homo politicus*. He breathes, eats, and lives politics *à la* Lyndon Johnson, but with perhaps a better sense of humor. He is capable of genuine laughter, occasionally even at himself, but like everything else that comes out of his mouth, even that can seem calculated or carefully controlled. The idea of an off-the-cuff comment is anathema to him. He rarely utters a word that is not well-considered beforehand and almost always says precisely what he wants to say with nary a surplus syllable.

McConnell's political style is not poetry, and is often not even prose, although he has given some very eloquent speeches on the Senate floor and to conservative groups. The better metaphor for his method may be that of the bullet-point memorandum or executive summary. He uses a few memorable phrases, perfect for relentless repetition, to drive his message home in a manner that makes the core concept automatic and unforgettable.

While he is confident in his own abilities, McConnell also recognizes, cultivates, and openly praises talent in others. This has yielded an abundance of young associates and staffers who are not only good, but also extremely loyal to "the Boss" or, now, "the Leader." He remembers and rewards his friends and supporters of long standing. Perhaps a rarity among highly placed politicians, he is acutely conscious that he has not done it all on his own, although aides suggest that he is prone to occasional forgetfulness on this topic.

On January 10, 2009, Mitch McConnell became the longest-serving senator in Kentucky history, passing his former Democratic colleague Wendell Ford. Ten days later, when George W. Bush vacated the White House, McConnell became the highest-ranking elected Republican in America. This book is the story, sometimes unlikely, of how it happened, and, to a lesser degree, what it means.

2

Portrait of the Senator as a Young Man
1956–1967

H OUSED IN A MASSIVE Collegiate Gothic structure on Second Street in downtown Louisville, duPont Manual High School was one of Kentucky's best, oldest, and largest secondary schools when the young Mitch McConnell entered it in 1957. Though an outsider who had moved from Alabama only a couple of years earlier, he made up his mind to become president of the student body, and in the spring of his junior year, at the end of a carefully plotted, multiyear campaign in which he focused on outworking and outplanning opponents, he was elected in a close race. The pattern—the ambition, the determination, the hard work, and the political talent to overcome considerable disadvantages—was set for the man who would become the foremost Republican politician and longest-serving U.S. Senator in Kentucky history.

McConnell's forebears immigrated to the colonies from Ireland in the mid-1700s. Ancestors on his father's side included a Revolutionary War veteran, a circuit-riding Presbyterian preacher, a Confederate soldier, a mortician, and a county judge. McConnell's maternal ancestors consisted mostly of subsistence farmers.

His parents, A. M. McConnell and the former Julia Odene Shockley—nicknamed "Dean"—met in Birmingham, Alabama. A. M. and Dean married in 1940 and soon set up house in the northern Alabama town of Athens in the Muscle Shoals region. They welcomed Mitch, their only child, born in a hospital at nearby Sheffield on February 20, 1942. Illness and war soon intruded upon the family, as they did on so many others in that era. In the summer of 1944, at about the same time his father left for the Army (he would serve in Europe roughly from the Battle of the Bulge to VE Day), polio partially paralyzed two-year-old Mitch's left leg.

Well before he became president, the stricken Franklin D. Roosevelt had established a polio treatment center in Warm Springs, Georgia. Dean took Mitch there for treatment, but because no room was available, the staff taught her the physical therapy regime her son needed. Hard as it was, she faithfully did that difficult regime with him for four forty-five minute sessions every day. Ordered by the doctors to keep Mitch off his leg lest he do permanent damage or become dependent on braces by walking prematurely, Dean read to him and they would color and draw "and create little towns on his bed with his toys," she recalled.[1]

"She watched me like a hawk twenty-four hours a day for two years," McConnell says. "But for her tenacity, I would not have been able to walk normally. The example of incredible discipline that she was teaching me during this period, I always felt had an impact on the rest of my life in terms of whatever discipline I may have been able to bring to bear on things I have been involved in."[2] It is impossible, of course, to fully fathom how the psychological inputs of infancy and youth influence a personality and form the finished product of adulthood, but this mother's single-minded focus surely shaped her son's character in a significant way.

Growing up deep in the heart of a segregated and thoroughly Democratic society also had an impact. The young Athenians enjoyed holidays from school on birthdays of Confederate heroes, and local boys had a hard time getting anyone to pretend to be a Yankee in the Civil War games they often played. Mitch's grandfather explained politics to him quite simply: "The Republican Party is the party of the North, and the Democratic Party is the party of the South." There was supposedly only one Republican in Athens, McConnell recalls, and the neighbors regarded him as a hopeless eccentric. Perhaps because of his father's respect for General Dwight D. Eisenhower, under whom he had served, McConnell resisted peer pressure and independently identified himself with the GOP at an early age.

His polio all but beaten, and his father home and working as a civilian employee at the Army's nearby Huntsville arsenal, Mitch could at last begin living the typical life of a small-town American boy. He attended the Saturday morning "picture shows," went swimming and fishing with his father, and played with his BB gun. Raised a Southern Baptist and baptized by immersion at age eight, McConnell recalls a distinct but relatively short-lived "fundamentalist" phase in his family's otherwise orthodox religious life.

In 1950, A. M. and Dean bundled eight-year-old Mitch and a pair of Boston bulldogs into the family's first car, a Plymouth purchased the previous year, and set off for Augusta, Georgia, where A. M. had accepted a new job. They set up house in a rented duplex, but in 1952, after a dozen years of marriage, they finally bought their first home and moved to what then passed for suburbs. Young Mitch's Republican leanings are confirmed by a school photo from that year which shows him proudly sporting an "I Like Ike" button.

Mitch made friends fairly quickly. Though he was a solid student, his real interest lay in sports, with baseball being his favorite. He was a determined player, and he liked to be, and usually found a way to be, the leader of the neighborhood children's games. McConnell thrived on the competition and the recognition that came with athletic achievement. He had found a niche.

But McConnell's life took a fateful turn in January 1956, midway through his eighth-grade year. His father, then in a managerial position with duPont, took a transfer to what seemed a very faraway place—Louisville, Kentucky. Whether he liked it or not, the young man had no choice but to go north.

The McConnells settled in Louisville's South End, then a middle-class enclave near one of the city's picturesque Frederick Law Olmsted parks. At first the new place seemed huge, northern, and not very

10

friendly. An only child already especially close to his mother since their shared struggle against his polio, he drew even closer to her as they both battled homesickness.

Baseball helped ease McConnell's transition to his new home, but he soon faced the fact that his future in the game was limited. So, still seeking status and an avenue for accomplishment, he shifted his ambitions from the baseball diamond to school politics.

Now an aspiring politician, he watched the 1956 presidential election with rapt attention. Not only did Eisenhower win again, but in Democratic-dominated Kentucky two Republicans, Thruston B. Morton and John Sherman Cooper, won hard-fought U.S. Senate races over a pair of former governors. It was almost always an upset when a Republican won a statewide race in Kentucky, but McConnell's rapidly developing political mind registered the fact that it could be done, and for the U.S. Senate, no less.

In his own political pursuits, McConnell had to settle for being student council vice president at his junior high school. As he now says, "I never liked being vice president of anything." With his mother's encouragement, he set his sights higher when he moved up to duPont Manual the following year. He was determined to become student body president.

McConnell enjoyed a reasonably active social life and was a solid student. He made good enough grades to gain National Honor Society admission, and placed in the 93rd percentile on a national college qualifying test. But the real keys to his scholastic political success were his efforts to secure early support from popular athletes and his systematic distribution of pamphlets into each and every student locker. These high school versions of celebrity endorsements and direct-mail marketing, along with his focus on winning votes in the often-overlooked lower grades, paid off at the end of his junior year, when he defeated the same fellow who had bested him for student council president in junior high.

In 1960, the year he graduated from high school, McConnell proudly put a Richard Nixon sticker on the bumper of the family's

1958 Oldsmobile, cast his first vote for the then–vice president,[3] and was disappointed by Kennedy's narrow victory.

Having already moved so often, McConnell chose not to go away for college. Instead he enrolled at the University of Louisville, then primarily a city-supported commuter school of 7,000 students, and lived at home with his parents. He ran for the freshman class presidency, but lost to a football player who had the added advantage of living on campus. Mitch at least secured a seat on the College of Arts & Sciences student council. He suffered the sting of political defeat twice more his second year, losing races for the presidency of the student Senate and of the College of Arts & Sciences student council, both by a single vote. Losing proved painful, but instructive. McConnell realized that he had not worked as hard as he should have, and vowed never to make that mistake again.

In 1962, U of L political science professor Grant Hicks—"the only conservative teacher" McConnell met in college, he now says—presided over a national organization called the United Association of Constitutional Conservatives. Hicks actively backed Senator Barry Goldwater of Arizona for the presidency in 1964. The professor exercised an enormous influence on his ambitious young charge.[4] With help from Hicks, McConnell, then president of the campus Republicans, brought Goldwater to the Louisville campus in October and introduced him at a speaking event. Despite, or perhaps because of, his close contact with Goldwater, McConnell soon sought and supported more moderate alternatives for the 1964 Republican presidential nomination.

Academically, McConnell excelled in history and political science classes, though they were taught by liberal professors. These topics excited him intellectually for the first time in his life, but he was never content with mere classroom theory or student government. Only the arena of real politics would do.

In 1961, Republican Marlow W. Cook had won the misleadingly named executive position of Jefferson County judge in the heavily Democratic county, while William O. Cowger became the first Republican mayor of Louisville since 1929. Cowger campaigned on a promise to pass a progressive public accommodations ordinance, which would be the first in an American city south of the Mason-Dixon line.[5]

Following the successes of Cooper and Morton five years earlier, these twin GOP wins fostered McConnell's growing belief that a certain kind of Republican could overcome the formidable obstacles to political success in Louisville and Kentucky. "Cook and Cowger were attractive young candidates promising change in a city whose Democratic Party had dominated local office long enough to have grown slack," McConnell recalls.[6] Moreover, neither man was a native of Kentucky, much less Louisville, which was another fact of which the Alabama-born McConnell made note.

Near the end of his junior year, McConnell ran again for president of the Arts & Sciences student council. This time he won. He was growing into a distinct variety of the big man on campus. He became vice president of his fraternity, was named an Outstanding Sophomore Man and an Outstanding Junior Man, and was elected to Pi Sigma Alpha, the National Political Science Honor Society; the Woodcock Society, a U of L academic honors club; and Omicron Delta Kappa, the National Leadership Honor Society. He even became business manager of the student newspaper, *The Cardinal*, leading to his induction (an event now rich with irony) into Pi Delta Epsilon, the campus journalism honorary society.

In the summer of 1963, McConnell served as an intern for ultra-conservative Kentucky congressman Gene Snyder, a job that included "reviewing hearings of the House Appropriations Committee in order to find areas which might be considered excessive government spending" and "boxing and mailing Government printed baby books to hospitals and cookbooks to ladies' groups," according to an article that appeared in *The Cardinal* upon his return.

Though Martin Luther King Jr.'s "I Have a Dream" speech on August 28, 1963, thrilled and inspired McConnell, he dared not let his enthusiasm show around Snyder's office. "I went outside to stand on the Capitol steps. I supported Dr. King and his cause, and wanted to witness what I knew would be a pivotal point in history. In the shadow of the Lincoln Memorial, Dr. King issued the greatest declaration of freedom since Lincoln signed the Emancipation Proclamation a century earlier. His words moved a nation."[7]

After returning to his studies in the early autumn of 1963, McConnell coauthored an article for *The Cardinal* advocating passage of President Kennedy's progressive civil rights legislation, then languishing in a Congress effectively controlled by segregationist Southern Democrats.[8] With the bold and broad moral certainty of youth, he indicted as "innately evil" any "strict interpretation" of the U.S. Constitution pursuant to which "basic rights are denied to any group." The Constitution, the article observed, was "a document adaptable to conditions of contemporary society." Responding to an argument often advanced by the bill's opponents, McConnell and his coauthor declared, "Property rights have always been, and will continue to be, an integral part of our heritage, but this does not absolve the property holder of his obligation to help insure [*sic*] the basic rights of all citizens."

McConnell was also among a group of U of L students who actively campaigned for a progressive statewide antidiscrimination statute in Kentucky. In the early spring of 1964, he spoke at a campus "Freedom Rally" urging students to march on the state capital in Frankfort with Martin Luther King Jr.[9]

After authoring his senior thesis about the great Kentucky senator Henry Clay and graduating *cum laude*, McConnell decided to attend the University of Kentucky's College of Law. He had considered more elite schools (to some of which one of his professors recommended him as someone "who *will* be a U.S. Senator"[10]), but while his academic record was very respectable, his score on the law school admission test was less so. Of equal or greater importance, he saw the state school as the best way to make new contacts from other parts of Kentucky, and as "the thing to do" for anyone interested in pursuing a career in politics in the commonwealth.

Before beginning his legal studies, McConnell returned to Washington for another summer on Capitol Hill, this time as an intern for Kentucky's moderate, sometimes even liberal, Republican senator John

Sherman Cooper. The times were extraordinary and historic, especially in the U.S. Senate, and McConnell was going to intern for an exceptional man who seemed made for just such moments. The genteel Cooper was the first great public person with whom McConnell had close contact for a sustained period. The impact was immediate and the effects long-lasting.

When he arrived at Cooper's office, the twenty-two-year-old McConnell was, by his own description, "long on desire but short on achievement and devoid of connections."[11] The sixty-two-year-old Cooper had thrice served out unexpired Senate terms before finally winning the first of three full ones of his own in 1960. That year, a *Newsweek* poll of fifty Washington news correspondents had named Cooper the ablest Republican in the Senate.[12] His reputation as a statesman was impeccable.

Cooper had been one of the first Republicans to denounce Senator Joseph McCarthy,[13] and, as a 1991 *New York Times* obituary noted, he generally followed the "liberal internationalist line of foreign policy." This often put him "in conflict with Old Guard Republicans" like Everett Dirksen of Illinois, who had bested Cooper by four votes in a 1959 contest to be Senate Republican leader.[14] But it was Cooper's efforts to pass the Civil Rights Act of 1964 that would provide McConnell with his most vivid memories.

Many of Cooper's constituents were conservative Democrats who had long felt an historic cultural kinship with their brethren futher South. This did not stop him from working hard to help assemble the Republican votes that, on June 10, helped break a filibuster that had occupied the Senate for fifty-seven working days, including six Saturdays. The obstructionist crusade had featured a fourteen-hour harangue by West Virginia Democrat Robert C. Byrd, a former Ku Klux Klan member and future Senate majority leader. The measure passed shortly thereafter.

McConnell was thrilled to see "his" senator "stand his ground" on such a controversial subject, but wondered how Cooper had managed to hold fast against such forceful opposition. So he asked him, "How do you take such a tough stand and square it with the fact that a considerable number of people who have chosen you have the opposite view?" Cooper responded, "I not only represent Kentucky, I represent the Nation, and there are times when you follow, and times when you lead."[15]

Cooper's courage and independent streak proved pivotal in both American history and the developing political character of young Mitch McConnell. Driving the lesson home the following summer, Cooper grabbed a visiting McConnell by the arm and spontaneously took him to the Capitol, where together they watched President Lyndon Johnson sign the Voting Rights Act of 1965.

While Cooper's moderate to liberal politics may have had only a marginal impact on McConnell over the long term, his conception of a legislator's function clearly made a lasting imprint. McConnell considers Cooper an outstanding example of the representative theory expressed by Edmund Burke in 1774: "Your representative owes you, not his industry only, but his judgment; and he betrays, instead of serving you, if he sacrifices it to your opinion."

Cooper, says McConnell, always "carried out his best judgment instead of pandering to the popular view." He was "sensitive to what his constituents were interested in, but not controlled by it." McConnell saw that it was possible for a legislator to stick to his principles and still have political success: Cooper won reelection in 1966 with 64.5 percent of the vote, a percentage that would stand as a record for a Kentucky Republican until McConnell eclipsed it in 2002.

Ironically, though, Cooper's example actually strengthened McConnell in the more conservative outlook to which he and the Republican Party soon moved. "I could have been a John Sherman Cooper Republican and been praised by the *Courier-Journal* and [Lexington] *Herald-Leader*," he notes, naming Kentucky's large, liberal daily newspapers. "That would have been a lot easier path to take for me, but that would have, frankly, not been consistent with my convictions, so I have chosen to do it the hard way."

Sticking to one's convictions in the face of public or party pressure is easier after a senator is mature and enjoys seniority, McConnell now realizes. He thus cites Cooper's career as an argument against term limits, which he has derided as "one of the most idiotic notions that has come on the American scene," saying that it would result in "revolving door novices." Cooper, he notes, became increasingly independent as he became more experienced and secure in the Senate and after he abandoned any ambitions of attaining a party leadership post there.

But Cooper was no role model in one important respect. He was never a party builder. Cooper was perhaps too liberal to transfer his immense personal popularity into a broader Republican movement in socially conservative Kentucky. McConnell would have to look elsewhere for examples of institutional and transformational party leadership to which he already aspired.

Of more immediate concern to McConnell in 1964, however, was the impending necessity of earning a living and doing so in a way that would allow him to start his own political climb. As with so many others then and now, that meant going to law school and low-level involvement in local politics.

At the University of Kentucky College of Law, he quickly concluded that he neither liked the law nor had any particular aptitude for it. He briefly considered pursuing a doctorate in history, but decided he would make an even worse professor than barrister. His desire was to make things happen, not to study, talk, or write about those who did.

Although only an average legal scholar, McConnell pursued law school politics with the same passion he had displayed in high school and college. He advocated adoption of an honor code and headed a group campaigning for a new constitution for Kentucky. These efforts failed at the ballot box, teaching McConnell an important political truth about getting too far in front of one's constituency. Although an established statesman like Cooper could take risks, most of the time a leader must know and heed the opinions of those he represents, especially on matters partaking more of preference than principle. The politician who wants to survive must choose carefully the occasions on which he can depart from popular sentiment.

In the 1966 primary campaign, McConnell worked against Gene Snyder, for whom he had interned. Snyder, who had lost his seat in the 1964 Democratic landslide, was seeking to return to Congress from another district. McConnell backed a candidate favored by the Louisville Republican establishment instead. The quintessential right-winger, Snyder won the primary and general elections and would hold the seat for two decades. Looking back, McConnell regrets his lack of loyalty to the man who had given him his first opportunity in Washington.

Snyder's personal abrasiveness and resistance to civil rights had moved the young McConnell toward his party's center and away from the sometimes reactionary conservatism of pre-Reagan Republicanism.[16] But by the time he was called on to eulogize Snyder in February 2007, he had gained some perspective. Snyder, he had come to realize, had shared some important qualities with Cooper despite their being ideological opposites:

> He was conservative before being conservative was cool. And he made no apologies for it. Most people would have excused him for moderating his views until he got his feet under him. But he wasn't the type to bend in the direction of the crowd. He stood still, and watched as the rest of the country bent toward him. . . . It was a difficult time, but it was exhilarating too. Young conservatives were quietly developing the ideas that would one day drive the political culture in Washington, and men like Gene Snyder, who dared to speak those ideas in a hostile crowd, gave all of them reason to hope.[17]

McConnell had not been among the young "movement" conservatives so instrumental in Goldwater's nomination, but he would eventually move in their direction just as the Republican political culture did, when the more pleasing personality of Ronald Reagan earned increasing respect for attitudes of the Right in the political mainstream.

Likewise, McConnell noted well how Snyder, "who had repeatedly denounced federal spending early in his career," had, as senior Republican on the Public Works and Transportation Committee, "evolved into a master at bringing federal funds to Kentucky."[18] Snyder's example of seeking the most for Kentucky from funds the federal government was going to spend anyway was one McConnell would later follow. While McConnell might proclaim the sainted Cooper as his primary political model, his political career clearly reflects plenty of the pugnacious Snyder's influence, too.

When McConnell finished law school in 1967, Vietnam was America's dominant political issue. He was against the war and knew very few people his age, Republican or Democrat, who supported it. He admits, however, that he does not know how much of his opposition flowed from his early, Cooper-inspired conclusion that the war was an exercise in geopolitical futility and how much came from his concern over the impact the conflict could have on his own life.

Facing a service obligation of some sort, McConnell decided to enlist in the Army reserves, which he later described as "a kind of 'honorable alternative' that wouldn't ruin my career or taint my advancement." Two days after finishing the bar exam, he began basic training at Fort Knox in early July. When he had trouble keeping up in the exercises, McConnell soon discovered for the first time that he suffered some residual effects from his childhood bout with polio. A physical exam also revealed that he had optic neuritis, a condition causing blurred vision. This qualified him for a medical discharge, which he gladly accepted.

When the Army's bureaucratic wheels turned too slowly, McConnell had his father call Senator Cooper's office, which helped expedite his discharge. Cooper wired the commander at Fort Knox asking "when final action can be expected." Sensitive to any hint of special treatment in connection with his military service, however, McConnell stresses that he used "no connections getting in" the reserves and "no connections getting out." Cooper never weighed in on the merits of McConnell's case, and his office was simply doing "routine case work" when it expedited the discharge, McConnell says. Future political foes would nonetheless try, without success, to turn this episode against him.[19]

A relieved McConnell returned home, moved in with his parents, was admitted to the Kentucky bar in September, and started looking for a job. His academic record left many of Louisville's major law firms uninterested, and Cooper politely advised him that he had no need for a novice attorney in his Washington office. So McConnell did not hesitate when came across a newspaper ad for a prominent pro-labor firm. He soon found himself moving into the office of a soon-to-be departing young attorney named Todd Hollenbach, whose path he would soon cross again.

As a beginning lawyer McConnell dealt with mundane debt collection and divorce matters. "I was not very happy doing this," he recalls. "It was not great fun." He was keenly alert for any opportunity to move out of law and into politics at the earliest possible moment.

3

Lukewarm Lawyer, Passionate for Politics
1968–1975

MCCONNELL'S OPPORTUNITY TO FORSAKE the law for politics came within a few months. When Thruston B. Morton surprisingly announced that he would not seek reelection to the Senate in 1968, the Jefferson County Republican Executive Committee declared for Marlow Cook, assuring that there would be but one GOP candidate from Kentucky's largest county. McConnell immediately signed on with the Cook campaign as its state youth chairman. It was a full-time paid position, and a relatively important one since Kentucky was then one of only two states allowing eighteen-year-olds to vote.

In March 1968, just as the primary campaign was heating up, McConnell and Sherrill Redmon were married. She was a former classmate at the University of Louisville then pursuing a Ph.D. in history from the University of Kentucky. The young couple named their first pet, a kitten, "Rocky" after Nelson Rockefeller, thus indicating that McConnell was on the left side of the right half of the ideological spectrum at the time.[1]

The newlywed McConnell worked nights and weekends, staging mock elections at college campuses and writing position papers and speeches for Cook, who had no writers of his own. This industry set him apart in what he recalls as a casual "nine to five" campaign culture.

After cruising to victory in the May primary, Cook won the general election by a fairly comfortable margin, but still significantly behind Richard Nixon's performance in the presidential race. The victory kept both Kentucky's U.S. Senate seats in Republican hands. When Cook offered him a spot on his Washington staff as a legislative assistant, paying about $17,000 per year, McConnell jumped at the chance.

Cook soon came into conflict with Cooper over the latter's efforts to block expansion of the Vietnam War through restrictive amendments to defense appropriations bills. The situation was an inherently uncomfortable one for McConnell, who explains that, "Cook was a hawk, and I was a dove."

Despite their differences on the war, Cooper, Cook, and McConnell all opposed deployment of an antiballistic missile system, another hotly debated defense issue of the day. Although McConnell now says he was wrong then, and that President Nixon's move to deploy such a system was the only way to obtain a treaty with the Soviets against deployment, the aide won considerable kudos on Capitol Hill for his work with Cook on the issue.

Cook sat on the Senate Judiciary Committee, and McConnell served as his point man on Nixon's ill-fated nominations of Clement F. Haynsworth Jr. and G. Harrold Carswell to the Supreme Court. Allegations of ethical improprieties doomed Haynsworth, but McConnell considered these charges mere pretense for opposition by northern Democrats and a politically hostile press. They perceived the nomination to be part of Nixon's so-called southern strategy of appealing to middle- and lower-class whites alienated by the Democrats' liberal policies on civil rights, crime, and welfare.[2]

Although Cook had led the pro-Haynsworth forces in the Judiciary Committee, he voted against Carswell. He thought Carswell was incompetent, had a "chronic inability" to "follow the law as laid down by higher courts," was short on professional achievement, and lacked a judicial temperament.[3] The nomination failed, 51–45. Nixon then nominated Harry M. Blackmun, who was confirmed by a Senate vote of 88–0, although, "If anything, Blackmun had much more flagrantly violated that standard used to defeat Judge Haynsworth than had Judge Haynsworth," McConnell later wrote.[4]

Cook encouraged McConnell to write a law review article with him in order to develop "a meaningful standard by which the Senate might judge future Supreme Court nominees."[5] The article foreshadowed many of the judicial confirmation controversies that McConnell would later confront as a U.S. senator. In the piece, he accused the Senate of employing "deception to achieve its partisan goals. This deception has been to ostensibly object to a nominee's fitness while in fact the opposition is born of political expedience." He wrote, prophetically, that the "inconsistent and sometimes unfair behavior of the Senate . . . [does] not lead one to be overly optimistic about its prospects for rendering equitable judgments about Supreme Court nominees in the future."[6]

A nominee, McConnell argued, must be competent, "have obtained some level of achievement or distinction," have a judicial temperament, "have violated no existing standard of ethical conduct," and "have a clean record in his life off the bench."[7] As a senator, he has consistently applied this standard to Supreme Court nominations by presidents of both parties.

Despite their cooperation on the article, however, McConnell never developed the kind of respect for Cook that he had for Cooper. Cook, he later recalled, "was not a deep thinker, was not particularly philosophical, and . . . kind of lumbered from one issue to another." He remembers "being more a good deal ambitious for him [Cook] than he was for himself, and being kind of frustrated that he did not work harder than he did." Cook "was afraid he was going to get in trouble politically. . . . And he did. In the early days he could have looked strong, acted strong, he could have done a lot, I thought, to kind of lock himself in. Instead he kind of floated."

Nor did Cook run the kind of office that McConnell admired. It lacked the seriousness and substantive approach he had seen in Cooper's shop. Of the friction between Cooper and Cook, he concluded that Cook was simply envious of Cooper's stature.

By mid-1970, McConnell decided he had been a staffer as long as he could given his own political ambitions. Despite an offer of employment in the Nixon White House, he wanted to come home, and did in 1971. Given the fate that was to befall so many Nixon insiders, this may be one of the most important decisions McConnell ever made.

With the backing of the local Republican Party apparatus, McConnell soon found himself running for the Kentucky House of Representatives. He moved into what would become a newly formed district two weeks before a legislative redistricting became effective. However, the Kentucky constitution required that candidates reside in "the county, town, or city for which he may be chosen" for at least a year before the election. After McConnell had campaigned for a few weeks, his Republican primary foes filed suit to disqualify him. McConnell argued that he could not have lived in the district *per se* for a year because the district was newly created and had not existed that long. He lost in the trial court and, just a week before the primary, Kentucky's highest appellate court also ruled against him despite his creative legal argument.[8]

Reflecting on his abortive first campaign for political office, McConnell concedes, "It was much too opportunistic. I had overreached. I had outsmarted myself, and it was really kind of embarrassing." He vowed to never repeat the mistake.

After his first effort as a candidate proved unsuccessful, McConnell soon jumped back into the campaign world, this time as a staffer on a gubernatorial campaign. In 1967, Louie B. Nunn had become the first Republican to win the Kentucky governorship since 1943. Kentucky law limited Nunn to a single term, but for all intents and purposes he would handpick the 1971 Republican candidate. Nunn settled on one of his administration's whiz kids, Tom Emberton.

In a bitter Republican primary battle in 1967, Nunn had attacked Cook as a "liberal former New Yorker," cast thinly veiled aspersions at Cook's Catholicism, and allowed his allies to criticize Cook's "Jewish backers."[9] As a result, McConnell, a Cook person, was never admitted to the Nunn inner circle. Nonetheless, Emberton needed some "Cook people" for his campaign and McConnell qualified. Nunn had been "so busy getting even" with those who had supported Cook in 1967, McConnell recalls, that the governor did little to build or unify the party. So Emberton put McConnell in charge of an amorphous category called "special groups" in hopes that he could help bridge the broad gap between the two factions.

"If the Cook campaign was laid back and lazy," McConnell remembers, the Emberton effort "was compulsive and burned out by two months before the election." There was enormous peer pressure to be at campaign headquarters whether or not there was anything to do. Emberton's team peaked too soon. McConnell filed away another important political lesson, this one about the proper pacing, tempo, and timing of a political campaign.

Emberton's campaign faced other obstacles as well, including most notably Nunn's broken campaign pledge not to raise taxes. Confronted with a budget crisis upon taking office, Nunn had pushed through an increase in Kentucky's sales tax from 3 percent to 5 percent. The tax hike hurt Emberton badly, even though he promised to exempt food and medicine from the levy. Emberton ended up losing to Democratic lieutenant governor Wendell Ford by 6 percent of the vote.

McConnell had not expected Emberton to lose, and needed a job. Before finding one, however, he made a brief foray back to Washington. While working on the Haynsworth, Carswell, and Blackmun nominations, McConnell had met William Rehnquist, then a promising young attorney in the Justice Department. In October of 1971, Nixon nominated the forty-seven-year-old Rehnquist to succeed Justice John Marshall Harlan, grandson of the eminent Kentucky jurist of the same name who had famously dissented from *Plessy v. Ferguson*'s "separate but equal" formulation in 1896. McConnell went to Washington at his own expense to help the nominee prepare for his confirmation hearings. The Senate confirmed Rehnquist in December by a vote of 68–26.

Returning to Kentucky, McConnell was in a near panic. He had no employment prospects and Sherrill was pregnant. He pinned his hopes on Barney Barnett, a lawyer turned entrepreneur who made a fortune in business. By early 1972, Barnett, whom McConnell had met while working with Cook, was ready to return to private practice. He asked McConnell to join him in a new firm and generously christened their decidedly unequal partnership Barnett & McConnell. A much relieved McConnell thus had gainful employment when, on July 15, 1972, Sherrill gave birth to their first child, Eleanor Hayes McConnell.

Barnett, who had an eye for and an interest in promising young Republican political talent, allowed him a "loose chain" to pursue it. After some significant successes in the 1960s, Jefferson County Republicans were now riding a losing streak, and a disenchanted group of "reform-minded dissidents" challenged the establishment for control of the local party organization.[10] McConnell managed the campaign for the "regular" slate, which managed to hold onto power. He had both chosen and performed well, and he emerged on the right side of a perpetually divided local party apparatus.

McConnell next set his sights on becoming Jefferson County Republican chairman. Because the local GOP then held almost no elected offices, the party chairmanship offered one of the few available avenues for him to become a familiar public figure. Preferring a more experienced hand on the helm, however, party leaders picked Kenneth A. Schmied, who had been mayor of Louisville from 1965 to 1969. McConnell, twenty-nine, settled for the slots of first vice chairman and chairman of the policy committee. He considered the latter post a mandate to speak out publicly on issues, and made the most of the opportunity.

In January 1972, Cooper announced that he would not run for reelection to the Senate. Nunn, not long out of the governor's office and still suffering the fallout from what had come to be called the "Nunn's Nickel" tax increase, took the Republican nomination. That fall, McConnell chaired the combined Nixon-Nunn effort in Jefferson County. Nixon ran up a record margin in Kentucky, but it was not big enough to carry Nunn into the Senate. Nunn ran a lackluster race and lost to Walter "Dee" Huddleston, a relatively obscure forty-six-year-old Elizabethtown radio station operator and state senator. The young

McConnell made another of those indelible mental notes for his own future benefit, observing the consequences that breaking campaign promises and raising taxes could have, especially on a Republican.

When Jefferson County GOP chairman Schmied died shortly after the election and in April, the thirty-one-year-old McConnell succeeded to the post. The next day a profile in the *Louisville Times*, an evening paper that was part of the media empire controlled by the city's liberal Bingham family, contained some revealing, and classically conservative, comments from the "self-described philosophical centrist." McConnell portrayed himself as "a strong believer in the art of the possible. To be effective, you have to superimpose over your idealism the realities of political life. . . . I have a very strong conviction that the best kind of change is gradual change. . . . you have to deal with what's possible and discourage those who advocate radical change."[11]

Within a few days, the new party chairman was making local news talking about the burgeoning Watergate scandal that was tainting all Republicans. McConnell called the situation "totally repugnant" and called on President Nixon "to rid the administration and the party of the stench of Watergate by cleaning house from top to bottom."[12]

That fall, Todd Hollenbach, who had been elected to Jefferson County's top executive office of county judge four years earlier at twenty-nine, won a landslide reelection. Harvey I. Sloane, an affluent doctor who had migrated to Louisville from the Northeast and quickly become the darling of the Bingham family's media empire, was elected mayor. After the GOP's poor showing, the local party was rife with recrimination and blame.

McConnell, eyeing a race of his own for county judge in 1977, decided he should get out of the chairmanship soon, but on his own terms. He also wanted to further separate himself and the local party from the Watergate scandal. He did so by expressing his first public opinions on an issue that would come to characterize his political career: campaign finance.

In a December op-ed piece in the Bingham's morning paper, the *Courier-Journal*, McConnell called for "truly effective campaign finance reform."[13] He claimed, "Many qualified and ethical persons are either totally priced out of the election market place or will not subject themselves to questionable, or downright illicit, practices that may accompany the current electoral process."

Focusing on local races, McConnell argued for reducing the limit on contributions from $2,500 to $300, complete disclosure of all donors, personal financial reporting by candidates, and a ceiling on campaign spending. "The lack of an overall limit on spending is an open invitation for special interests to circumvent this ordinance and lavishly finance future candidates, regardless of the limitations on amounts of individual contributions." A city-controlled campaign trust fund was, he wrote, "one of the most progressive proposals" then under consideration. Invoking the name of Theodore Roosevelt, McConnell also advocated public financing for presidential elections and "serious consideration" of a bill to publicly finance gubernatorial campaigns.

His views on this subject would evolve considerably, of course. Reflecting on the period recently, he explains that he was "playing for headlines" and trying to deflect attention from Watergate. His comments were part of a plan to set himself up as the loyal opposition, and position himself for a race against Hollenbach for county judge.

McConnell continued to engage in what he now describes as "calculated résumé-building activities," like accepting a presidential appointment to a largely symbolic air quality advisory board. To make extra money, he taught a class in "American Political Parties and Elections" at the University of Louisville during the 1974 spring semester. He cites this detour into academia as a turning point in his political thinking. After studying and teaching how parties operated and elections were won, he began to believe that much of what he had been saying about campaign finance was radically wrong. This epiphany would become an important part of his political philosophy and a focal point of his future career.

All Republicans were under a cloud after Nixon's resignation in August 1974. Given the public mood, McConnell decided he had to get out of the limelight for awhile. The Barnett law firm had grown considerably, and McConnell could feel a distinct tugging on that long leash Barnett had allowed him to indulge in political pursuits at the expense of the billable hour. This provided him a legitimate reason for resigning the party chairmanship. He announced his decision "with sadness and reluctance" in mid-July 1974.[14]

With his own impending campaign perhaps in mind, McConnell reiterated that he was "philosophically opposed to the current system of campaign finance which relies exclusively on private contributions," but "until that system is changed I am convinced that fund-raising to be done effectively must be done professionally."[15] About this latter point his views would not evolve.

McConnell hated the practice of law, but made himself do it to feed his family. However, one morning at 4:30 a.m., while monitoring a run-of-the-mill union election in rural Louisiana, he decided that he simply could not and would not continue. That day, he called a friend in the new Ford administration's Justice Department about a job. That night, he flew to Washington to interview with an Assistant to the Attorney General he had known during his days with Cook. Offered a job as a Deputy Assistant Attorney General for Legislative Affairs, he accepted on the spot. The post paid $33,000 a year. His responsibilities would include acting as a liaison to Congress on federal judicial nominations.

McConnell resigned from the law firm in October 1974 and went back to Washington "to kill some time" before running for Jefferson County judge. He stayed in D.C. until December of 1975, eventually becoming Acting Assistant Attorney General under Edward Levi. On weekends, he would come home to Louisville, and was there for the birth of his second child, Claire Redmon McConnell, on September 15, 1975.

During his fairly uneventful tenure at the Justice Department, McConnell formed some important impressions that he says helped hasten the transformation of his political philosophy in a more conservative direction. He had always considered himself a moderate Republican, but once inside the belly of the government beast, he became increasingly dismayed at just how big and unresponsive the federal bureaucracy actually was. McConnell concluded that the administrative machinery of big government was very often entirely beyond the influence of elected policymakers. Although he would support Gerald Ford against Ronald Reagan for the 1976 Republican presidential nomination, the latter's critique of bloated government was beginning to resonate with him as he headed back to Louisville to run the first real political campaign of his own.

The political situation there was by no means encouraging. In November 1974, then-governor Ford easily ousted Cook from the Senate. Lieutenant Governor Julian Carroll served out Ford's term and then, in 1975, easily won a full one of his own.

The only good news in this Democratic deluge was that Hollenbach, the incumbent county judge and McConnell's likely opponent for that post in 1977, had challenged Carroll for the Democratic gubernatorial nomination and lost by a big margin. Although McConnell's future foe had weakened himself, Hollenbach still enjoyed enormous advantages of incumbency, name recognition, and organizational strength in heavily Democratic Jefferson County. Against these obstacles, McConnell would soon make the political move for which he had been preparing his entire life.

4

"Horse Sense"
1976–1981

Back in Louisville, McConnell scraped by financially on some retainers Barney Barnett directed his way. In the meantime, he poured his excess energies into politics.

That spring, Jefferson County Republicans had another of their periodic internecine spats. As in the past, McConnell remained loyal to the "regulars," but this time he did so behind the scenes to avoid making enemies among the insurgents. His prospective Republican rival in the upcoming race for the Jefferson County judgeship endorsed the dissident slate. The establishment held onto power once again, and McConnell reaped the benefits of being on the victorious side without having had to take a public position.

McConnell systematically scheduled "get acquainted" lunches with potential campaign contributors. He often held these intimate discussions at Louisville's exclusive, indeed exclusionary, Pendennis Club, which he had joined in 1968 (but would ultimately leave for reasons of both frugality and political prudence).[1] The bluebloods and businessmen he solicited liked his ambition, energy, and obvious organizational skills. They also detested the ethically challenged environment of administration of the two-term incumbent, Todd Hollenbach, which McConnell characterized as "the whole aura of cronyism and people getting into trouble and the lifestyle thing."[2]

In the summer, McConnell formally filed a county judge campaign committee and announced an impressive group of supporters, including former senator Thruston B. Morton and a dynamic young former Nunn administration staffer, Larry Forgy. A week after Jimmy Carter won the 1976 presidential election, McConnell formally announced his candidacy for county judge. "He did it," observed one postelection analysis, "in the living room of his house, with his wife Sherrill at his side and a crackling fire in the fireplace behind them. The carefully constructed picture of the McConnells at home suggested the unstated: Hollenbach's domestic problems." (Hollenbach's wife had filed for divorce in February).[3] Employing a tactic that would later be used against him, McConnell sought to turn attention to his opponent's family life by running an early ad in which he described himself as a "lucky guy" with a "great wife" and "two kids."

The handsome Hollenbach had lost his luster as a Democratic political prodigy. His defeat at the hands Julian Carroll in the preceding year's Democratic gubernatorial primary had hurt him badly. McConnell remembers being "blown away," but delighted, when Hollenbach "decided on that suicidal venture against Carroll."[4]

McConnell's friend and political confidant Joe Schiff resigned as chairman of the county GOP to serve as the unpaid manager of McConnell's campaign. The pair had met in 1968, when Schiff was working for congressman William O. Cowger, and since late 1975 they had been meeting in McConnell's basement to "plot and scheme" about politics.[5] Determined to run a campaign characterized by the most modern and sophisticated methods, McConnell hired seasoned professionals Bob Goodman, a Baltimore television producer, and Tully Plesser, a New York pollster, to provide the necessary national experience and expertise.

Since Democrats enjoyed an approximate two-to-one registration advantage, McConnell decided to "de-link" himself from the Republican label. Breaking with local tradition, he ran his campaign independently from the Jefferson County GOP apparatus and refused to share a slate with the Republican candidates in other races down the ballot.

This upset some in the local party establishment, which was used to running such "team" slates and financing them from a single fund,[6] but designing the campaign to produce ticket-splitting on the county's top race proved to be a critical and correct tactical decision.

McConnell's initial commercials targeted working-class Democrats. He described himself as "one of us" and a product of Louisville's increasingly blue-collar South End, where, "We came up the hard way, the right way, like a lot of you." When he appeared in neighborhoods to address their particular problems, his aides compiled a list of his promises so he would be sure to fulfill them once in office.

Aggressively seeking "earned media," or free news coverage, McConnell's campaign cranked out rafts of announcements, and issued eighteen position papers in hopes of building a policy-based case he considered essential to securing editorial support from the powerful local press, which, while liberal, had tired of Hollenbach.[7] Among these initiatives, he called for a county ethics code and backed a new basketball arena for the University of Louisville.[8] The campaign craftily focused on areas where political reporters lived in order to create an illusion in malleable media minds that it was deeper and more formidable than it actually was.[9]

McConnell recalls that he "went after everything" in the campaign, including support from traditionally Democratic organized labor. The effort paid off in April when he captured the endorsement of the Greater Louisville Central Labor Council, the blessing of which signaled to rank and file Democrats that it was alright to split their tickets and support *this particular* Republican. The county's Fraternal Order of Police, which had never before endorsed a candidate for county judge, also came out for McConnell. These influential nods from labor and law enforcement gave the campaign a kind of bipartisan credibility it badly needed.

To win them, however, McConnell cynically declared his support for a state law allowing collective bargaining by public employees. He never really supported such a measure, but knew he would never have to honor the commitment because its actual advocates could not get it to a vote in the state General Assembly. This instance of what he concedes to have been "open pandering" is one of the few things in McConnell's public career to which he now openly admits being ashamed.

Despite his hard work, by April almost half of the voters had still never even heard of McConnell,[10] and Hollenbach held a 44-point lead. This affected fundraising because, as Schiff observed, "It was always Mitch because he didn't have the public identity to allow other people to solicit major contributions for him."[11] Although he won praise as being bright, ambitious, hardworking, thorough, and determined, and his campaign was considered by some observers as a model of organization and initiative, McConnell still needed money in order to compete.

No other Republican filed for the May primary so McConnell did not have to devote scarce resources to winning the party's nomination and could concentrate on the general election. Hollenbach was not so lucky. In the Democratic primary he garnered only around 60 percent of the vote against two much lesser known challengers, one of whom he suspected, and not without reason, of being a GOP stalking horse.

School busing to achieve racial integration had burst upon Jefferson County in 1975 courtesy of a controversial federal court order. Although it was not actually a county government concern, it was by far the biggest issue facing the community in 1977. Hollenbach had waded into the emotionally charged dispute when he did not have to, and bought himself considerable political trouble as a result. He criticized the court order, which had produced street demonstrations and other unrest, but had very limited ability to do anything about it.

Alarmed by McConnell's apparent rise and reeling from his own hard primary, Hollenbach did something unusual for an incumbent. He challenged McConnell to debate. While McConnell's campaign tactics had managed to create a perception in the media and many minds that the race was close, he knew he was still running considerably behind and leaped at the chance to tangle with Hollenbach side-by-side on television. Once in office, he would seldom be so accommodating to any of his opponents.

The debate was set for the end of October. In the meantime McConnell continued making almost daily policy proposals, kept focusing on particular concerns of individual neighborhoods, went to "a gazillion Catholic picnics," spent six days working every shift at every entrance of General Electric's large Appliance Park, and personally worked the parking lots after University of Louisville sporting events. McConnell's father assured him that he would provide financial help if the campaign did not work out. This safety net buoyed McConnell both personally and politically, since it provided the freedom he needed to immerse himself fully in the campaign without worrying about what might happen if he lost.

By September, polling showed Hollenbach's lead had fallen from April's "enormously depressing" 44 points to a still significant 16 points. 18 percent remained undecided.[12] It was a race, but not yet a close one. Settling intra-party scores with Hollenbach, Democratic governor Carroll described McConnell as "an attractive, well-qualified candidate." McConnell tried to capitalize on these unusually kind words from the other party's leader by brazenly announcing a transition team and publishing instructions on how to apply for a job in his soon-to-be administration.

McConnell also began running television ads. One featured him strolling around Washington's Lafayette Park with the beloved Cooper, who had recently returned from a stint as ambassador to East Germany. Cooper, a former county judge, said he had limited himself to two terms and thought that was enough for any such chief executive. Another ad called the county's new jail "Freedom Hall," a play on the name of the renowned local basketball arena, ridiculing Hollenbach's management for a rash of recent escapes. Still another featured a man in a clerical collar saying, "*Speaking for myself,* I think that Mitch McConnell has the character that's been missing." Hollenbach was Catholic, and the spot suggested a seal of approval from the church that McConnell did not actually have.

But it was a humorous negative ad that had the biggest impact on the campaign and can be credibly said to have launched McConnell's political career. Entitled "Horse Sense," it featured a plain-speaking farmer expressing earthy contempt for Hollenbach's claim to have cut county taxes four times. While mucking out a stall, the farmer scoffed, "When Hollenbach says he cut my taxes he doesn't credit me with any more sense than old Nell here." As the farmer said, "Maybe Hollenbach ought to have my job, because in my business, I deal with that kind of stuff every day," and pitched a shovel of manure directly at the camera.

The ad made its debut during the first game of the World Series on October 11, 1977, and had an immediate impact. Schiff staked out a working class bar in order to gauge the reaction of the target audience. The response was overwhelmingly positive there, but some of McConnell's more refined supporters from Louisville's affluent areas urged him to pull the spot because it was undignified. He wisely ignored them. Schiff credits the controversial ad with changing McConnell's image from "a stand-offish guy to someone who is willing to mix it up."[13] Hollenbach says the Horse Sense ad was the "only thing that really changed this race," and was "the only time we saw movement in the polls."[14] The ad's success convinced McConnell that "if you can make 'em laugh at the other guy, he's gone,"[15] a maxim he has heeded in his campaigns ever since.

In the much-anticipated debate, McConnell came off as confident and qualified, while a defensive Hollenbach depended heavily on note cards and failed to convey the command of issues voters might expect from a man who had held the office for eight years. Afterward, campaign polling showed that McConnell had closed to within 4 points. He followed the conventional wisdom and aired only positive ads during the campaign's last two weeks. One of them prominently featured his endorsement by the *Courier-Journal*, which had become hostile to Hollenbach after he repeatedly disappointed or failed to toe the line of its editorial board and other local left-wing elites. The newspaper's surprising support further encouraged potential ticket-splitters.

In a critical pre-election development, the United States Supreme Court declined to hear an appeal of the federal court order that had imposed forced busing on Jefferson County.[16] Hollenbach had filed an optional "friend of the court" brief and could have claimed credit if the high court had opted to review the case. When the justices took a pass, however, it looked to some locals as if he had failed.

McConnell's campaign had prepared an ad that showed him standing before a school bus and simply stating, "Some say Judge Hollenbach could have done something about this. Some say he couldn't." But an increasingly cautious McConnell deemed the issue too dangerous to touch and never ran the spot. Looking back, Hollenbach says, "If not for busing, Mitch McConnell would not have been close."[17]

On November 8, McConnell won his first election for public office by a surprisingly large margin—101,653 votes to 89,818 (53 percent to 47 percent). His was the only Republican win in Louisville or Jefferson County that night. The campaign's strategy of promoting ticket-splitting so as to isolate Hollenbach from other Democrats before "lopping him off like the cherry on the top of a sundae" had worked just as McConnell has planned.

It had been the most expensive race in Louisville's political history. McConnell spent $355,000, and the candidates combined to pay $325,000 to campaign consultants alone.[18] Recognizing the financial reality he had just personally experienced, McConnell acknowledged the importance of campaign fundraising: "Everything else is in second place. Paid television commercials are an indispensable part of winning a modern campaign in an urban area. This is not to say that I like that or am happy about it, or that I think it's the most informed way to make a decision. It is nevertheless a fact of life." Sending a signal to future foes, the erstwhile campaign finance reformer added for good measure that, "I will always be well financed, and I'll be well financed early."[19]

The three-member Fiscal Court was Jefferson County's legislature, but the county's chief executive, the county judge, also had a vote. All three commissioners of the Fiscal Court were Democrats, and they immediately moved to limit McConnell's power. McConnell would take the oath of office on January 1, but before he took office and without consulting him, the commissioners threatened to reorganize the county government and cut his staff considerably. This preemptive strike was a sign of partisan strife to come, but opposition in the local press dissuaded the Democrats from carrying it out.

As county judge, McConnell's first budget was about $60 million, and he oversaw about two thousand employees. The Kentucky constitution set the salary for the office at $17,000 (or about $60,000 in inflation-adjusted 2009 dollars). He received a $3,600 state supplement and, later, gave some speeches to justify $25,000 that local business leaders funded anonymously. Sherrill worked at the University of Louisville archives to help the family make ends meet. Aping Jimmy Carter's post-Watergate fondness for symbolic gestures of solidarity with the common man, McConnell rejected the chauffeur-driven Lincoln Continental favored by his predecessor and instead drove himself in a 1978 Ford Granada.

McConnell recalls thinking that, "I was surrounded when I came to county government with the largest group of fools and knaves I have ever seen." Determined to run a scandal-free administration, he put trusted friends in the most important posts. Schiff became assistant county judge and McConnell's college friend and fellow former Cook staffer Dave Huber served as chief of staff. To provide much-needed help across party lines, McConnell even persuaded a few respected Democrats to serve in his administration. He also abolished the venerable and bipartisan practice of informally "assessing" county employees a percentage of their salary as political contributions (although some credit him only with increased subtlety in securing the money).[20]

In mid-May, a *Louisville Times* article said McConnell "shines as a source of hope for [the] Kentucky GOP."[21] Believing he had "some responsibility to the party as the only breathing winner from last year," he began building his identity and laying the foundation for a future statewide race almost immediately after taking office. McConnell eagerly accepted almost every invitation he received to speak in Kentucky. Using sign-up sheets from such excursions to build a mailing list, he made a conscious effort to keep in touch with the people he met. With a primary or general election about every six months under

Kentucky's election calendar (since reformed), there was always a race somewhere. That meant there were always voters he could reach.

By the birth of his third and last child, Marian Porter McConnell, on October 6, 1978, McConnell had been in 30 of Kentucky's 120 counties. While he "let himself be mentioned" as a potential Republican candidate for governor in 1979, he never seriously considered running. Kentucky's governor was limited by law to a single four-year term and the state government at Frankfort was still considered a "wholly owned subsidiary of the Democrats." A gubernatorial race was simply not a prudent career plan for a Republican in Kentucky.

McConnell had already set his sights firmly on the Senate. Republicans had won eight of fifteen Kentucky Senate races since World War II, five of them in presidential election years. "I was running for the Senate in '84 from the moment I was sworn in as county judge on January 1, 1978," McConnell admits.

That fall, voters rejected a proposal to change the Fiscal Court by increasing the number of commissioners and electing them on an at-large basis instead of by district. Neither McConnell nor the Republican organization had supported the plan, both believing they had a better chance of capturing the court by winning two of the three seats under the existing structure. For the present, McConnell used citizen advisory boards and task forces to circumvent and pressure the hostile Fiscal Court as much as he could.

Over time, McConnell managed to establish a working relationship with Sylvia Watson, one of the Democratic commissioners. The blocking power their informal two-vote alliance provided, and the fact that the county judge could break ties on hiring decisions, helped him cut deals necessary to get some things done despite the opposition of the other two Democrats. Although the city of Louisville and Jefferson County were often at loggerheads over the revenue implications of city annexations of county territory, McConnell also got along reasonably well with Mayor William Stansbury. Or at least he did until the Democrat lost public confidence after being found frolicking in New Orleans with a girlfriend as local firefighters went on strike.

McConnell enjoyed some wins and suffered some defeats as his term progressed. Doubtful that a "garbage-to-steam" plant that Democrats and the *Courier-Journal* strongly supported was financially sound, he helped kill it. He also questioned the economic viability of an ambitious industrial project called Riverport, but, in a move he would later deem a mistake, reluctantly went along with it anyway. He began to use mostly federal money to buy land that would ultimately double the size of the Jefferson Memorial Forest. He would later list this as his proudest accomplishment as county judge. At the end of his first year, *Courier-Journal* political reporter Mike Brown wrote, "Even Democrats agree privately that McConnell in his first year has been smart and energetic and certainly far more capable than his adversaries in capturing public opinion."[22]

Nevertheless, controversy was a constant companion during McConnell's second year in office. Invoking a new state statute, he changed the county budgeting process by excluding the commissioners from meetings he held with department heads to develop his executive spending proposal. Excluded Democrats howled in protest. The local NAACP lodged complaints about changes in management and staffing at the county's jail, though McConnell claims he actually increased the percentage of minorities and women in county government. His working relationship with the Fraternal Order of Police and law enforcement became strained after he concluded that it would be futile to resist a federal court consent decree that had the practical effect of establishing racial hiring and promotion quotas for county police to remedy past discrimination.[23] McConnell also lost a legal battle over a county cable television ordinance.

He also managed to get away from Louisville politics for almost a month when, in the spring, the American Council of Young Political Leaders sent him to the Middle East for three-and-a-half weeks. It was his first foreign trip, and he spent time in Saudi Arabia, Sudan, Egypt, and Israel. His roommate on the sojourn was future senator and U.S. attorney general John Ashcroft.

Closer to home, after barely besting popular former Louisville mayor Harvey Sloane in a hard-fought Democratic primary, millionaire fried chicken magnate John Y. Brown Jr. decisively ended Louie Nunn's dreams of political comeback by capturing almost 60 percent of the general election vote for governor in 1979. The Nunn debacle did not hurt the GOP in Jefferson County, however. There, a promising newcomer named Carl W. Brown (no relation to the newly elected governor) captured a Democratic seat on the Fiscal Court. McConnell had raised money for Brown and helped him run a sophisticated media campaign.

Realizing how much Brown's election would reduce their power by giving McConnell another vote on the Fiscal Court, Democrats resorted to litigation. Brown had promised to reduce his own salary if elected and Democrats claimed that this violated Kentucky's corrupt practices act. Brown proceeded to serve as a commissioner as the suit wound its way up the federal judiciary for almost three years, until April 1982, when the U.S. Supreme Court ruled for him on First Amendment grounds.[24] The constitutional priority the high court accorded to political speech was not lost on McConnell, who filed it away for future use in connection with campaign finance.

To send a strong political signal to anyone thinking of running against him, at the end of 1979 McConnell declared his intention to raise a half-million dollars for his 1981 reelection campaign. He could list plenty of major accomplishments in his first term—the selection of professional department heads, creation of an office of historic preservation, spending a million dollars a year on drainage improvements, standardizing the compensation scheme for county employees, and improving jail conditions. Nonetheless, he conceded at the time that "the voters—myself included—are sick and tired of costly, big-time broad-reaching programs that they have to pay for."[25]

On the Democratic side, Governor Brown correctly considered Sloane a potential foe in future Democratic races. He therefore encouraged Sloane to run against McConnell, perhaps believing he could eliminate one of his political nemeses if he could orchestrate a race between the two of them. McConnell doubted he could defeat Sloane and hoped the well-heeled darling of the *Courier-Journal* would opt for an easier race for another mayoral term, so as to better position himself to run for governor again in 1983.

Nationally, McConnell was still aligned with the moderate wing of the GOP. He would attend the party's national convention that year, his first as a delegate, and preferred the then little-known George H. W. Bush over Ronald Reagan for president in 1980. While Reagan's effectiveness and popularity as president would eventually help move McConnell rightward, he then ranked him no better than his fourth choice to be the GOP nominee.

Despite McConnell's growing public prominence, one observer noted that his wife, Sherrill, and his aides, Huber and Schiff, were the "only three people in the world who really know him." Sherrill described him as "kind of civilized," the "same from day to day" without "hots and colds," and "a self-contained person." The *Louisville Times* said he was "by nature a prudent man." As for self-assessment, McConnell conceded, "I'm not exactly a Renaissance Man. Modern society is increasingly pushing you and pushing you toward specialization."[26]

Others were harshly critical. The pastor of a large Baptist Church with whom McConnell had clashed characterized him as a "schemer" who lacked courage and warned him, "Your damned arrogance is going to destroy you. You're not God." One critic denounced McConnell's "reckless ambition," while another described him as "a warmed over vanilla milkshake."

A newspaper article claimed that "once loyal" McConnell aides were leaving his administration "disenchanted." A number of people who had helped him in the campaign did indeed depart for a variety of reasons. One said he was leaving because McConnell wanted to be surrounded with sycophantic "yes people." McConnell responded that some of the people who left his administration "just weren't that good and moved on."[27]

By October 1980 McConnell had raised $280,000 for his reelection. He hoped the hefty total would help scare off Sloane, who still carried a significant debt from his unsuccessful gubernatorial bid the year before. A *Louisville Times* poll put McConnell's approval numbers at 6 percent "excellent," 41 percent "good," 27 percent "fair," and 10 percent "poor," comparable to that of Governor Brown and Senators

Ford and Huddleston, but well ahead of both President Carter and the lame duck Mayor Stansbury.

In the midst of all this ambition, governance, and partisan strife, McConnell's twelve-year marriage to Sherrill was coming to an end. Their parting was amicable, but the situation was personally unpleasant and politically delicate. Recently divorced and facing fierce Democratic determination to recapture control of county government, McConnell now turned his attention to the formidable task of getting reelected. It would prove harder than he expected.

5

From One Campaign to Another
1981–1984

O N FEBRUARY 20, 1981, his thirty-ninth birthday, McConnell formally announced his candidacy for reelection as county judge with a flashy event featuring a large American flag, a balloon drop, and a fourteen-piece band. McConnell, who was being taped for campaign ads, declared, "Three years ago we brought Jefferson County government home. We made it fair, we made it clean, we made it open, and we made it work."

As the end of his first term neared, McConnell had become frustrated at trying to govern "surrounded by a sea of hostility" in the form of Democratic county officials.[1] So, desperate for help and support during his hoped-for second term, he put together a Republican slate instead of running his own campaign as he had successfully done in 1977. However, he quickly realized that his decision to campaign atop a Republican ticket was an "absurd" tactical error.

Much to his relief, Harvey Sloane had announced in late 1980 that he would run for another term as mayor and not the judgeship. After considerable dithering, the Democrats settled on an uninspiring first-term commissioner, Jim "Pop" Malone, as their candidate. It looked like McConnell's reelection might be easy, and his campaign may have developed an attitude that the race was but an inconvenient prelude to the 1984 Senate contest on which the candidate had long ago focused.

That May, however, the *Louisville Times* hit McConnell hard for running his political operation out of the courthouse at public expense.[2] A citizen even filed suit against him, but McConnell mitigated the impact by bringing the Democratic commissioners into the case. With the prospect of wide-ranging legal discovery of both parties' political purity, the proceeding quietly went away. But the campaign's rough-and-tumble tone had been set.

The economy was weak, and McConnell had to recommend some unpopular budget cuts. To make matters worse, the county police labor contract expired, and negotiations over a new one were going nowhere. Other county employees wanted to organize, too, a prospect that was anathema to McConnell. By this time he had lost almost all the hard-earned labor support he had earned in his first campaign. Joe Schiff, who again managed McConnell's campaign, notes that there was "no burning issue" to rally supporters as busing and corruption had before, so it was matters like these that might decide the election.

In an ill-conceived attempt to appear dynamic and enliven his bland public image, McConnell ran an ad that showed him racing across the Ohio River in a speedboat with the wind blowing through his thinning hair. Malone effectively ridiculed the spot with a cartoon parody that depicted McConnell as captain of a ship slowly sinking to the tune of "Blow the Man Down." McConnell found out how it felt to be on the receiving end of a hard-hitting but humorous ad for a change.

Despite these difficulties, a local television station's polling still showed McConnell comfortably ahead, 52 percent to 36 percent, just a week before the election. He again earned the *Courier-Journal*'s endorsement, a considerable accomplishment for a Republican. And he had raised almost $600,000, which he believed to be four times as much as Malone had amassed.

Nevertheless, McConnell recalls that he could practically feel the race slipping away fast.[3] Because of slating, many voters began to view the contest as one between Sloane's Democratic ticket and McConnell's Republican. Some folks were beginning to ask themselves, "This is a Democratic county so why do we have this Republican county judge?" Schiff admits that he was "a little bit asleep," making a "major miscalculation" of the effect the popular Sloane's mayoral campaign would have on the race.[4] The campaign's polling also apparently overstated McConnell's support in the minority community. Relying on this inaccurate information, the Republicans made a major get-out-the-vote effort there that had the unintended consequence of turning out Sloane-Malone voters by the droves.

McConnell could not claim victory until very late on election night.[5] Despite the advantage of incumbency and outspending his opponent by about four to one, he had held on to win by only 6,844 votes, a mere 1.5 percent of the total ballots cast. The rest of the Republican slate lost badly. At least one of them—John Yarmuth, who had replaced McConnell on Marlow Cook's staff before coming home to run for commissioner—felt "totally used" at the campaign's end because McConnell had enjoyed the use of a common fund while doing little to help others on the GOP ticket.[6] "Captain Mitch did not sink in the surf," McConnell joked to his relieved supporters. He had, however, learned hard lessons about looking beyond the race at hand and linking himself too closely either to other candidates or to his own party.

The day after the election, Walter "Dee" Huddleston, the Democratic senator whom McConnell planned to challenge in three years, scoffed, "An incumbent who does no better than that is not a statewide candidate." Political observers agreed that McConnell was weakened. Mustering his formidable focus, however, he began working hard to climb out of what he accurately perceived as a self-dug political pit.

The medical maxim "First, do no harm" was on McConnell's mind as he began his second term as Jefferson County judge in January 1982. He sought to avoid controversies that could compromise his efforts to position himself for the 1984 Senate campaign, but trouble erupted almost immediately. Shortly after winning reelection, McConnell had taken a vacation to the Mexican resort of Cancun courtesy of a Louisville television station from which his campaign had purchased considerable advertising time. Although the trip was part of a promotion that had been open to all the station's advertisers, it did not look good when reported. The embarrassing brouhaha did not die down completely until the summer.

Unable to avoid making tough decisions, McConnell opted to end county-financed transportation subsidies for parochial schools, voted against a gun-control ordinance, and supported legalizing Sunday liquor sales. Then, under the pressure of potentially losing federal highway funds, he had little choice but to implement a mandatory air pollution testing program for all cars registered in Jefferson County. The measure aroused less public hostility than he had feared, and may even have burnished his environmental credentials a bit. But none of these things made McConnell's political life any easier.

Not all hard choices were forced on him. Although both McConnell and Sloane had their sights set on higher office, they decided to team up to tackle the touchy issue of merging the Louisville and Jefferson County governments. McConnell strongly believed that combining the two often-overlapping bureaucracies was in the community's best interests, but it was only with considerable difficulty and discipline that he could divorce the merger issue from his senatorial ambitions and pursue it with the necessary passion. He did his best to pass the controversial plan despite its very real potential to hurt him politically.

In negotiations over the substance of the merger proposal McConnell managed to get many of the features he wanted most. Local legislators would be elected by districts, not at large. This would give badly outnumbered Republicans a better chance at representation reflecting their countywide registration. Collective bargaining for public employees would not be mandatory, thus minimizing the clout of pro-Democratic organized labor.

Despite being bipartisan, well-financed, and well-organized, the measure still failed by a mere 1,600 votes, largely because of a lack of support in the minority and working-class white areas west of Interstate 65, the highway artery that bisects downtown Louisville and more or less divides the community along lines of class, race, and party affiliation.

Recognizing his weakened political position and eager to sew up the Republican Senate nomination as early as possible, McConnell filed papers with the Federal Election Commission in April 1982 so he could begin fundraising immediately. To solidify his support outside Louisville he announced a distinguished supporting committee that included a former state party chairman, a former congressman, and a GOP national committeewoman, all strong in the state's heavily Republican southeast.

The year offered a few unexpected obstacles. In the summer, the *Courier-Journal's* Mike Brown wrote a profile of Huddleston that featured extremely flattering remarks about him by Senate majority leader Howard Baker, a Republican from the neighboring state of Tennessee. Infuriated, McConnell fired off what he now describes as a "snotty" letter to Baker. Making amends with money, Baker's political action committee promptly contributed $10,000 to McConnell's campaign.

Carl Brown, who with McConnell's help had been elected the only Republican among the county's three commissioners with McConnell's help, decided to mount a quixotic campaign for Congress against popular Democratic incumbent Romano Mazzoli. This annoyed McConnell, who needed Brown as an ally on the Fiscal Court, saw him as his logical successor as county judge, and considered the congressional campaign counterproductive in the extreme. Brown rebelled and publicly attacked McConnell for doing "more to hurt my candidacy than Mazzoli ever did." The relationship between the two quickly deteriorated. Brown not only lost to Mazzoli, but declared he would not run for reelection as commissioner and later suffered a highly public schizophrenic episode that effectively ended his political career.

That fall, Jim Bunning, a former major league pitcher who was then a state senator, made some noises about running for the Senate in 1984, but opted to run for governor in 1983 instead. McConnell feared that even an unsuccessful gubernatorial campaign might make Bunning the Republican frontrunner for the Senate race the following year. So he refused to support Bunning in the Republican gubernatorial primary until Bunning made a public commitment to back him for the Senate. McConnell then agreed to suspend his fundraising for six months in 1983 so Bunning could have the financial field to himself. This not only hurt McConnell, but proved a futile gesture when Bunning lost badly.

In 1982, McConnell raised $250,000—more than the incumbent Huddleston—for the 1984 race. He saw superior fundraising as absolutely essential for any Republican seeking election in Kentucky. Not only did Democrats outnumber Republicans but the latter had to run in an extremely hostile media atmosphere. The state's two biggest newspapers, the *Courier-Journal* and the *Herald-Leader*, seemed to compete to have the most consistently and dramatically liberal editorial policy. In Kentucky, McConnell later explained, "The only way a relatively conservative candidate can ever win is to be able to market his own message in his own way to his own voters." His use of "relatively" before "conservative" in describing himself was perhaps as revealing as was his reason for his famous fundraising ferocity.

Being a Republican challenging a well-regarded Democratic incumbent, McConnell knew he did not stand a chance unless he was well funded. To him this meant banking "as much as you can raise." He did most of the asking himself, because it cost less and he got more that way. He tried to "max out" major donors as early as possible in a campaign cycle so he could be earn as much interest as possible on their donations.

Predictably, the media criticized his aggressive fundraising. They did so, McConnell said, because "the liberals do not like to lose, and they know that if conservatives are adequately funded, those who comment on the campaign are less significant." Referring to his ideological rivals in the left-leaning press, McConnell has repeatedly declared his adamant refusal to let "them define the environment in which I am going to compete."

After Sloane lost the Democratic gubernatorial primary in 1983, he and McConnell made another attempt at merging the Louisville and Jefferson County governments. McConnell thought they should simply put the same plan on the ballot again since it had come so close the previous year, but Sloane insisted on making some structural changes. The Democrat wanted to be able to pitch the plan to voters as a "new charter." The merger lost again, this time by an even bigger margin.[7]

Throughout his second term, McConnell had made the most of the issue of missing and exploited children. Working with widely known national spokesperson John Walsh (whose six-year-old son had been abducted and decapitated), he championed an initiative to fingerprint children, held statewide hearings, and created a task force that helped him develop legislation that would publicize the issue, enhance prevention, and strengthen penalties. McConnell took the plan to Frankfort, secured the sponsorship of Democratic Speaker of the House, and lobbied for its passage, which happened in 1984.

He sincerely believed in the issue, but it did not hurt that it was also politically popular. His efforts in the field drew national attention, won praise from the press, and gave him a good reason to travel widely across Kentucky. He visited every one of Kentucky's 120 far-flung counties over the course of 1982 and 1983.

All this travel educated McConnell in the culture of rural Kentucky and gave him plenty of time to think and plan. As 1984 arrived, his aides assumed ever-increasing responsibility for running the county government as he turned almost all his attention and energy to the Senate campaign. He was beginning far behind Huddleston and saw no readily apparent prospects for catching up. McConnell knew he had to do something to change the dynamic, so he set his mind to finding an issue with the potential to be a turning point.

6

Hound Dogs
1984

IN AUGUST 1983, SENATOR Huddleston released a poll showing him ahead of McConnell by 52 points. Huddleston's margin included a lead of 64 percent to 24 percent in McConnell's home county. McConnell knew the poll was accurate.

Despite being warned that McConnell "would be a formidable opponent because of his dedication to it and his analytical abilities of finding out any weaknesses and exploiting them," Huddleston recalls that he "didn't take it too seriously for the first several months." He knew very little about McConnell, whom he saw as "pretty much an unknown, which was probably to his advantage so he could say anything he wanted to."[1]

McConnell officially announced his Senate candidacy in a mid-January "fly around" of five Kentucky cities. He attacked Huddleston's record as "mediocre at best" and blasted him for everything from the federal deficit to the "giveaway" of the Panama Canal. Taking aim at Huddleston's low profile in Washington, McConnell promised, "When I am in the Senate representing Kentucky's interests, you won't call me a shadow senator. You'll know I'm there."[2] He also declared his support for the Reagan defense buildup in doomsday terms: "If we spend too much on defense we lose some money. If we spend too little, we lose America."[3]

After Jim Bunning's loss in the previous year's governor's race, McConnell had resumed fundraising at a furious pace and reached $450,000 by the end of that November. He put the cash to use immediately. With former Nixon consultant and future Fox News president Roger Ailes as his media guru, McConnell began airing television ads the day after his announcement. These spots carried the tagline "Kentucky's Next Great Senator." He also ran a rare and expensive two-minute commercial tracing his life and career. Looking back, McConnell believes these early and expensive efforts were a waste of money because voters had not yet focused on the race.

By February, McConnell and Huddleston had raised about $800,000 each. At the end of the year's first quarter Huddleston had outraised McConnell by only about $100,000. McConnell went to extraordinary lengths to get the money he knew he needed. For example, Nelson Bunker Hunt, best known for his late 1970s effort to corner the world silver market, hosted a successful fundraiser for him in Texas.

Under the leadership of Senator Richard Lugar of Indiana, the National Republican Senatorial Committee (NRSC) put top priority on protecting GOP incumbents. The committee would give significant support to challengers like McConnell only if thoroughly convinced it would not be wasting resources. At this stage of the campaign, neither Lugar nor his young right-hand man, future Indiana governor Mitch Daniels, gave McConnell much of a chance.[4]

In a surprise move, former governor John Y. Brown Jr. filed against Huddleston for the Democratic nomination. Privately, McConnell feared that their primary might hurt him if the winner emerged with a "bounce," but he publicly professed pleasure at the fight, claiming that Brown evidently saw the same weak target in Huddleston that he did. Brown never got traction and soon dropped out of the race. Yet Brown had, McConnell recalls, at least campaigned "long enough to get some negatives out there against" Huddleston and made the incumbent spend "about half a million dollars that I would not have had to spend."[5] McConnell immediately tried to capitalize on Brown's abortive campaign by running a television ad stating that they stood for many of the same things, like "reducing the size of government, controlling taxes, and ending political patronage." He told the press that Brown's withdrawal was a good thing, but privately worried that it had made Huddleston appear stronger.

In late May, after trouncing three token Republican primary opponents, McConnell attacked Huddleston for poor Senate attendance and for frequently voting against the popular President Reagan. McConnell also tried to make Huddleston's occasional changes of position an issue, calling him "The Washington Waffle." In July, however, a Huddleston poll showed him still holding a commanding lead of 67 percent to 23 percent.

Huddleston had on hand $511,000 to McConnell's $197,000. Using two secretaries so he could make twice as many contacts, McConnell spent countless hours cold-calling past Republican donors to ask for money. An aide who built a donor database on three-by-five cards would schedule appointments for McConnell at forty-five-minute intervals. As soon as McConnell got in the car after a meeting, he would write a thank you note to the person with whom he had just spoken, always taking care to confirm the commitment, the amount, and the date of payment.[6] He could be incredibly persuasive. During one visit to coal-rich Pike County, McConnell quickly realized that he was in the wrong house, but still managed to wrangle a $4,000 donation from his accidental hosts and $2,000 more from a relative who lived next door.[7]

On the first Saturday in August, McConnell made his maiden appearance at the annual Fancy Farm picnic in the Jackson Purchase, the region of far western Kentucky extending to the Mississippi River that was then known as the Gibraltar of the Kentucky Democratic Party. Sponsored by the tiny local Catholic parish since 1880, the Fancy Farm picnic had evolved into Kentucky's premier political event. The stump-style speechmaking drew intense statewide media coverage, and the raucous atmosphere and boisterous audience participation made the experience a daunting rite of political passage for inexperienced orators.

McConnell's team knew it was deep in the Democratic lions' den as they drove into the single-traffic-light hamlet along curvy roads lined with Huddleston signs.[8] With his supporters brandishing posters bearing the campaign's "Switch to Mitch" slogan, McConnell spoke from notes he had jotted down that morning on the backs of some envelopes. He did well, ridiculing Huddleston as "good ole' Dee" and criticizing him as "totally anti-business," "consistently against a strong national defense," and the bearer of "a twelve-year record of indecisiveness, big spending, and absenteeism."

When Huddleston took to the bunting-draped stage he shrugged off McConnell's attacks as "juvenile" and reminded the audience that the Republican challenger was not a Kentucky native. He said McConnell could not be expected to know much about the commonwealth after a few months of campaigning. Stressing his seniority, Huddleston said that "tobacco price supports and other farm programs wouldn't be safe in the hands of an urban freshman who will have to stand in line until everybody else is finished before he gets to speak in the Senate."

Kentucky's other senator, Wendell Ford, followed Huddleston. He did to McConnell what McConnell had done to Hollenbach in 1977 by not-so-subtly raising the issue of McConnell's recent divorce. Ford said senators needed a strong family life and proceeded to make a major production out of introducing Huddleston's wife. To McConnell's dismay, the next day's papers did not highlight his aggressive speech, but focused instead on an exchange between Ford and a heckler.[9] This "irritated the living hell" out of McConnell, since Ford was not even on the ballot that year, and confirmed the challenger's suspicions that he would not get favorable attention from the state's left-of-center press corps even when he performed well.

The next Monday, McConnell started running radio ads. Thanks to his Herculean fundraising, he managed to stay on the airwaves without interruption through Election Day. On Ailes's advice, the spots were almost exclusively negative, focusing mainly on Huddleston's spotty Senate attendance.

At McConnell's urging, his campaign manager, Janet Mullins, had compared the dates of Senate votes Huddleston had missed with the dates of speaking fees he had reported on his financial disclosure forms. She knew that the staffers who usually filled out the forms used the dates the checks came in, not the date of the speech. But Huddleston apparently filled out the forms himself, and he listed the dates of his speaking appearances instead of the dates he actually received his honoraria. Mullins was "absolutely stunned" to discover that Huddleston had missed Senate votes on the same day he had been paid to make a speech no fewer than twenty-four times.[10] With this information in hand, the campaign was about to change dramatically.

Mullins remembers the bearded, Buddha-like Ailes, his head wreathed in pipe smoke, saying, "Dogs! I see hound dogs."[11] Thus was born the "bloodhound ads," which remain among the best known and most effective campaign commercials in the history of U.S. Senate races, if not all of American politics. The spots showed a hunter and a pack of baying dogs searching for Huddleston in a series of exotic locales like the ones where he had made paid speeches while the Senate was voting. The hunter finally abandoned his quest and decided to "Switch to Mitch."

Expensive to produce, the ads were a major gamble for the McConnell campaign.[12] They began airing around Labor Day and, like the "Horse Sense" spot in McConnell's first county judge campaign, had an immediate impact. McConnell, whose only creative contribution to the commercials had been his insistence that the ads feature the right kind of dog lest he lose credibility among Kentucky's many hunters, started hearing about the hounds wherever he went in the state. According to Huddleston, the bloodhound ad changed the "theme of the campaign" into "pretty much the opposite" of what he had wanted it to be, making it difficult for the incumbent to project himself as "on the job, doing the job, not in a flashy sort of way but there at committee meetings, representing every part of Kentucky."[13]

McConnell intensified his fundraising to keep the ads running. Throughout the remainder of the campaign McConnell's advertising continued to be almost all negative because he did not believe he had enough time or money to build himself up while also tearing Huddleston down. In retrospect, McConnell admits that at least one of these spots, a radio ad dealing with Huddleston's attendance at committee meetings, was "fundamentally unfair" and "kind of ridiculous."[14] But the challenger was more than 30 points down, the race was "asleep," and he could not afford to let it stay that way. Unfair or not, the ad kept running.

Doubting he could win by much of a margin in his home county of Jefferson, McConnell did what once seemed unthinkable for a Kentucky Republican—he targeted traditionally Democratic territory in western Kentucky's two congressional districts. Appealing to the conservative "Reagan Democrats" who resided there in abundance, his ads focused on subjects like the Panama Canal and school prayer. This effort not only proved successful against Huddleston, but would mark the beginning of a new era of partisan realignment in Kentucky politics.

McConnell was there when the national Republicans convened in Dallas in late August to nominate Reagan for reelection. He hoped to raise money, garner attention from Kentucky's political press, and link himself to Reagan in the popular mind, but his success was marginal at best.

Realizing that he could not continue essentially to ignore his pesky foe, Huddleston finally started attacking McConnell on the stump. His ads accused McConnell of "hysterical, negative mudslinging," stealth tax increases, and increased spending as county judge. Huddleston told rural audiences that a freshman from the city could not protect Kentucky's farm interests in a clubby Senate that put a premium on seniority. In response, McConnell curtly called Huddleston "a liar."

In mid-September, Huddleston claimed that his polling showed him ahead 60 percent to 27 percent. But former president Gerald Ford campaigned for McConnell in Lexington that month, signaling that some national Republicans were finally taking an interest in the race. An NRSC poll taken in early October showed Huddleston's lead down to 52 percent to 40 percent, with a generic "new person" actually running ahead of him for the first time. The race was starting to move McConnell's way.

The day after that poll was taken, President Reagan came to Louisville to debate the Democratic presidential nominee, Walter Mondale. The Gipper put in one of the worst public performances of his presidential career, and at a post-debate rally, with McConnell's cameras running to preserve a hoped-for magical moment for use in an ad, Reagan mistakenly referred to the Kentuckian as "Mitch O'Donnell." It was embarrassing for both.

The next night, McConnell and Huddleston debated on statewide television. An aggressive McConnell attacked Huddleston for helping Louisville-based Dairyman, Inc. by getting the federal government to buy a large quantity of powdered milk, for voting to create new bureaucracies, and for supporting higher taxes. He questioned Huddleston's Senate attendance record, belittled his impact and influence, and argued that a Republican could do more for Kentucky by working with the Reagan White House.

An indignant Huddleston found himself playing defense and stressing the advantages of seniority. Referring to Reagan's "Mitch O'Donnell" gaffe, Huddleston said the president did not even know who McConnell was. Using a line Ailes had prepared in advance, McConnell responded, "The president knows who you are, Dee, and that's why he is supporting me." Overall, McConnell was clearly the sharper of the two candidates, and the debate showed voters that he could hold his own against Huddleston. Once again, McConnell saw how debates could help a trailing challenger achieve instant parity with a better-known incumbent.

By this point, McConnell's campaign had established a regular routine. He attended local fundraising events and called prospective contributors during the week and campaigned on weekends. Although he flew around Kentucky to appear in as many local festivals and parades as possible, he treated the campaign mainly as a "television event" in which the influence of local politicians and personal campaigning would make only a marginal difference. He also brazenly used his office as county judge to maximum benefit. Although the media gave him some heat for making mass mailings at public expense to tout his accomplishments, he did not back off.

Staffers agree that McConnell was a true conservative when it came to campaign money. While traveling, he would place "person-to-person" calls from pay phones to his campaign headquarters, which would reject the charges and then call him back to save money. Lest any bumper sticker be wasted, McConnell insisted that volunteers wielding Windex and paper towels personally clean the vehicle's surface before applying the pricey items to willing people's cars. McConnell preferred to return home to Louisville each night, but when his schedule would not permit that he economized by staying in someone's home instead of a hotel.[15] He nonetheless spent a few nights spent in small town hostelries where "dial-out phones" and "tile bathrooms" were still advertised as luxury features.[16]

Yet Huddleston enjoyed a financial advantage. From July 1 through September 30, he spent $503,000 and raised $335,000, whereas McConnell spent $363,000 while raising $280,000. Most of McConnell's money came from Kentucky donations of $500 or more, with $1 million of his $1.8 million total raised in Jefferson County. But with the race tightening two weeks before the vote, national Republicans at last started steering significant sums his way.

The *Courier-Journal*, the *Herald-Leader*, and most other Kentucky papers endorsed Huddleston. And just as McConnell's momentum was building, the *Herald-Leader* released a survey showing Huddleston ahead 59 percent to 36 percent. McConnell knew those numbers were not accurate, but their publication hurt nonetheless. Ailes and McConnell decided to spend $20,000 to produce a sequel to the bloodhound ad. This one featured a Huddleston look-alike being symbolically treed by the Republican hounds. "Dee Huddleston has been running from his record, but now Kentucky is closing in," it said.

After national Republican tracking polls put Huddleston ahead by just 45 percent to 41 percent with less than a week to go, money started coming in "by the truckload," McConnell recalls. On the Friday before the election, the campaign made a $50,000 deposit, far and away its biggest financial day. This inflow allowed McConnell to quickly produce more ads and send aides fanning out across the commonwealth carrying blank checks to buy as much weekend radio time as needed to counter an anticipated last-minute Huddleston attack. Long resistant, President Reagan's advisers finally relented and let their boss tape an ad.[17] McConnell ran the spot in heavily Catholic and socially conservative northern Kentucky, the only area of the state where the campaign's internal polling indicated that it would have significant impact. Huddleston, in contrast, coasted to the campaign's conclusion, apparently leaving around a quarter of a million dollars in the bank.[18]

On election night, NBC projected McConnell as the victor by a substantial margin shortly after 7 P.M., but the race tightened as results rolled in from east to west.[19] Flanked by his parents and his daughters,[20] McConnell claimed victory in time to make the 11 P.M. newscasts,[21] but was queasy even then. "We had just a little bit to overcome," McConnell said, speaking to cheering supporters at Louisville's downtown YMCA. "We had against us the big labor, big business, the two largest newspapers in the state, the state administration, and the county courthouses. But we did it!" Recalling his boyhood move to Kentucky, McConnell said he used to wonder if he and his family would ever fit in. "I guess we've been accepted!" he crowed.[22]

Just after he finished speaking, however, aides informed him that his margin had shrunk to a few thousand votes. Badly wounded by his ally's impending defeat, Senator Ford blustered about getting a court order to reopen polls in one heavily Democratic county in the eastern Kentucky mountains because they had opened late.[23] Huddleston finally conceded and, blaming liberals like Mondale for his defeat, said, "It's time for our party, the Democratic Party, to redefine itself at the national level so that these good Democrats in Kentucky can identify with the party."[24] But the next morning Huddleston nonetheless called for a recanvass of the votes. Although such a review would be less exacting than an actual recount, it would still take two weeks to complete.

The Republicans feared that the state's long dominant Democrats would somehow steal the election. Louie Nunn called to reassure McConnell that the Democrats had stolen all their votes before the voting machines were sealed and could not swipe any more. Still, McConnell had a lawyer send a letter to statewide officials detailing the penalties for election fraud.

The recanvass ultimately confirmed McConnell's victory. He won by a mere 644,990 votes to 639,821, or 49.8 percent to 49.5 percent, which amounted to about one vote per precinct. Huddleston had won in the state's far eastern and western congressional districts, but not by nearly as much as he needed in the latter. McConnell made up the ground in suburban Cincinnati areas of northern Kentucky, the Bluegrass region around Lexington, and in his home county of Jefferson, which he won by about 9,000 votes out of 287,000 cast.

Schiff believes the bloodhound ads changed a significant loss into a narrow win.[25] Early in the campaign their creator, Ailes, had told McConnell, "If Dee dies you'll still lose by 6, but I'm prepared to fight if you are." Looking back, Ailes marvels at McConnell's determination to win, his "stomach to keep fighting, and his unusual ability to raise money despite being fairly far behind."

In reflection, Huddleston says some in his campaign overconfidently concluded that "this little guy in Louisville is not going to be any problem" and voters "just thought it was no battle, no contest, and the polls showed that right up until the last." McConnell was "a student of political campaigns" and "ahead of the curve when it came to using the negative type approach."[26]

There is a lingering debate about whether and to what extent Reagan's coattails contributed to McConnell's upset. Reporting on the race the next day, the *Courier-Journal* began its story by stating that McConnell was "swept along by a strong Reagan tide."[27] McConnell resents such contentions. He calls 1984 a "confirming election" in which voters were generally happy with what they had, and notes that Republicans actually lost two Senate seats nationally. Huddleston was the only Democrat incumbent who lost in 1984, whereas a dozen had gone down to defeat when Reagan was elected four years before. To McConnell, this suggests that Reagan lacked down-ballot influence elsewhere, and there is no reason to think that Kentucky was an exception.

But Reagan did carry Kentucky by 283,193 votes. Huddleston believes "the Reagan influence had to be probably the most prominent" cause of his defeat.[28] Political correspondent Al Cross of the *Courier-Journal* believes that a presidential landslide inevitably affects any Senate race decided by less than 5,000 votes, and he notes that McConnell himself had, at the beginning of the campaign, acknowledged the benefits of running on a ticket with Reagan.[29]

In December 1984, McConnell presided over his final Jefferson County Fiscal Court meeting. The commissioners unveiled his official portrait and announced the naming of the "Mitch McConnell Loop Trail" in the Jefferson Memorial Forest he had expanded. One explained that they chose to honor him in this way because the trail "went from the bottom straight to the top."

With this victory McConnell would be the only Republican to win a race for statewide office in Kentucky during the thirty-year period from 1968 through 1998. As he left Louisville for Washington, McConnell was convinced that he would not have been elected if the sort of campaign finance restrictions he had previously advocated had been in place for his race.[30] As he began to look for issues on which he could make his mark as a senator, this lesson loomed large in his mind.

7

Rookie
1985–1986

MITCH MCCONNELL, THE VERY model of a moderate Republican, began his career as a senator just as the quintessential conservative Republican, Ronald Reagan, was at the peak of his popularity and power as president. The Capitol Hill rookie did not need a political compass to notice that the GOP had enjoyed considerable electoral success as it had moved rightward. Having gone with that flow, he now found himself in Washington.

McConnell was perhaps the most obscure member of an incoming class that included Republican Phil Gramm of Texas and Democrats Al Gore of Tennessee, John Kerry of Massachusetts, Jay Rockefeller of West Virginia, Tom Harkin of Iowa, and Paul Simon of Illinois. Because of his lack of seniority, McConnell's desk was in a dimly lit back corner of the Senate chamber. He recalls "looking around and thinking to myself, 'None of these people is ever going to die, retire, or be defeated.'"[1]

According to one veteran Washington observer, McConnell "didn't have much going for him" and "clearly was not a man of the world" when he arrived in the Senate.[2] Given that he had never been a congressman, which would have given him a better understanding of Washington issues and legislative politics, McConnell admits to having wondered,

"Now what do I do?" The obvious initial answer was to follow the Republican leadership.

"He had won, and that was as far as the plan went," recalls Mullins (now Mullins Grissom), an "old Washington hand" who became McConnell's chief of staff after managing his campaign.[3] He put trusted aide Larry Cox in charge of Kentucky operations. In addition to his headquarters in Louisville, McConnell set up field offices in Paducah and Bowling Green—all the better to expand the political bridgehead he was building into Democratic western Kentucky—and in Covington, Lexington, and London along the Interstate 75 corridor that runs north-south through the state.

McConnell's first major vote as a member of the Ninety-ninth Congress took place in the Republican conference, or caucus. Howard Baker had retired, and Kansas's Bob Dole, Indiana's Richard Lugar, New Mexico's Pete Domenici, Idaho's Jim McClure, and Alaska's Ted Stevens were seeking to succeed him as leader of the recently reduced fifty-three-member Republican majority. Although he did not announce it publicly at the time, McConnell voted for Dole, the eventual fourth-ballot victor, who had been cultivating the Kentuckian since coming to the commonwealth to campaign for him late in the 1984 Senate race.

Although McConnell lobbied hard for a seat on the tax-writing Finance Committee,[4] Dole assigned him to the Intelligence Committee instead. McConnell also took seats on the Agriculture and Judiciary Committees.

The newcomer kept a wary distance from Kentucky's senior senator, Wendell Ford, with one major exception. Known as "Mr. Tobacco," Ford had doggedly protected the interests of those involved in all aspects of Kentucky's most lucrative crop. As an urban Louisvillian, McConnell knew he had to demonstrate some interest and expertise in agricultural matters. So the first bill he introduced as a senator was a piece of farm legislation, albeit an insignificant one. Still, he found working on the session's major farm bill to be "extraordinarily boring, and arcane, and difficult to understand." Commentators correctly concluded that he was not a player on it.

A 1983 drought had hurt the burley industry and farmers were demanding help. Yet some Reagan administration officials and legislators from non-tobacco states were talking seriously about abolishing the New Deal–era federal tobacco price support program for reasons both budgetary and philosophical. Ford pushed a reform requiring manufacturers to buy from existing federal stocks to pump up prices and making market-oriented modifications to the price support and quota formulas. Although the effort bogged down in a prolonged budget battle, McConnell deferentially followed Ford's lead on this issue that was so important to his state and political future.

McConnell realized he would have to do more, and proved to be a quick study when it came to learning how. For instance, he took an official trip to Korea the following year as part of an attempt to open Asian markets to American cigarettes. Upon returning, he introduced a bill to impose quotas on Korean products until the situation changed.

From the outset, McConnell considered his first term as being mainly about getting elected to a second, and did everything he could to solidify his standing back home.[5] To this end he made, honored, but soon came to regret, a pledge to visit all of Kentucky's 120 counties over the next two years. He discovered that town meetings tended to bring out "malcontents" and generate bad press, but did not provide him with useful information or insight into issues of broad popular concern. He was soon exhausting himself with statewide travel that produced more negative media than political benefit or policy fodder. He also worked hard to build strong connections with the military and civilian communities associated with Kentucky's two major army bases, Fort Knox and Fort Campbell, both full of conservative-leaning voters.

McConnell knew he would face a tough reelection fight in 1990. His internal polling showed him behind his most likely opponent, Harvey Sloane. In 1984 McConnell had convinced voters to "fire" Huddleston, but he believed they still "really didn't know who they had hired" as a replacement. He admits that he had "no real public persona in those days," enjoyed no room for error, and "had to work like hell for the full six years both on the political side and on the governmental side to win."

Recognizing these political realities, McConnell believed that he needed at least to look bipartisan and not to "spend any time trying to do the undoable and thereby weaken myself any further." So he announced that defeating Wendell Ford in 1986 was not a priority for him.[6] He also sought to demonstrate his political independence by breaking with Reagan to support trade sanctions against the apartheid regime of South Africa. But on two big issues, McConnell took solidly conservative positions, strongly backing the Gramm-Rudman-Hollings deficit reduction measure and Reagan's controversial policy of aiding the Nicaraguan contras against the Cuban-backed Sandinistas.

"To be listened to in the Senate," McConnell quickly realized, "you have to pick a few areas [and] learn a lot about them, because knowledge is power. The person who knows the most about a subject is most likely to achieve a result." Reflecting on a new senator's place in the process, he notes that "you can be a very effective legislator and still be open to the charge the next time you run that you have never passed a bill," because authoring a bill "with your name on it" that becomes law is relatively rare. Senators usually accomplish the most by amending others' legislation "that could be very, very significant, yet you would have to argue with some reporter or some opponent over whether or not it was really your bill because it was stuck to something else."

McConnell discovered that learning how to effectively "massage the system" takes time. Looking back from the perspective of multiple reelections, he says, "In the first term I wasn't particularly effective. I think it took a while to get good, and I don't think I even came close to beginning to hit my stride until some time into the second term. And I am much more effective now than I used to be because I understand parliamentary procedure better, I understand the rhythm of the Senate better." He uses his own learning curve as yet another argument against term limits, which has occasionally put him at odds with some other prominent conservatives and Republicans.[7]

McConnell indeed made his share of mistakes in his first term. He blundered in late 1985 by announcing that a large Toyota plant was coming to Kentucky when he actually had little to do with the project.

The stunt rightly earned him statewide criticism and ridicule. "I think it was a stupid mistake," he concedes. "It made me look opportunistic and overreaching. It was embarrassing, and I should have been embarrassed by it, and I was. I ended up getting creamed by the press, which I richly deserved."

McConnell recalls that "1985 was not a terrific year." It had become painfully clear to him that he "was not ready for this job," and that it was going to take considerable time for him to become effective. Always a long-range planner, he continued putting more emphasis on reelection than legislation. He had banked $325,000 by year's end, which, with interest, would mount to almost a half million dollars by the time the next campaign came around.

Feeling the need for some extra money of his own, McConnell made some paid speeches, just as Huddleston had. In January 1986, he earned $10,500 for seven speeches and panel discussions during an eleven-day trip to the West Coast. He reported it all, but the sponsoring groups had paid not only his expenses but also those of his then-fiancée. Taking care not to repeat his predecessor's mistake of missing official business in order to make paid speeches, McConnell returned to Washington on the day the Senate reconvened.[8] The trip was over and the engagement soon was, too, but their political repercussions were not.

McConnell got his first national notice for Senate work when the venerable conservative pundit James J. Kilpatrick mentioned his tort reform efforts in a column. Shortly thereafter, self-proclaimed consumer advocate Ralph Nader blasted McConnell on the same subject in a speech at the University of Louisville. He welcomed Nader's criticism because it garnered him publicity while enhancing his conservative credentials in the process.

1986 also marked McConnell's first major involvement in the cause that would become his signature issue: campaign finance. The previous December, David Boren, an Oklahoma Democrat, and Republican icon Barry Goldwater had introduced a measure to limit the amount of political action committee (PAC) contributions that Senate and House candidates could accept. The bill passed the Senate 69–30 the next

August, but died in the House. McConnell spoke and voted against the measure. His objections at this stage were more political than constitutional, as he believed the limit would cripple the ability of Republicans like him to win elections.

McConnell also asserted himself on another issue of increasing conservative-liberal friction, the selection of federal judges. Ford and Huddleston had created a judicial nominating commission for Kentucky's federal district court vacancies with the ostensible objective of producing the best qualified nominees. Each senator appointed three members, as did the Kentucky Bar Association. McConnell initially acquiesced in the arrangement, but after a couple of battles with Ford he quickly concluded that the composition of the federal judiciary was just too important an issue for him to sacrifice any of his actual or potential influence to some Democratic scheme. He soon took steps to regain what he considered his rightful priority over Kentucky federal judicial nominations while a Republican occupied the White House.

Tax policy is the defining issue for many conservatives, McConnell voted for the big and controversial Tax Reform Act of 1986, perhaps the most important piece of legislation to pass during his second year in the Senate.[9] The act was designed to be revenue neutral over a five-year period by offsetting large reductions in individual and corporate income tax rates with a broadening of the tax base by eliminating various deductions, tax shelters, and preferential treatment for capital gains.[10] Ever mindful of the fate that befell Governor Nunn in Kentucky after he backed a tax increase, McConnell would rarely again come this close to supporting a bill that could be so characterized.

Tax reform was not enough to prevent significant Republican losses in midterm elections the following month. Democrats defeated six first-term GOP senators, made a net gain of eight Senate seats, and—with a fifty-five to forty-five majority—took control of the Senate for the first time since the Reagan landslide of 1980. Winning almost three-quarters of the vote, Ford easily earned reelection.

Although McConnell's next campaign was four years in the future, it was never far from his mind. He had $642,000 in campaign funds on hand at year's end. His strategy was, as always, not only to raise money, but also to trumpet the fact of his financial strength in the hope of discouraging opposition. As the new year dawned and a reconfigured Congress convened, he had plenty of reason to be concerned.

8

In the Minority
1987–1988

MᶜCONNELL QUICKLY LEARNED HOW very different life would be in the 100th Congress. As his party moved to minority status he surrendered a still-new subcommittee chairmanship and cut his staff.

He also left the Judiciary and Intelligence Committees to take a seat on the prestigious Foreign Relations Committee. It was there that Cooper had made his name as an influential minority member. McConnell hoped he might do likewise, but soon came to believe that the committee was "increasingly irrelevant" and not a very good fit for him. Making the most of the post nonetheless, in early 1987 he took his second trip to Israel. He had unsuccessfully sought the support of the powerful American Israel Public Affairs Committee (AIPAC) in his 1984 race, hoping to win the group's endorsement as payback for Huddleston's support for selling sophisticated military aircraft to Saudi Arabia over Israeli opposition. So from the outset of his Senate career he set about proving himself a staunch friend and supporter of Israel.

That spring found President Reagan weakened by the Iran-contra scandal and wanting to demonstrate his continued clout and relevance. To this end, he vetoed what seemed to some conservatives as an excessively expensive and earmark-laden $87.5 billion highway bill.[1] Support for the bill was strong in Kentucky, so McConnell resisted Reagan's intense personal lobbying and voted with twelve other Republicans to override the veto, which was done by a margin of one.[2] Again, he took solace from the fact that in a Democratic state like Kentucky such occasional displays of independence from his party and its then-embattled leader would not hurt him politically.

Led again by Boren and the new majority leader, the former civil rights obstructionist Robert Byrd, the emboldened Democrats renewed their push for campaign finance reform. Starting that spring and continuing into the next session of Congress, McConnell teamed with Oregon's Bob Packwood to block the Democratic bill from coming to a floor vote It was a difficult struggle and, reluctantly, McConnell concluded that Republicans had to offer some "reforms" that their own members could support if they hoped to keep fending off the Democrats' even more unpalatable initiatives.

So he started offering some proposals that he did not like. One prohibited political action committee contributions to congressional candidates, mandated lower rates for political advertising in the last thirty days of a campaign, lifted contribution limits from $1,000 to $3,000, and relaxed those levels further for candidates opposing wealthy self-funded rivals. McConnell was not proud of these mostly "bad ideas," and believed several of them were unconstitutional, but was convinced such ploys were required to keep the Republicans together. This made for votes that would be difficult for him to defend later and gave some critics reason to claim that he changed his position on campaign finance reform only after Republicans claimed majorities in both houses of Congress in 1994 and were in a position to capitalize on their power.[3]

The Republican opposition held firm through eight cloture votes attempting to terminate their filibuster. For the final effort in February 1988, Byrd mustered only fifty-three votes, seven fewer than he needed.[4] McConnell and Packwood had held the line.

This was McConnell's most visible role as a senator thus far. It was, he recalls, "the first time I had understood an issue well enough to feel very comfortable out on the floor engaged in debate, talking a lot."

In the meantime, the battle for the 1988 Republican presidential nomination had begun in earnest. Dole was planning to challenge the favorite, Vice President George Bush. Kentuckians John Sherman Cooper and Representatives Jim Bunning and Hal Rogers came out for Bush. Risking Dole's wrath, McConnell did likewise. He felt underappreciated by Dole, found him difficult to deal with on campaign finance issues, and thought backing Bush from the Senate would be a way to build clout. McConnell proceeded to stump for Bush in a few southern states, once crossing paths with a snarling Dole in Louisiana.

Always attentive to his own political situation, he sought to make life as difficult as possible for Sloane, his probable opponent in 1990. Sloane's term as Jefferson County judge would end in 1989. McConnell wanted to deter him from running for reelection so that he would not enjoy the benefits of incumbency, or would at least be forced to run two hard races back to back. He encouraged John G. Heyburn, scion of a prominent Louisville Republican family, to run. Heyburn announced his candidacy the following April and began attacking Sloane almost immediately. This episode was a textbook example of a favorite McConnell tactic—using surrogates and "down ballot" races to protect himself and make life difficult for potential foes.

In May, a poll published in the *Courier-Journal* showed McConnell's approval rating at 67 percent and his disapproval at 10 percent (Ford stood at 69 percent to 12 percent). Nonetheless, he worked hard to insert into the highway appropriations bill a popular provision allowing Kentucky to raise speed limits on its parkways and toll roads to sixty-five miles per hour to make them compatible with the newly increased limits on interstate highways. "I was beginning to learn how to pass a bill," he remembers, which was important from a political perspective as well as a legislative one.

A month later, the *Washington Post* ran a front-page story about lobbyist-paid travel by legislators.[5] Although the piece discussed many members of Congress, it gave the most prominence, including an illustrative map, to McConnell's West Coast speaking tour from the preceding year. The article said McConnell's trip "epitomizes the explosive growth for House and Senate members of honoraria and expense-paid trips to luxury resorts financed by corporations, associations and law firms that lobby Capitol Hill." The *Post* conceded that McConnell had missed no votes and that he had complied with Senate rules limiting speaking fees to 40 percent of his $75,100 salary by donating his over-age of $16,600 to charity, including $7,360 to his church, Crescent Hill Baptist. He was quoted as saying that "many of us are not millionaires" and "it's nice to have some option."

All this was perfectly legal and properly disclosed, but the payment of his then-fiancée's expenses presented a problem. McConnell had obtained a supportive Senate Ethics Committee opinion, but, to his chagrin, later learned that the matter was actually within the jurisdiction of the Federal Election Commission, which forbade senators from accepting such expense payments. He quietly reimbursed the trip's sponsors for his fiancée's costs for that excursion as well as an earlier, much more expensive one to Japan. He carried copies of these checks throughout his reelection campaign in case the issue ever came up.

It was a costly and embarrassing mistake, which McConnell characterizes as "one of the low points" of his public career. Though the bad press did not stop him from traveling, he became scrupulously careful about it from that point on. In August he embarked on an official trip to Turkey, Greece, and the Soviet Union, after which he introduced a resolution calling on the secretary of state to dispatch a senior U.S. official to Greece and Turkey to consult on possible solutions to Greek-Turkish tensions that he said had diminished the strength of the North Atlantic Treaty Organization (NATO). Ever attentive to issues relating to Israel, he also offered a resolution supporting B'nai B'rith's cooperation with the Soviet Union.

In October, McConnell was one of the forty-two senators voting to confirm Reagan's controversial nomination of Robert Bork to the Supreme Court. Once again, he argued that the Senate should concern itself only with the nominee's qualifications, not with his judicial philosophy. But McConnell was no rubber stamp for Reagan nominations that required the advice and consent of the Senate. After having repeated problems with free-market apostles in the Department of Agriculture who were hostile to the tobacco program, he put a "hold" on certain nominees and prevented their confirmation. The situation quickly improved, so he lifted the hold and allowed the nominations to go forward.

Back in Kentucky, a political newcomer named Wallace Wilkinson trounced a GOP sacrificial lamb in the 1987 governor's race. McConnell intensified his speaking schedule at party events, hoping to rebuild shattered Republican morale.

His Senate leadership aspirations led him to attend weekly lunches with GOP senators of both the conservative and moderate camps, but he had undeniably migrated rightward since his arrival in Washington.[6] Although he had come of age among them, he now sometimes dismissively described the moderates as *"New York Times* Republicans."

McConnell cites several reasons for his evolution toward conservative orthodoxy. Dealing with labor unions as county judge and battling the federal bureaucracy as a Justice Department staffer had started this shift. Ronald Reagan then provided a powerful example that conservatism could work both in practice and politically. He saw its adherents endure both bad polls and bad press and still win. Conservative columnists like George Will and Paul Gigot also influenced him, as did his intellectual Senate colleague Phil Gramm, a brainy economics Ph.D. whom he found consistently impressive and persuasive in the Senate's substantive policy debates.

The year 1987 ended as a decidedly mixed one for McConnell. He had made headway as a senator, especially in the area of campaign finance reform, but had suffered some significant bad publicity. He was in the minority, but was steadily building his legislative skills. Perhaps best of all, his campaign war chest bulged with a million dollars—the product of consistent and determined asking over a broad spectrum of individual givers, industries, and interest groups.

In February 1988, Vice President Bush finished behind both Bob Dole and television evangelist Pat Robertson in the Iowa caucuses. Concerned, McConnell did more campaigning for Bush in the South.

Bush rebounded in New Hampshire and South Carolina and virtually swept the March 8 Super Tuesday primaries, including winning Kentucky's by an almost three-to-one margin over Dole. Despite the initial scare, it looked like McConnell had won his risky presidential wager. In the meantime, he defended Bush in the Senate Foreign Relations Committee, engaging in what he called political "hand-to-hand combat" with Massachusetts Democrat John Kerry, who was trying to tar the vice president with accusations of involvement in the Iran-contra scandal.

In gratitude for his support, Bush invited McConnell to spend the Fourth of July holiday at the family compound in Kennebunkport, Maine. It was a personal and professional milestone for McConnell, who had arrived in the Senate as a virtual unknown fewer than four years before.

Not everything worked out so well, however. In an attempt to draw attention to his efforts for tort reform, McConnell launched the "Sue for a Million Award." Much as former Wisconsin Democratic senator William Proxmire's "Golden Fleece Award" brought attention to notorious examples of government waste, McConnell's award was meant to spotlight egregious instances of trial attorneys out of control. The idea never got off the ground, however. The press was not that interested in a conservative angle or an obscure junior senator whose publicity-seeking was fairly transparent. McConnell soon dropped the idea altogether.

In Kentucky, Sloane released a poll showing McConnell leading him for the Senate by only 44 percent to 40 percent. Although these numbers were close, McConnell was actually relieved that they were no worse. In response, he tried to subtly put Governor Wilkinson's name in play for the Senate race to make it harder for Sloane to raise money.

McConnell served as a Republican voice available to the media during the Democratic National Convention at Atlanta in July. He harassed the vice-presidential nominee, Lloyd Bentsen of Texas, for simultaneously running to retain his Senate seat. At the Republican

National Convention in New Orleans the following month, McConnell served in the largely symbolic role as a deputy floor manager for Bush, introduced a speech by the secretary of labor, and acted as chairman of the Kentucky delegation. At Bush's request, he sounded out almost every Republican senator about prospective running mates. Most favored Dole for the sake of party unity, and none mentioned their colleague Dan Quayle. When McConnell reported to Bush, however, the nominee appeared to have already settled on the very junior senator from Indiana. Bush would go on to win the election, capturing Kentucky by a comfortable 56 percent to 44 percent in the process.

In late November, Sloane announced that he would not seek reelection as county judge. Perhaps McConnell's gambit with Heyburn had paid off, although the latter still lost in November to another Democrat. A few years later, a grateful McConnell backed Heyburn for a federal district judgeship.

By the end of the year McConnell had amassed about $1.2 million in campaign money and hoped to raise $2 million the next. As a sitting senator he could tap into a national fundraising base, which he would surely need against the well-connected Sloane. Employing a political misdirection play to confuse the opposition, McConnell claimed that he expected to run against Wilkinson and suggested, not entirely without basis, that the governor was trying to stir up Republican primary opposition for him.

Whomever he faced, McConnell knew he was in for a tough fight over the next two years. It turned out to be even harder than he could have imagined.

9

Fighting for Reelection
1989–1990

A MARCH 1989 POLL showed McConnell leading the major Democrats who might challenge him the next year. He was ahead of Governor Wilkinson, 45 percent to 33 percent; Harvey Sloane, 48 percent to 28 percent; and Lieutenant Governor Brereton Jones, 55 percent to 18 percent. Running a dozen points ahead of a sitting Democratic governor told McConnell that he had made significant political progress.

In mid-May, President Bush repaid McConnell's early support by coming to Kentucky for his first fundraiser since moving into the White House. Bush described McConnell as "a man of principle and character" and told the crowd, "In a very short time in the U.S. Senate, he's gained the kind of clout that Kentucky needs in Washington."[1] This marked the first invocation of a theme to which McConnell would return throughout his career. The evening grossed $1.3 million, a political fundraising record for a single event in Kentucky at the time, and netted $1 million. The success stunned McConnell. Even the *Courier-Journal* admitted that "McConnell continues to amaze," and "has gone far on a combination of shrewdness and luck."[2]

In the Senate, Wendell Ford had introduced a "motor voter" bill to strongly encourage states to register people to vote when they got a driver's license or conducted other business at various government offices. It also limited the circumstances in which states could purge voters from the rolls. McConnell opposed the measure as an unfunded mandate that would put poorly informed voters on the registration lists, thus opening the door to fraud, while having no effect on voter turnout. He also felt that it favored Democrats by making registration easier and more permanent. Foes sustained a filibuster by five votes in September 1990.

McConnell thought Ford's "hand-wringing about low voter turnout" was misplaced, if not altogether phony. It is, he has argued, "a sign of the health of our democracy that people feel secure enough about the health of the country and about its leaders where they don't have to obsess about politics all the time." He has professed not being troubled "in the least that the people having the most influence on the political process are the ones who are the most knowledgeable and the most interested."

In June, the U.S. Supreme Court held that burning an American flag was a form of free speech protected by the First Amendment.[3] That fall, and again the following year, McConnell cosponsored a constitutional amendment authorizing the federal and state governments to prohibit physical desecration of the flag. As his First Amendment thinking continued to develop, however, McConnell would change both his mind and his vote on this issue. The switch would dog him throughout his future campaigns.

At the annual Fancy Farm festivities in August, McConnell savaged Sloane as "the wimp from the East" and a "Northeast establishment liberal" whose "mommy left him a million dollars." Now, he continued, Sloane has come "down here to save us from ourselves." Describing himself as "moderate to conservative," McConnell warned that Sloane "hasn't gotten over his elitist behavior even yet because one of his lovely children is now in a private school up East" and he has a vacation home in "a foreign country." He did not mention that the house was in Canada, not some exotic locale.[4]

This all-out rhetorical assault on Sloane may be the most aggressive and inflammatory public speaking of McConnell's entire career. It perhaps reflected some authentic, Nixonian class resentment of the affluent and patrician Sloane. McConnell had none of the things for which he strafed Sloane, although his oldest daughter would soon be the first of the three to enroll at exclusive New England private colleges. Mainly, however, he wanted to make sure that western Kentucky's "Reagan Democrats" and agricultural yeomanry would not buy into Sloane's claims to "better represent the working men and women of Kentucky."

In what he now describes as one of his "most ridiculous" political moves, McConnell introduced an amendment to the defense spending bill to allow law enforcement to shoot down planes suspected of smuggling drugs. Senator John Kerry was a cosponsor, but Senator John Glenn ridiculed the measure. Larry Hopkins, a Republican congressman from Lexington, called it "goofy" and "irresponsible" and vowed to defeat it in conference committee.[5] That is exactly what happened, "as it should have," McConnell now acknowledges.

More prudently, in November he opposed a congressional pay raise that increased a senator's salary 9.7 percent, to $98,400, but reduced the permitted amount of honoraria from $35,800 to $26,568.[6] Although McConnell voted against it, this measure helped fuel an anti-incumbent sentiment in the electorate that would soon come to complicate his political life.

The year ended with the epochal events associated with the collapse of the Soviet communist empire in Eastern Europe. The Berlin Wall came down in Germany, the "Velvet Revolution" ousted Czechoslovakia's communist regime without bloodshed, and Romanian revolutionaries executed the tyrannical leader Ceauşescu and his wife on Christmas Day. These unexpectedly sudden American victories in the Cold War were exhilarating, as was President Bush's successful year-end military action to depose the corrupt Panamanian strongman Manuel Noriega. But the good feelings did not last long. The post–Cold War euphoria gave way with astonishing rapidity to what McConnell characterized as a "depressed America."

The year ended on a somber note for McConnell personally as well. His father was fighting for his life against colon cancer. The shadow of this old soldier's battle would darken his son's reelection campaign.

Although he had been running hard for reelection since the day of his election, McConnell officially announced his 1990 Senate candidacy in a January 16 state fly-around. Less than six years earlier he had strenuously argued that Huddleston's experience in office was irrelevant, or worse. Now, of necessity, he claimed that he had the "clout" required to help Kentucky. This was, as McConnell admits, "kind of a weak case." He was only a one-term senator, though he did have a good relationship with President Bush. It had, among other things, helped him persuade the president to nominate a Kentuckian as head of the Office of Surface Mining Reclamation and Enforcement, a critical position for the coal-rich commonwealth. But he did not have any extraordinary influence or standing in Washington.

McConnell knew that he had to capture between 20 percent and 30 percent of voting Democrats to win. Concluding that an endorsement strategy would work best, he went after three big ones.

The first, boldly, was the Fraternal Order of Police (FOP), an organization that had "hated his guts" when he was county judge. But neither had the FOP liked Sloane when he held the same office. At a crucial meeting of the Jefferson County lodge, a member told McConnell, "I don't like you, but I don't like Sloane either." Parried McConnell, "You ought to be happy because in this election you're gonna get rid of one of those son-of-a-bitches!" He won the Jefferson County FOP's public endorsement just days after announcing his candidacy, and others, including the statewide organization, followed suit. He thus enjoyed a decided advantage over Sloane on the crime issue.

Newspapers were McConnell's second endorsement source. He personally visited editorial boards around Kentucky and asked for their support. By the campaign's end, he had received almost every endorsement Kentucky newspapers made, including that of the *Herald-Leader*. That pillar of liberalism apparently deemed Sloane "too cozy with the coal industry" when it came to clean-air issues. The *Courier-Journal* endorsed Sloane, but after interviewing McConnell said as much or more that was complimentary of him than of their anointed one.

Of the *Courier-Journal* editorial board's meeting with McConnell, chief editorial writer Bert Emke recalls:

> He assumed we were not going to endorse him. What he was looking for was at least something that was sort of respectful. He talked about the race, how it had gone. He did it like a really good chess player. He talked about how, had he been Harvey, he would have run against himself, Mitch. He had thought it out a lot better than Harvey Sloane ever did. He just talked about tactics and strategy and, basically, how you win a race. I thought it was a brilliant performance. As a matter of fact, afterward, everybody just shook their heads and said, "This guy is incredible."[7]

The third endorsement target was a strong "Democrats for McConnell" organization, through which he hoped to show Democrats that it was okay to cross over and vote for a Republican. It included a former Democratic state chairman, a former U.S. attorney, and several Democratic mayors.

Firearms issues, like a proposed ban on assault weapons, were politically sensitive even in pro-gun Kentucky, especially after a deadly mass shooting at a Louisville plant the previous year. McConnell opposed gun control, but nonetheless declined contributions from the National Rifle Association (NRA) to make his independence clear. The NRA endorsed him anyway, and his relations with that influential group have continued to be good.

Sloane, a doctor, saw national health insurance as his biggest issue in the campaign,[8] but McConnell moved aggressively to take it away by introducing a five-year, $21.1 billion comprehensive health-care bill in April. The measure was more tactic than substance and went nowhere in the Senate, but it allowed McConnell to run an ad claiming, in a tagline he developed himself, "You don't have to be a doctor to deliver health care to Kentucky."[9] He also worked hard for, and won, the Kentucky Hospital Association's endorsement. To top off his successful strategy, McConnell also garnered endorsements from some agricultural groups.

Concerned that Democrats might try to make an issue out of his television adviser Roger Ailes, whom hostile national media regularly portrayed negatively, McConnell had his campaign manager, Steven J. Law, launch a preemptive strike against Sloane's media consultant, Frank Greer, by showing some of his harsh, negative ads at a Lexington press conference. Vowing never to let his adversary on the airwaves alone, McConnell countered an early Sloane ad with an aesthetically pleasing "accomplishment-type" spot about how he had helped the state's walking horse industry.

In March, Sloane made the mistake of saying he wanted to "rekindle the activism of the '60s." McConnell immediately seized on this comment to portray Sloane as unreliable on the military issues so crucial to counties around Fort Knox and Fort Campbell. McConnell's campaign went to considerable, even questionable, lengths to reinforce the perception of Sloane as a radical left-winger. For example, when Sloane appeared on a television call-in show, a staffer phoned in and, assuming the persona of a '60s liberal, thanked him for making Louisville a "nuclear-free zone." Sloane responded with criticism of nuclear power. McConnell used a tape of Sloane's comments to win over western Kentucky voters, for whom Paducah's uranium-enrichment plant was economically vital. After McConnell played the tape at a joint appearance with a squirming Sloane in front of workers at that plant, the union local quickly endorsed him, but the national union just as quickly ordered a retraction.

Campaign finance reform was back on the agenda at Capitol Hill. Thirty-five of forty-four Senate Republicans signed onto a McConnell campaign finance measure providing an alternative to Democratic proposals. He was becoming a national figure on the issue, but often in what he considered "a pejorative way." Pro-regulation elite media like the *New York Times* began to criticize him by name. Even some who saw him as courageous thought he might be making a politically stupid mistake to persist in his controversial position during a tough reelection campaign. But he believed that campaign finance was simply too arcane an issue to sway a Senate election in Kentucky, a conclusion in which he has been proved correct time and again.

An April newspaper poll showed McConnell beating Sloane 45 percent to 37 percent. His number, being less than the 50 percent believed so significant for an incumbent, worried McConnell. Both McConnell and Sloane easily won their May primaries, and in June, Sloane released a poll showing McConnell ahead only 42 percent to 37 percent. A few weeks later, a McConnell survey put his lead at 51 percent to 42 percent. McConnell thought these samplings were probably pretty accurate and was happy just to be ahead in both. He was especially relieved to be over 50 percent in his own sampling.

In the meantime, McConnell had to cast votes while Sloane did not. Family-leave legislation that would entitle employees to unpaid time off from work for births, adoptions, or serious health conditions was among the high profile issues. McConnell initially opposed it, but admits that he finally just "chickened out" politically and voted for it "to deny Sloane that issue." The Senate approved the measure in June, but President Bush vetoed it and the House of Representatives failed to override. McConnell had gotten the best of both worlds by voting for family leave without it becoming law.

By mid-summer, McConnell had amassed a $4.5 million campaign war chest, thrice Sloane's $1.5 million. Sloane says that McConnell's pro-Israel voting record made AIPAC "ruthless," with the pro-Israel group's head discouraging Jewish contributors who might have otherwise lent support to a Democrat.

Confident that he could handle Sloane in debate, McConnell insisted that any such encounter consist of a one-on-one format with no reporters, notes, or props. He did not want anyone coming between him and his prey.[10] His instincts were sound. He began an early September debate by asking Sloane to explain the 1985 farm bill. When Sloane predictably had trouble, McConnell tweaked, "Obviously they don't teach agriculture at Yale." Democrats typically appealed to the working class, but McConnell once again "decided to engage in ridicule" to prevent Sloane from doing so. He repeatedly called attention to Sloane's blueblood pedigree. Sloane "had inherited a million dollars" in contrast to McConnell himself, who claimed he "thought squash was something you ate." Belittling Sloane's status as a physician, McConnell needled, "He hasn't lanced a boil since medical school." Sloane concedes that McConnell "pretty well clobbered" him in the confrontation.[11]

The McConnell campaign moved aggressively and effectively to neutralize two potentially troublesome issues. To head off any attack by Sloane on contributions from sources associated with the troubled savings and loan industry, Law had surrogates and supporters criticize Sloane for his connections with an embattled real estate developer. When Sloane attacked McConnell over oil industry contributions in the wake of the high gasoline prices that followed on Iraq's invasion of Kuwait, McConnell had a response ad ready that called on Sloane to sell his significant personal holdings in Exxon.

Not all McConnell ads were negative, however. In August, he ran a "casework" spot about how he had helped a Vietnam veteran navigate the bureaucracy to get an artificial leg. Such pieces became staples of McConnell's subsequent campaigns.

An early September internal poll showed McConnell ahead by 15 points, 51 percent to 36 percent. Sloane's internal polling showed him 27 points behind.[12] A newspaper poll in late September had McConnell leading by 53 percent to 33 percent.

Things were looking good. But fresh from the emotional experience of taking his oldest daughter, Elly, to Smith College in Massachusetts, McConnell faced the death of his father, who succumbed to cancer on September 28. It was a tough time for McConnell emotionally, even though he had known it was coming for some time. The funeral forced him to cancel a second debate with Sloane, which was never rescheduled.

A month before the balloting, *Courier-Journal* columnist Robert T. Garrett wrote: "The McConnell campaign apparatus is nationally renowned. A marvel. A high-tech marriage of big bucks and political cunning. Its voter targeting is so sophisticated that, and I kid you not, it probably can tell you who in McLean County uses Crest and who uses Colgate. The vast gap between the two campaigns in sophistication, discipline, and ruthlessness was obvious from the beginning. McConnell is ready for almost any desperate move Sloane may make."[13]

That was the perception, and it was accurate. The race looked like a landslide in the making. Yet things had already begun to turn by the time President Bush reneged on his infamous "Read my lips: no new taxes" pledge. According to McConnell, "If Republicans are not about lower taxes, they are not about anything. It is the core issue that separates the Republicans and the Democrats." He immediately distanced himself from Bush's budget and tax deal, but the president's turnabout hurt all Republicans.

In the last month of the campaign, the political landscape shifted dramatically. An anti-incumbent sentiment took hold of the country. McConnell had been touting his relationship with Bush, but, suddenly, close to the president was the last place he wanted to be. So he pulled a television spot featuring First Lady Barbara Bush from the air and instead ran multiple ads highlighting his opposition to the Bush tax hike.

By late October the campaign turned into a war of television attack ads. McConnell ran one that characterized Sloane as a big spender. Sloane countered, assailing McConnell on health care. Sloane called McConnell a puppet of special interests and attacked him for voting to forgive Egyptian debt, as had been done to secure that country's involvement in the Gulf War coalition. In the all-out ad battle that followed, growing anti-Bush sentiment compelled McConnell to act as if he were a Democrat on many important issues.

An October 27 poll showed McConnell's lead down to 10 points, 44 percent to 34 percent. The next day, the *Courier-Journal* issued its endorsement of Sloane and followed up with a harsh profile of McConnell entitled "Low Profile but High Ambitions."[14] One of the most unfavorable preelection features ever written about McConnell, it pointed to his sometimes spotty attendance record for certain committee meetings and characterized him as generally ineffective. It also hit McConnell for sending too much franked mail to constituents.

Then McConnell's campaign discovered that Sloane had used an expired Drug Enforcement Agency registration number when prescribing sleeping pills for himself. McConnell had long thought that the crime issue might be decisive, so he drove this episode home with hard-hitting ads that showed pills and vials as an ominous voice intoned about Sloane's prescribing "powerful depressant" and "mood-altering" drugs for himself "at double the safe dose without a legal permit."

Congress was still in session sorting out the compromise budget bill containing Bush's tax increase. McConnell ran an ad saying voters could trust him to keep his promises and oppose it. Trying to steal Sloane's key theme, he added that everyone should pay their fair share, "including the rich." Even so, the issue was still taking its toll on all Republicans, including those, like McConnell, who had broken with Bush.

McConnell categorically ruled out a second debate with Sloane, saying that all his opponent had done lately was call him names. In truth, he did not want to risk giving Sloane a significant audience so close to the vote. Sloane was secretly relieved.

A week before the election McConnell's one-night internal tracking poll showed him behind for the first time. Somehow Senator Ford knew about this the next morning, which made it clear to McConnell that someone in the NRSC was "leaking numbers in order to lower expectations" about how many Senate seats Republicans would win. A "palpable dark cloud" was now hanging over the campaign and staff morale started sagging.[15] Publicly, McConnell denied that his lead had shrunk.

Sensing the momentum swing, Sloane shifted to an anti-Washington campaign theme. He told voters, "If you're sick and tired of the mess in Washington, of politicians that vote tax breaks for the rich and take huge pay increases and then sock it to the middle class and seniors, you can send 'em a message. I want to go to Washington to take the fat cats on and fight for you.... I've never been a slick politician and I know I'm not perfect, but I do care deeply. I've spent my whole life fighting for the people of Kentucky."

The Democratic Party complemented these spots with ones featuring a McConnell marionette dancing like a puppet on strings pulled by "special interests." It later came to light that Mary Bingham, the matriarch of the wealthy first family of Kentucky's liberal media, had funded these ads by routing over $200,000 through the Democratic National Committee into Sloane's campaign to circumvent legal contribution limits. This was ironic (not to mention illegal) since the Binghams and Sloane supported such limits and enjoyed an image of being the clean campaign and good government crowd. The Federal Election Commission found reason to believe Bingham and Sloane had violated federal law, but exercised its discretion not to prosecute.

McConnell was relying heavily on a sophisticated mail and phone operation. On the Friday before the election, McConnell, over Ailes's strenuous objection in an "angry phone call,"[16] announced that he was "going positive" for the rest of the campaign. His instincts told him that the public was simply sick of all the attacks. So he opted for ads featuring endorsements from newspapers and prominent Democrats. He was rebounding in his internal tracking polls, and he hoped that by backing off on the attacks he could entice Sloane into going positive, too. It didn't work.

During the campaign's last weekend McConnell endured some particularly ugly Democratic smears.[17] Still hurting from his father's death, McConnell recalls it as "the worst last ten days of a campaign" he has ever endured. He spoke with his pastor often. At a final airport rally in Louisville he put on a karate robe to symbolize the beating he had been taking.

When the votes were at last counted, McConnell defeated Sloane 52.5 percent to 47.5 percent. Sloane won their heavily Democratic home county of Jefferson by only 10,000 votes. McConnell broke even in the state's two western congressional districts and won all the others. He had narrowly escaped political disaster. After pulling even or ahead near the campaign's end, the Democrat simply had not had enough dollars to counter McConnell's media blitz.[18]

It had been "a helluva tough race" that sated Sloane's appetite for politics forever. Of his opponent, Sloane now says, "Senator McConnell is someone who knows himself. He's got a good compass. . . . Mitch's motto is to win. He looks for your underbelly."[19]

With good reason, McConnell considered his campaign as the best run in America that year. Having secured reelection, he felt he could afford to start looking beyond his own political future toward both building his national profile and helping other Kentucky Republicans emulate his winning example. He also made his first major move for national leadership by seeking the highly coveted chairmanship of the NRSC. The chairman wields considerable power in directing resources to campaigns across the country, often earning gratitude and loyalty from recipients that can prove quite useful in future leadership races and political fights. Texan Phil Gramm won the position, 26–17, but McConnell would both befriend him and keep pursuing the post.

The same day, Senate Democrats, who had increased their margin by one, elected Ford to be their whip. McConnell had not lost an election of any sort since his sophomore year of college. Ford's success made it especially galling for him to have done so now, if only within the GOP conference. Another hard session in the Senate minority had just been made a little harder.

10

New Term and New Wife
1991–1992

AFTER TAKING THE OATH to begin his second Senate term in January 1991, Mitch McConnell left for a vacation in the Virgin Islands. It was a short-lived respite. President Bush called the new Congress back to Washington for a special session to debate a resolution authorizing military action to oust Iraq from Kuwait, which it had invaded and occupied the previous August. The resolution passed the House, 250–83. Few in the Senate foresaw what would turn out to be a relatively easy military victory and the resolution barely passed, 52–47, with McConnell voting for what he considered "a war worth fighting."

After accomplishing the declared objective of expelling the Iraqi invasion forces, Bush decided to stop at the border instead of going on to Baghdad to depose the dictator Saddam Hussein. McConnell again backed Bush. "My inclination was that his decision was correct," McConnell explained in a 1999 interview. "I'm not sure that occupying a country as large as Iraq would have been in any way a pleasant experience for us. We would have been subject to all sorts of terrorist activities." McConnell's words would prove prescient, but his position on invading and occupying Iraq would later change with the circumstances.

After celebrating its military success, America soon lapsed into what McConnell called a "funky mood." Focus shifted from the international crisis to economic recession and domestic issues favorable to Democrats. Bush's unprecedented postwar popularity faded fast.

John Sherman Cooper died on February 21, 1991, the day after McConnell's forty-ninth birthday. McConnell spoke at a Somerset memorial service, extolling his role model's gentle ways, independence of mind, and courage of conviction.

McConnell was not much involved in the furor over Bush's nomination of Clarence Thomas to the Supreme Court. He voted to confirm Thomas and considers him "a thoughtful, articulate, and consistent conservative" who "will go down in history as one of the better Supreme Court justices."

On the year's major legislative issues, McConnell returned to his original position of opposing family-leave legislation, which passed both chambers before the House failed to override President Bush's veto. He also opposed the "Brady Bill," which imposed background checks and waiting periods for firearm purchases and the bill was successfully filibustered in the Senate. He supported "fast track" authority to expedite and simplify the negotiation and passage of trade treaties, and most-favored-nation trade status for China, both of which passed and were signed into law.

McConnell's foreign travel included a trip to Hong Kong, an experience which prompted him to sponsor the U.S.-Hong Kong Policy Act. The bill sought to support the Hong Kong Chinese by incorporating the Sino-British declaration on Hong Kong into American law and allowing the United States to treat Hong Kong separately from China on economic and trade matters after the British handover to the People's Republic. The bill became law on October 5, 1992. It was the first measure of which McConnell was primary sponsor ever to make it all the way through the legislative process, and it annoyed the Chinese, who saw it as interference in their domestic affairs.

Not all his legislative efforts were so successful, however. McConnell was not proud of his proposed Pornography Victims Compensation Act. It provided for civil suits against pornographers by any victims of violence who could prove that the smut caused the crime. The measure may have appealed to some social conservatives, but by creating a new legal cause of action, it stood in striking contrast to McConnell's other tort-reform efforts intended to limit the litigation explosion. The bill went nowhere.

Democrats were once again pushing campaign finance reform, this time calling for spending limits and taxpayer funding of elections. McConnell was floor manager for the opposition during a bruising two-week Senate debate. In this instance Republicans could not maintain a filibuster. The measure passed, 56–42, but met with a presidential veto almost a year later. Once again, McConnell and like-minded Republicans had held the line.

With two daughters now in expensive private colleges and no income except his Senate salary, McConnell found himself financially strapped. So he took a second job teaching a course on "American Political Parties and Elections" on Saturdays at Bellarmine University, a Catholic college close to his Louisville home. As before, teaching helped him gain additional perspective on the relationship between campaign finance and free speech under the First Amendment, as well as on the important role that political parties play in the American political system.

Teaching was not McConnell's only, nor his most significant, involvement with higher education in 1991. Having seen some of his Senate colleagues creating legacies that would outlive their legislative work,[1] he raised $2 million from private sources to create and endow what would become the McConnell Center for Political Leadership at the University of Louisville. The project began as a four-year scholarship program for ten undergraduate students from Kentucky per year, but quickly grew to include a distinguished lecture series, annual trips abroad—including a month in China during the students' junior summer—and to Washington and other parts of Kentucky, a series of seminars and internships, and an ambitious civics education program.

As it expanded and matured over the next fifteen years, the Center would host an impressive bipartisan array of speakers. Those who have either visited Louisville to meet with McConnell scholars include both Presidents Bush, former Soviet leader Mikhail Gorbachev, former British prime minister Margaret Thatcher, five secretaries of state, and several senators of both parties. McConnell always attends the events and helps ensure that programs provide a broad range of political perspectives.

The next year, 1992, brought another presidential campaign, and as McConnell says now, it "was clearly the year of the angry voter." President Bush's stratospheric 1991 poll numbers had deterred several strong Democratic candidates from starting a presidential campaign. Of those who did run, however, Governor Bill Clinton of Arkansas soon showed the innate political skills and acute Darwinian instinct for self-preservation with which America would become intimately familiar.

On the Republican side, traditional conservative and former Nixon speechwriter Patrick Buchanan ran a populist campaign that embarrassed Bush with a surprisingly strong showing in the New Hampshire primary. Texas billionaire Ross Perot joined the fray under the banner of the Reform Party and focused attention on America's enormous budget deficits and debt. Bush was also still paying a political price, especially with his conservative base, for having broken his "no new taxes" pledge. Everything was, McConnell recalls, "listing off in the wrong direction" for Republicans, whom he saw as having "lost our edge" after twelve years in power. It was a phenomenon he would serve long enough to experience again.

Come November, Bush lost, capturing what McConnell called an "embarrassingly low" 37 percent of the popular vote. The peculiar Perot garnered 19 percent. Yet McConnell rejects the conventional wisdom that this surprisingly strong third-party showing is why Clinton won. He places more emphasis on the shift in public concern from foreign affairs to domestic ones, where Democrats had a more activist agenda and had maneuvered Bush into several controversial vetoes. Republicans also lost a seat in the Senate.

It was during the 1992 campaign that McConnell first became significantly involved in a Kentucky congressional race. Feeling more politically secure after his recent reelection, he had dispatched a staffer to work on the campaign that moderate Republican Susan Stokes was running against Democratic incumbent Romano Mazzoli. Stokes lost, but McConnell now considered the seat as winnable with the right candidate.

He also got involved with a bill in the state legislature for the first time. Earlier in the year, the Kentucky General Assembly, reeling from the effects of a corruption scandal, sought to impose spending limits and partial public financing on gubernatorial campaigns. McConnell thought this measure would hurt the prospects of commonwealth Republicans and lobbied hard, but unsuccessfully, against it. Twice upheld against constitutional challenges, the reforms would hamstring Republican efforts in the next two campaigns for the Kentucky statehouse.

At the urging of Senate Republican leader Bob Dole, McConnell again sought the chairmanship of the NRSC. Then-chairman Phil Gramm was planning to run for president four years hence and Dole, who had the same desire, hoped to deny a potential rival the influential platform the NRSC provided. McConnell ran hard but lost again, this time by a single vote, 20–19. Despite their two tough races for this post, McConnell's affection and respect for Gramm continued to increase.

The lame duck President Bush received the first class of the University of Louisville's McConnell scholars at the White House. It was a bittersweet moment for McConnell, who was proud, but sobered by the fact that for the first time in his Senate career a Democrat would be sitting at the other end of Pennsylvania Avenue. He would be more than ever in the opposition and would find himself moving somewhat more to the political right as a result.

The otherwise dark year had at least one bright moment for McConnell. Having been single for thirteen years since his divorce, he had finally found a personal, and political, soul mate. Late in the year he became engaged to Elaine Chao, then thirty-nine and a remarkable person in her own right. Her family had immigrated to America from Taiwan when she was eight and spoke no English. Her family settled in a tiny apartment in Queens, New York, before moving to Long Island, where Elaine attended high school. She went on to earn an undergraduate degree from Mount Holyoke and an MBA from Harvard. A White House fellow for Reagan in 1983, she rose to be deputy secretary of transportation. In 1991, she was appointed director of the Peace Corps, and the next year she became president of the United Way, where her four-year tenure won plaudits for successfully restoring the scandal-tainted reputation of America's largest institution of private charitable giving.

Chao and McConnell would marry, fittingly for a pair of increasingly powerful conservatives, on Ronald Reagan's birthday, February 6, 1993. She brought much-needed affection, companionship, and intellectual stimulation to McConnell's life, and each proved an asset to the other in their ongoing political ascents. But for now, they found themselves confronting a distinctly inhospitable environment in a newly all-Democratic Washington.

11

Resistance and Revolution
1993–1994

W ITH DEMOCRATS CONTROLLING BOTH the White House and Congress for the first time in a dozen years, the filibuster was the
only way McConnell and his colleagues could stop Democratic initiatives from becoming law. But the forty-two Senate Republicans had
but a single-vote margin above the minimum required to block cloture.
Looking back later, (but well before he would lead an even smaller
COP contingent) McConnell called it "a formula for disaster."

Constantly searching for ways to increase his influence, McConnell changed his committee assignments. Disenchanted after six unful-
filling years on the Foreign Relations Committee, he moved to Appropriations and immediately became the ranking minority member on
the influential Foreign Operations Subcommittee, which exercised
jurisdiction over most foreign aid. This switch instantly made him
more powerful in the area of international affairs than he had ever
been during his tenure as a majority member on the Foreign Relations
panel. He also became the ranking Republican member on the Ethics
Committee, a move which would soon prove significant for both his
public and peer group profiles.

Although America was already coming out of the relatively mild
recession that had contributed to Bush's loss, President Clinton's first

big initiative was a $16 billion public-works "stimulus package." Senate Republicans stayed united through four cloture votes and eventually killed the proposal. Such was not the case with either Wendell Ford's "motor voter" measure or a campaign finance reform bill, both of which passed.

The former withstood a filibuster by four votes and became law on May 20. Democrats did not try to move the latter to a conference committee for more than a year after it passed, however. They coveted it more as a campaign issue in the upcoming 1994 elections than as an actual accomplishment. McConnell would make them regret their cynical decision to delay.

On October 28, 1993, McConnell's mother, Dean, died after a massive stroke. She had lavished attention on his upbringing, and her passing caused him to ponder the potential impact that the increased number of working mothers would have on contemporary and future generations.

In November, popular Louisville mayor Jerry Abramson announced that he would not run for governor in 1995, but indicated that he was considering challenging McConnell for the Senate in 1996. McConnell immediately set about subtly making Abramson's political life as difficult as possible to dissuade him from making the race.

Later that month McConnell was among the sixty senators who voted for the North American Free Trade Agreement (NAFTA), a measure that eliminated certain tariffs and moved the United States, Canada, and Mexico toward a single integrated market. NAFTA was so controversial in Kentucky that Senator Ford broke with President Clinton and voted against it. A firm believer in freer and more open trade, McConnell would also support the General Agreement on Tariffs and Trade (GATT) in a lame-duck session after the 1994 elections.

From his post on the Foreign Operations Subcommittee, McConnell opposed what he saw as a "Moscow-centric" focus on the former Soviet Union and excessive personalization of America's relationship with Russia. He believed America's goals in the region should include not only preventing Russia from reemerging as a threat, but also aggressively supporting the democratic development of other post-Soviet states, including Ukraine, Armenia, and Georgia in particular. He therefore did his best to earmark foreign assistance bills to help those nations, and his efforts were as successful as they could be given that he was toiling in the minority.

Perhaps the biggest foreign policy challenge of 1994 was in Bosnia, which had descended into crisis after the predominately Muslim population declared its independence from the former Yugoslavia in 1992. Bosnian Serbs sought to break away and form an ethnically separate "Greater Serbia." McConnell supported a resolution to lift the American arms embargo against the breakaway Bosnians so they could better defend themselves, but the measure failed when Vice President Al Gore broke a 50–50 tie by voting against the measure. The issue would continue to simmer, and occasionally boil, well into the next year and beyond.

In May, McConnell spoke against a gift ban that would have, among other things, severely limited senators' ability to have meals with constituents and others seeking to have input on issues and legislation. He deemed the ban and the larger lobbying reform measure to which it was attached to be inconsistent with the First Amendment and dangerous to the sort of ordinary social intercourse essential to the legislative process. McConnell proposed an amendment to modify the gift provisions while enhancing penalties for violations, a move that the liberal organization Common Cause correctly said would gut the bill. The amendment failed and the ban passed, 59–39, only to die later along with the broader Democratic campaign finance reform efforts.

That summer Ralph Nader visited Louisville to renew his long-running attack on McConnell for having what the advocate considered one of the worst anti-consumer voting records in modern history. McConnell fired back that Nader was a hack for rich plaintiffs' lawyers who funded his organization. Each man seemed to relish their ritual of recrimination, which had no noticeable impact on either of them or on public policy.

Earlier in the year, on March 29, the legendary Kentucky congressman William Natcher had died at the age of eighty-four. Natcher, from Kentucky's Second District, had made 18,401 consecutive roll call votes since coming to Congress in 1953, and had served as the chairman of the powerful House Appropriations Committee since 1992. His death opened a political door through which McConnell would lead Kentucky Republicans to power and, in the process, pioneering campaign themes that the national party would use that fall to capture the House for the first time in forty years.

In a misguided attempt to save money, Kentucky's Democratic governor, Brereton Jones, scheduled the special election to fill Natcher's seat for the same day as the primary election for the full term that would begin in 1995. Under the law, the election could have been held two weeks earlier. The additional time would prove to be pivotal to Kentucky's political future, and perhaps to America's.[1]

The district was 68 percent Democratic by registration and no Republican had represented it in the House since the Civil War. But McConnell had carried it in his two races and thought it was ripe for Republican picking. A GOP district convention nominated Ron Lewis, a Baptist minister disdained by some sophisticates because he owned a Christian bookstore, to run in the special election. McConnell immediately arranged to meet with Lewis and emerged convinced that the political novice was "thoroughly electable."[2] He decided on the spot that he "was going to go all out for this guy."

The Democrats nominated Joe Prather, a well-known and respected state senator, whose votes for tax increases made him vulnerable in McConnell's opinion. Because of the compressed campaign timeframe it was impossible for either candidate to develop his personality or his issues. McConnell quickly recognized that the race must be made into a referendum on something or someone in order for Lewis to win, and President Clinton presented the most obvious opportunity.

Not yet two years into his term, Clinton was already immensely unpopular in the socially conservative and tobacco-oriented district. He had pressed for gays in the military, passed the largest tax increase in American history, pushed a bureaucratic national health plan, and was tarnished by the tawdry-looking Arkansas land deal known as Whitewater. Moreover, as then-Republican House leader Newt Gingrich later recalled, people in the district "were deeply disturbed by the decay in Washington and thought a congressman with moral values might be a good thing."[3] Polling showed a majority of likely voters opposed to Clinton. Thus, the campaign strategy was set.[4]

On a plane to Richard Nixon's funeral in California, McConnell assured Republican National Committee chairman Haley Barbour that the seat was within the GOP's grasp. He urged Barbour to provide party financial support for the effort. Gingrich got interested, too, and soon national party money started flowing into Kentucky, especially after another Republican won a special election in Oklahoma.

Lewis's campaign raised $225,000, about $40,000 more than Prather, but held back until nine days before the election before taking to the airwaves. Since there was not enough time to run ads "introducing" Lewis to voters as is typically done in regular campaigns, McConnell called for an attack-only campaign built around a memorable television spot that used new video technology to show Prather's face morphing into Clinton's and back. Another ad featured back-to-back photos of Clinton and Prather on a spindle that spun faster and faster until the two images appeared to be one.[5]

The effect was devastating. Lewis won big—55 percent to 45 percent. The victory took on national significance as a template that Republicans could use to capture Congress in the fall. Senator Ford, humiliated by the loss of his long-Democratic home district, declared that Lewis would lose the seat a few months later against David Adkisson, a Harvard-educated mayor and his handpicked candidate for the full term.

By then McConnell had become convinced that Republicans could not only hold that seat, but also do what was once unthinkable and capture the First District in far western Kentucky, too. Tom Barlow, an unimpressive one-term incumbent Democrat, was not a formidable figure, but there was no obvious Republican challenger.

A few months earlier, Ed Whitfield, a man who had served a single term in the Kentucky state legislature as a Democrat before becoming a Washington lobbyist, had shown up in McConnell's office. Whitfield was a resident of Florida, but he told McConnell that he wanted to run for Congress from Kentucky's First District as a Republican.[6] McConnell's reaction was tepid. Undeterred, Whitfield later flew to Kentucky, registered as a Republican, and filed for the office, all on the same day. He then won the primary, though by only 405 votes out of 8,022 cast.

Most would have thought that this minuscule margin and turnout reflected the meager Republican prospects in the district, but McConnell was determined to pull off another major upset in a Kentucky congressional race. He told Whitfield he would need a minimum of $250,000 for a Lewis-style television blitz during the final three weeks of campaign. He advised Barbour and Bill Paxon, chairman of the National Republican Congressional Committee, "We've got another investment here that's worth making." They concurred, and national party help again poured into the Bluegrass State.

To emphasize the president's unpopularity, McConnell brought a life-sized cardboard cutout of Clinton to that year's Fancy Farm picnic in August and dared Democratic candidates to have their picture taken with it. None but the hapless Barlow would do so. The photo of the pair soon appeared in a Whitfield ad.

These congressional campaigns were being conducted against a backdrop of increasing bitterness between the two parties in Washington. For instance, McConnell had learned that the Senate would have to pass three motions subject to filibuster before conferees could be sent to sort out differences between the House and Senate's campaign finance bills. In a provocation to Democrats that he would deem his "proudest legislative accomplishment" up to that point, he successfully mounted the first-ever filibusters of these heretofore routine motions.[7] By doing so, he was also able to consume much of the limited time remaining in the Democrat-controlled 103rd Congress.

The Republican resistance featured old-fashioned tag-team talk-a-thons that kept the Senate in session overnight. McConnell set up a cot outside the Senate chamber, spoke for seven hours straight at one point, and persuaded twenty-three colleagues to help him.[8] Many Republicans feared the political fallout from blocking the much-ballyhooed reform, but he was confident that such concerns were wildly off the mark. In critical cloture votes in late September, he managed to secure enough Democratic votes against cutting off debate to effectively kill the bill. He had pulled off this parliamentary coup with almost no assistance from his party's leadership, and while being vilified on influential national editorial pages.

Having won that battle, McConnell made his way back home to Kentucky and laid it on the line for both Lewis and Whitfield, acting as de facto campaign manager for the latter.[9] On election night, Kentucky played a pivotal part in the Republican Revolution that reshaped the American political landscape for years to come. Whitfield beat Barlow 64,849 to 62,387. Lewis won in a landslide over Adkisson, 90,535 to 60,867.

Elsewhere in Kentucky, incumbent Republican congressmen Harold Rogers and Jim Bunning won easily over token opponents. McConnell could relish his role in putting Republicans in four of Kentucky's six House seats and giving the GOP a majority in the state's congressional delegation for the first time in modern memory. *Courier-Journal* political writer Al Cross christened McConnell "king of Kentucky politics" for "authoring" the Lewis and Whitfield wins.[10]

Kentucky's political mood had palpably changed. The state Democratic Party chairman called McConnell "the meanest junkyard dog in the Republican Party in Kentucky."[11] "It was a very exciting election, but one election does not a two-party system make," McConnell observed.[12]

Nationally, Republicans celebrated an unprecedented triumph. Republicans had won fifty-two House seats to take the majority for the first time in forty years. No Republican incumbent lost. The GOP also gained eight Senate seats to retake the majority in that chamber as well. The party topped off its stunning midterm success by taking twelve governorships, too.

McConnell put responsibility for the Democratic debacle squarely on Clinton. "For the first two years of the Clinton presidency we saw the real Bill Clinton—the Bill Clinton he wanted to be, philosophically." This hurt Democrats, especially in socially conservative Kentucky. But he knew that political highs never last too long, and the politically adept president promptly started tacking back to the center. The postelection Republican euphoria would vanish by the end of the next year.

As if anyone might doubt it, McConnell admitted after the 1994 election that, "I'm interested in tactics, and polling . . . the mechanics of it. I do have an interest in the techniques of modern campaigning." Despite having suspended some in-state fundraising in deference to Lewis and Whitfield, he still had a million dollars in the bank.[13] He was already preparing for his own campaign two years hence.

12

The Packwood Case
1995

NEWLY ENERGIZED, REPUBLICANS RETURNED to the Senate majority from which they had been banished by the election losses of 1986. For the first time in any of their Senate careers, their party also controlled the House of Representatives. Both chambers began by considering the items in the platform document on which GOP House candidates campaigned, the Contract with America. The House Republicans had promised a vote on each of the ten Contract items in the session's first hundred days.

As previously noted, McConnell was a vocal foe of one of the most prominent measures—a constitutional amendment to limit congressional terms. Calling term limits "a ridiculous idea," he explained, "The presumption is that if you learn more about something you are going to get worse. In fact it's just the opposite." He argued, "We have term limits now—they're called elections. And anybody can end our terms any time they want to." So adamant was McConnell's opposition to term limits that he introduced a symbolic resolution to repeal the Twenty-second Amendment, which provides that no person shall be elected president more than twice. He was therefore gratified when, in March, the proposed term-limits amendment failed to garner the necessary two-thirds majority to pass even the House.

Despite his belief that the House Republicans had advocated "too many constitutional amendments" in the Contract with America, McConnell did support one requiring a balanced federal budget. It passed the House, but fell a single vote short of the required supermajority in the Senate. All Senate Republicans voted in favor, but thirty-five Democrats, including Wendell Ford, stopped it from going to the states for ratification.

Although generally sympathetic to efforts to rein in federal spending, McConnell occasionally felt compelled to compromise on conservative consistency for reasons that were sometimes philosophical, but more often purely political. For example, when the House "zeroed out" the budget of the Appalachian Regional Commission, a Great Society agency extremely popular in some of the poorer parts of Kentucky, he offered an amendment to restore the funding. He made similar efforts to save funding for western Kentucky's Land Between the Lakes recreation area. He also sought to temper reductions other Republicans wanted in child nutrition programs, tried to increase funding for foreign aid, and began what would become a sustained campaign to impose sanctions against the reppressive regime in Burma.

A March Bluegrass Poll showed McConnell's approval rating at 60 percent and Ford's at 64 percent. But as the year progressed, McConnell had to deal with two matters that would have been politically difficult in the best of times, but were even more so in the year before a reelection campaign. One was another attempt to amend the Constitution to ban flag desecration, and the other was a series of sexual harassment charges against Oregon Republican and Senate Finance Committee chairman Bob Packwood.

In the five years since McConnell had cosponsored a constitutional amendment to ban flag desecration his First Amendment philosophy had matured, largely as a result of his leading role in the campaign finance reform debates. Seeing the need to be consistent in his support of the First Amendment rights and free speech generally, he voted against the flag amendment this time around. To mitigate the political fallout in his highly patriotic home state, he sponsored a largely symbolic bill providing for the protection of the flag. It would not be the end of the issue, however.

McConnell's role in the Packwood matter arose as a result of his service on the Senate Select Committee on Ethics, to which he had been appointed in 1993. Although he was not thrilled by the assignment, he thought that the Senate had an important responsibility to police its own. He had also developed an ever-increasing interest in institutional issues, such as campaign finance and term limits, and the new post fit in well with what, as the *New York Times* reported, "friends say its Mr. McConnell's plan to become not just a senator but a party figure and statesman, like Mr. Cooper."[1] In fact, Cooper had proposed creation of a permanent ethics committee in 1964, the year McConnell had interned for him.

McConnell saw the committee's primary purpose as preventative. Comprised of three members from each party, with four votes required for any action, it mainly issued advice and guidance to keep senators out of trouble. But it also investigated senators and recommended sanctions as appropriate.

The Packwood case had come to the Ethics Committee just before McConnell did, in response to allegations published in the *Washington Post*. The newspaper reported that he had made a series of what the Ethics Committee would ultimately characterize as "aggressive, blatantly sexual advances, mostly directed at members of his own staff or others whose livelihoods were connected in some way to his power and authority as a Senator."[2] Packwood promptly issued a generalized apology for causing "any individual discomfort or embarrassment" and checked himself into an alcoholism treatment program for a few days.[3]

McConnell had known Packwood longer than he had any other senator, having first met him while working as a congressional staffer in the late 1960s. He appreciated the Oregon moderate as a consistent free trader and an expert in tax and entitlement programs. They had also worked well together against Democratic campaign finance reform proposals.

The committee pursued all leads, believing that its reputation and that of the Senate dictated a thorough investigation. After almost a year, Packwood mentioned some recorded personal diaries during a deposition. The committee voted unanimously to seek the diary tapes, but Packwood reneged on a promise to produce them until, many months later, the courts forced him to give them up.[4] Once Packwood turned over the diaries, however, it was clear that he had tried to record over incriminating parts after the investigation had begun.

McConnell assumed the chairmanship of the Ethics Committee when Republicans returned to the majority after the 1994 elections. Shortly thereafter, the committee announced that it had substantial credible evidence against Packwood in three areas: trying to get jobs from lobbyists for his former wife in order to reduce his alimony obligations; sexual misconduct, including at least eighteen separate unwanted advances by Packwood against women between 1969 and 1990; and tampering with evidence in the form of his diaries.

Packwood declined a public hearing, and the Ethics Committee split evenly on the issue after Senator Barbara Boxer, a California Democrat, said she would seek a vote in the full Senate. McConnell opposed this effort to force the committee's hand or, as he saw it, to have the full Senate micromanage the committee. With most of America's attention riveted on the O. J. Simpson murder trial, the matter proceeded to the Senate floor. McConnell's position prevailed, 52–48, with Daniel Patrick Moynihan of New York as the only Democrat voting against public hearings.

On August 25, during the Senate's summer recess, a desperately scrambling Packwood reversed himself and requested public hearings. He criticized the committee as "an Inquisition." Republicans, having already cast tough votes against a public hearing, were outraged by his about-face.

McConnell had already concluded that the evidence-tampering charge was so serious that it constituted a crime against the Senate in the nature of obstruction of justice. It was a direct attempt to frustrate the investigation, and it appeared to him that the only appropriate penalty would be to expel Packwood. All committee members concurred, so McConnell and Nevada's Richard Bryan, the ranking Democrat, told Packwood of the recommendation.

Majority leader Bob Dole was shocked when McConnell informed him of the proposed punishment, saying it seemed overly harsh. McConnell advised him to wait for the next day's release of evidence. Then he introduced a resolution calling for Packwood's expulsion.

On September 7 the committee released a supporting report that laid out the overwhelming evidence in thousands of pages of damning detail.[5] Dismissing Packwood's protests, McConnell declared, "As happens with increasing frequency these days the victimizer is now claiming the mantle of the victim. The one who deliberately abused the process now wants to manipulate it to his advantage. That won't wash."[6] Packwood emotionally announced his resignation on the Senate floor that afternoon.

While McConnell had achieved the outcome he sought—Packwood was no longer a member of the U.S. Senate—his committee came under criticism for its handling of the case. Arizona Republican John McCain was one senator who derided the committee's work. McCain had endured a fourteen-month Ethics Committee investigation of his own after helping a corrupt savings and loan figure, Charles Keating Jr., who had contributed $112,000 to his campaigns. He was merely admonished for exercising poor judgment, but said the ordeal was "more painful than being held as a prisoner of war in North Vietnam."[7] Wyoming's Alan Simpson was also critical, saying that the committee had been created "to avoid a public hanging, frontier justice and vigilante justice," but "something surely has gone awry."[8]

McConnell strongly disagreed. He saw the outcome as a triumphant moment for the institution. "The handling of the Packwood case enhanced the stature of the Senate," he said, believing that it dispelled the notion that the body could not or would not police itself. He believed that the public was satisfied with the result and that faith in the Senate had been fortified.

McConnell's growing national reputation was enhanced as well. In a major profile piece, the *New York Times* described him as a "blend of understatement and ambition" and "a sober-sided legislator with a subterranean profile from a not-very-influential state" who had "landed with a thump on the national political scene." Calling the Packwood saga perhaps "the most contentious investigation" in Senate history, the *Times* noted of McConnell that "even many Democrats who otherwise hold him in low regard allow that he has run the inquiry in a generally fair and honest way."[9]

McConnell was quoted as following what he calls a "Jeffersonian" (although it might be better described as Burkean) approach to public office "where you were elected to follow your best judgment and if your judgment falls out of favor with the people, they have an opportunity at the next election to do something about it." As evidence of McConnell's "streaks of independence" and ignoring of "party dogma," the *Times* cited his resistance to North Carolina Republican Jesse Helms's efforts to "sharply reduce foreign aid" and his opposition to "both term limits and a constitutional amendment against flag burning."

According to the article, McConnell's "willingness to shoulder unpopular causes," such as campaign finance reform and the Ethics Committee assignment, "has won him considerable regard among fellow Republicans, who gave him a spontaneous standing ovation at a party luncheon this summer." A former aide to Todd Hollenbach was quoted as saying that politicians like McConnell "exist to demonstrate their mastery of the political process." McConnell regarded this as a compliment.

That fall featured Kentucky's first governor's race under the state's new campaign finance law. McConnell had strongly opposed the measure, which offered candidates a relatively small sum of public dollars as an incentive to limit their overall spending. Larry Forgy, the Republican nominee, opted to accept the new law's free money and submit to its spending limit. McConnell considered this a tremendous tactical blunder and remained largely aloof from Forgy's campaign.

The Democratic candidate, Lieutenant Governor Paul Patton, prevailed over Forgy by a mere 20,378-vote margin out of 983,797 ballots cast. It was ironic, McConnell thought, that Forgy's support for the spending limit law had probably cost him his last chance to win the office he had so long coveted. Having willingly submitted to stay on an equal financial footing with his foe, Forgy simply had no way to overcome the many built-in advantages that the more numerous Democrats enjoyed. A Republican in Kentucky just had to have enough money to deal with a hostile political environment produced by decades of Democratic dominance and the liberal media in Kentucky's largest cities.

But Forgy did not go gently into the good night of political obscurity. He claimed Democratic fraud and corruption. A prosecution of some Patton pals and labor cronies for violating a state law against coordinated activities would continue for years, as would Forgy's colorful brand of bitterness. McConnell earned some of Forgy's ire after filing a friend-of-the-court brief challenging the constitutionality of the campaign finance laws under which the Democrats had been charged. He did so not out of hostility to Forgy, however, but on the belief that protecting First Amendment rights trumped party loyalty.

Back in Washington, the battles over the budget and Medicare that shut down the federal government dominated the year-end news. The substance of the disputes became largely irrelevant as President Bill Clinton clearly won the public relations battle against his Republican rival Gingrich, improving the Democrats' political prospects in the process. The change in the American political climate was immediate and palpable.

McConnell considered the Contract with America to have been a tactical mistake. He thought it had "overpromised" and raised public expectations unrealistically high given that the presidency remained in the hands of the other party. Gingrich had been a "great revolutionary," but proved less adept at governing. Clinton was now making a radical recovery from the dire straits in which he had found himself a mere twelve months before.

Just a year after the joyous 1994 elections and despite their congressional majorities, Republicans found themselves on the defensive again. Against this sobering backdrop, McConnell began his campaign for a third Senate term.

13

Third Term's a Charm
1996

M CCONNELL HAD NOT PURSUED fundraising as early or as vigorously during his second Senate term as he had in his first, when he had been a top target of national Democrats.[1] He had suspended most of his efforts in 1995 to help the gubernatorial campaign of Larry Forgy, who had needed to raise a certain amount of money to qualify for public largesse under Kentucky's new campaign finance law so as the year began McConnell had a little more than $2 million in his campaign kitty, about $1 million less than at the same point in 1990.

The Democratic establishment did not settle on a standard bearer until late in 1995. Before that, as was his custom, McConnell had tried to influence the other party's decision in his favor.

Still suspecting that Louisville mayor Jerry Abramson would run against him, he had his former aide and then–state Republican chairman, Terry Carmack, stage some public events to take some of the bloom off Abramson's rose. One was a press conference at which Carmack questioned how and why Abramson's wife had become director of a savings and loan and profited handsomely from a lucrative stock transaction. McConnell also drew on his connections in the American Jewish community to undermine Abramson's support. In late 1994, after an extended public performance as a political Hamlet, the risk-averse Abramson finally announced that he would skip the Senate race.

Charlie Owen was perhaps McConnell's most dangerous potential Democratic foe for the 1996 race. Owen had won bipartisan praise as director of the Kentucky Crime Commission and had made a fortune in cable television and real estate. He had spent around $800,000 in losing the Democratic primary for Louisville's congressional seat in 1994, but that defeat made barely a dent in his bank account. To McConnell's relief, however, Owen also opted out of the Senate race in late 1995.

Jim Squires, a former editor of the *Chicago Tribune* who came to Kentucky in 1990 to become a horseman, had also made some noises about running. McConnell had his staff research Squires's newspaper writing and send letters to the editor of the *Herald-Leader* pointing out some of the more controversial gleanings. But Squires ultimately decided to stay in the barn, too.

McConnell sometimes wondered if he had outsmarted himself by running off these potential challengers only to open the door for a stronger one. Desperate to find a credible Democratic candidate, Senator Wendell Ford and Governor Paul Patton settled on Steve Beshear, a former Kentucky attorney general and lieutenant governor, promising him that they would raise a million dollars each if he would make the race. Beshear had no illusions about his chances of success, but for the sake of his party, and hoping to ride the coattails of President Clinton's likely reelection, he got in the race.[2]

The campaign got off to an ominous start for McConnell. After formally announcing his reelection campaign on January 17, 1996, he boarded a small plane for his traditional state fly-around. The aircraft sputtered after starting and stalled on the runway. Someone had mistakenly filled its tank with the wrong kind of fuel, an error that could have been fatal if the flight had gotten off the ground before the fuel cycled into the engine. Badly shaken but undaunted, McConnell changed planes and was belatedly airborne to Frankfort to file his candidacy papers.

In so doing, McConnell once again sought to emulate John Sherman Cooper, who was then the only Kentucky Republican to have won three statewide races. Although by 1996 McConnell was clearly more conservative than Cooper, he explained, "My politics are more like Ronald Reagan's, but my aspirations are more like John Sherman Cooper's."[3] So he stood without reservation before Cooper's bronze bust in the State Capitol to remind voters that he was every bit as courageous as the beloved Kentucky icon had been. To support his case, McConnell gave examples of independence such as his defense of the First Amendment in the campaign finance debate, his role in the Packwood proceedings, and his opposition to the flag-burning amendment.

According to *Courier-Journal* reporter Al Cross, McConnell created a campaign profile as a "strong leader who advanced Kentucky's interests."[4] He had attained political power, and repeatedly promised to use it for the moderate-sounding purpose of taking "some of the rough edges off the Republican revolution when Kentucky's vital interests are at stake." In a state where Democrats still held a decided registration advantage, he emphasized bipartisanship and made it clear that he was a Kentuckian first and a conservative Republican second. He wanted to make it difficult for Democrats to depict him as a heartless partisan the way they had done to the beleaguered Gingrich.[5]

But while wooing the political middle, McConnell could still attack the Clinton administration's efforts to regulate tobacco. He also sounded some popular conservative themes, saying he was running "to finish the job of balancing the budget, reforming the welfare culture, shrinking the government, and saving Medicare from financial collapse." And he promised to stay on the offensive during a campaign stressing "courage, clout, and independence."

Never one to apologize for bringing home federal projects, McConnell was determined to burnish the conservationist credentials he had earned as county judge. Invoking the progressive Republican legacy of Theodore Roosevelt, he overcame resistance from Ford to win something for Kentucky that every other state already had—a federal wildlife refuge.

A February newspaper poll showed McConnell leading Beshear by only 50 percent to 36 percent despite enjoying a much larger 83 percent to 49 percent advantage in name recognition. A group supporting a constitutional amendment banning flag burning released a poll showing more support for replacing McConnell than returning him to office. The Republican pollster who had performed this work resigned from the account after receiving a blistering call from McConnell.

In April, McConnell delivered the Republican response to one of President Clinton's weekly radio addresses. He criticized the president for overly personalizing diplomacy with Russian president Boris Yeltsin, just as he had faulted President Bush for doing the same thing with Mikhail Gorbachev. McConnell believed that both presidents had paid insufficient attention to advancing freedom in the former Soviet republics, with which he advocated stronger relationships. He called Deputy Secretary of State Strobe Talbott, the Clinton administration's point man for Russia policy, "the brightest, best-educated man I've ever met [who's] been most consistently wrong."[6]

By then, McConnell had concluded that, as the *New York Times* put it, his "real opportunity to influence [foreign] policy lay where the money was."[7] To this end, he made the absolute most of his chairmanship of the Foreign Operations Subcommittee of the Appropriations Committee. As one commentator observed, the controversial chairman of the Foreign Relations Committee, Jesse Helms, "may have the megaphone, but McConnell has the money."[8] To the more than occasional consternation of Clinton's foreign policy team, McConnell used his subcommittee post to earmark funds in ways that frustrated administration objectives while favoring his own, such as more aggressive American involvement in mediating a dispute between Armenia and Azerbaijan.

Most Kentuckians were blissfully unaware that their senator was a leading advocate for the citizens of central Asia, but they were indirect beneficiaries of his burgeoning influence. McConnell's power of the purse in international affairs became a form of legislative currency that he could exchange or spend on accomplishments helpful to the homefolk and, politically, to himself.

Much to McConnell's surprise, former Democratic governor Wallace Wilkinson endorsed him in April, probably out of animus for Beshear. Wilkinson was controversial, if not corrupt, and McConnell was not even assembling a "Democrats for McConnell" organization for this campaign. Still, he welcomed the support from such a prominent Democrat.

Steven Law, who had managed McConnell's 1990 campaign, was in Washington serving as his chief of staff and was not enthusiastic about an extended stint back in the Bluegrass running another campaign. So McConnell tapped Kyle Simmons, a savvy former press secretary, for the job. Roger Ailes had left the political wars to head up the new Fox News network, but McConnell retained his former firm and, as he had since the 1984 campaign, relied on trusted pollster Jan R. van Lohuizen.

Bob Dole, then seventy-three, was at long last the Republican presidential standard bearer, but there was not much optimism about his chances. McConnell backed Dole but ran his own race with complete independence from the Kansan's national campaign. When Dole resigned from the Senate to focus on his presidential bid, Trent Lott of Mississippi, with whom McConnell considered himself "closely allied," succeeded to the position of majority leader.

One of McConnell's favorite campaign maxims is "If someone flicks a pebble at you, hurl a boulder back." His response to any attack is not merely to counterattack, but to escalate. So when Beshear ran a rather benign pre-primary ad linking McConnell to the much-maligned Gingrich, McConnell fired back with an immediate radio response that referred to Beshear as "a lawyer-lobbyist for hire, bankrolled by personal injury and corporate lawyers," and made an issue out of the Democrat's lucrative role in the controversial liquidation of a large Kentucky insurance company. The campaign's tone was set.

Like Sloane before him, Beshear believed that campaign finance could be a key to beating McConnell in November. As if to evidence his disagreement, and his confidence, McConnell proceeded to lead another successful filibuster against the first incarnation of what would come to be called the McCain-Feingold bill to ban "soft money," or unlimited contributions to political parties, and set campaign spending limits. Recalling how Clinton had gotten the best of Gingrich the previous year, however, McConnell worried much more about Medicare's potential power as a campaign issue.

In McConnell's mind, there are always two categories of issues in a campaign. One is "walking-around issues," which he discusses freely with citizens and the press. The other is "real issues," which have the potential to actually affect the outcome. McConnell plays the latter quite close to the vest, guarding his comments closely and timing them for maximum impact when revealed in television ads against an unprepared opponent. Most campaigns err, he believes, by talking too freely with media about matters they should be keeping confidential or under more calculated control.

When Elaine Chao decided to step down as leader of the United Way, the organization's board proposed to pay her a generous bonus for having successfully rehabilitated the agency's public image and operations. Michael Gartner, a former *Courier-Journal* editor who had been deposed as head of NBC News after the network rigged tests in a report about General Motors trucks, wrote a column for Gannett newspapers harshly criticizing her. "Mad as hell," McConnell responded with a hard-hitting piece of his own that garroted Gartner as a "peddler of tabloid trash" guilty of "producing phony film footage of news stories and then covering up his unethical actions." Despite her husband's gallant defense, Chao declined the money. Freed to stump for McConnell, however, she proved to be a major political asset, and her presence made the campaign trail a much more pleasant place for him than it had been in 1990.

From the opening of the McConnell Center for Political Leadership at the University of Louisville in 1991, the press had attacked its founder for refusing to disclose the identities of donors. McConnell and the university took the position that the school, which was the entity that actually received the donated funds, could grant anonymity to charitable givers. In June 1996, as the Senate campaign heated up, the *Courier-Journal* rekindled this issue with an article and open-records request. This battle would be fought out in the courts over the next several years, with the newspaper ultimately winning, but went nowhere as a campaign issue.

As he had with family-leave legislation in 1990, McConnell in July made a purely political decision to vote for an increase in the minimum wage despite believing it was bad policy if enacted without corresponding business tax relief. Such exercises in expedience exemplified another McConnell campaign axiom: "You've got to get elected before you can be a statesman." Beshear saw it differently, observing that McConnell has "never let any issue stand in the way of getting elected or reelected."[9]

McConnell's minimum-wage concession also reflected his concern about the "gender gap" that had helped bring down President Bush four years before. He moved early and effectively to close that gap. The Olympics then under way in Atlanta drew an extremely large audience comprised of more women than men. McConnell ran expensive sixty-second ads during the games that highlighted his political independence and role in the Packwood case. Later in the campaign, a female Democratic operative upon whom Packwood had preyed would come to Kentucky and tearfully call McConnell "a hero." Beshear vainly tried to claim that McConnell was among senators who had protected Packwood far too long before acting, but such claims were ineffective.

Democrats, McConnell believed, were both attacking his marital history and trying to send discreetly racist messages about his Chinese-American wife. Beshear spoke often about his long marriage, and at a rural Kentucky Fourth of July celebration that Chao attended, former governor Edward T. Breathitt, a Beshear campaign surrogate, urged the crowd to send "a real all-American family to represent Kentucky in Washington." Furious, McConnell decided to call attention to these tactics in hopes of ending them. He said, to the apparent agreement of most Kentuckians, that Chao's inspiring life story made her the personification of the American dream.

July campaign finance reports revealed that McConnell had raised $3.7 million. Appearing beside his foe at a Kentucky Farm Bureau function that month, McConnell turned Beshear's frequent invocations of Wendell Ford back against him by noting that Ford had voted with the bureau on only six of fifteen major issues in the past session of Congress. McConnell also pointed out that he had been with the bureau on all fifteen, thus proving himself a friend of the farmer. It was a difficult point for Beshear to parry.

In August, McConnell's outnumbered but imaginative shock troops descended on the annual Fancy Farm picnic. As he had with Harvey Sloane in the 1990 campaign, McConnell once again used ridicule to brand Beshear as a hypocrite for his pretensions of solidarity with ordinary working Kentuckians. Mocking the Democrat for membership in an exclusive Lexington hunt club, the Republican crowd responded with shouts of "Tally-Ho!" whenever Beshear uttered any form of the word "working."

"Steve's been pretending to be a folksy, shotgun-totin,' pickup-drivin' defender of the working class," McConnell needled. "The problem is, can you imagine a working-class hero who wears a hunting pink and brandishes a riding crop?"[10] Having discovered a photo of Beshear in full British-style fox-hunting regalia, the McConnell forces started sending a similarly attired character called "Hunt Man" to some of the Democrat's public appearances. Similar derision would soon force Beshear to spend about $80,000 of desperately needed campaign money to discharge a lingering debt from his unsuccessful gubernatorial campaign of almost a decade earlier.

McConnell again chaired Kentucky's delegation to the Republican National Convention, which was held in San Diego in mid-August. He thought Dick Cheney of Wyoming made the most sense as Dole's running mate, but Jack Kemp, the former quarterback, congressman, and secretary of Housing and Urban Development, got the nod. McConnell thought that Dole and Kemp failed to mesh, although there may have been nothing either man could actually do to impede Clinton's march to reelection.

Having again won the state Fraternal Order of Police endorsement in March despite some adverse reactions to his vote on the flag-burning amendment, McConnell next moved to solidify support from veterans' organizations. During a meeting with a large group in Louisville, he expected and took flak for his controversial stance. But even the military men seemed to give him some credit for courage, and a few even said his position reflected the values for which they had fought.

An internal poll released in late August showed McConnell up 51 percent to 34 percent. It was a good margin, but not necessarily a great one, for an incumbent seeking reelection. After Labor Day, he went on the air with an award-winning sixty-second ad about his efforts to help residents of Hickman, Kentucky, after part of their little town fell off a bluff and into the Mississippi River. The spots featured an appealing little old lady named Anna Belle Newton and (although the project to stabilize Hickman on its precarious perch turned out to be extraordinarily difficult and expensive), painted a compelling picture of both McConnell's clout and his commitment to constituent service. Beshear began running ads in early September, one biographical and another attacking McConnell along the same lines as Sloane had in 1990.

In mid-September, McConnell launched a preemptive strike on the Medicare issue by running a television spot rebutting some of Beshear's accusations and hitting him back on Social Security. Working to capture all-important Democratic votes, McConnell also ran positive ads touting his support for school lunch programs and tax breaks for college tuition. Beshear countered with yet another ad linking McConnell to Gingrich and claiming, as President Clinton had during the prior year's government shutdown, that Republicans were out to cut Medicare.

Later that month, McConnell and Beshear debated one-on-one with only a moderator between them. McConnell challenged Beshear to quit his hunt club, which had no black members. Beshear criticized McConnell for not releasing his tax returns, to which McConnell responded with a request that Beshear release his law firm's billing records for its government work. He also attacked Beshear for appearing with the anti-tobacco Clinton during a western Kentucky trip instead of attending a pro-tobacco rally that was held the same day.

Neither the ads nor the debate noticeably changed the race. A poll published on October 5 gave McConnell the lead 50 percent to

38 percent. He led among women 49 percent to 38 percent, probably because of his Packwood and education ads. *Courier-Journal* columnist Robert T. Garrett referred to "the feminized McConnell" and wrote, "It's pretty obvious what the strategy is in McConnell's bid to get his third six-year ticket to the Senate dining room punched. He's looked into the abyss known as 'the gender gap' and he's gotten religion. He can't do enough for those women."[11] Beshear tried to counter with what McConnell considered "an excellent ad" featuring two women criticizing his votes against certain programs for children and senior citizens, but it did not seem to move the meter much, if any.

President Clinton came to Louisville on October 11 to campaign for both himself and Beshear. He had been to the hotly contested state twice before and would return on election eve, before barely carrying it, with 636,614 votes to Dole's 623,283. It was the narrowest winning margin in any state he won, and at no time leading up to the election did anyone see evidence of presidential coattails that could benefit Beshear in the Senate contest.

Down the campaign homestretch, Beshear tried to use NAFTA and McConnell's international travel to depict him as favoring foreign interests over Kentucky's own. McConnell called Beshear "reckless and extreme" on crime. Playing on his opponent's last name, McConnell ran two of his trademark humorous, animal-oriented spots. One accused Beshear of "fleecing" taxpayers and showed footage of sheep while warning, "Don't get 'besheared.'" Another, written by Steven Law to counterattack on NAFTA, showed sheep wearing sunglasses in various locations around the world to illustrate foreign investments held in Beshear's mutual funds, and said that Beshear "thinks 'ewe' should pay more." At best, McConnell recalls, it succeeded "in futzing up the issue."

On October 17, McConnell and Beshear had another "debate," this time in the joint press conference format. There was a presidential debate that same evening, so Beshear requested rescheduling. Naturally McConnell refused, unwilling to give his adversary any larger an audience than he absolutely had to.

Beshear estimates that he had to spend almost 90 percent of his campaign time trying to raise money to offset the nearly two-to-one financial advantage of McConnell's $5 million war chest.[12] Aside from the big-city dailies, the *Courier-Journal* and the *Herald-Leader*, McConnell once again earned endorsements from most Kentucky newspapers. Even his pollster, the ever-cautious van Lohuizen, was beginning to hint that the victory margin could be big.

McConnell's was the first race television networks called that night. He won going away, 724,794 to 560,012, or 55 percent to 43 percent. Dole's loss to Clinton did not prevent McConnell from carrying every Kentucky congressional district, 88 of the state's 120 counties, including heavily Democratic Jefferson County with 53 percent of its vote, winning a majority of senior citizens, and running well in heavily Democratic western Kentucky counties. Republican representatives Ron Lewis and Ed Whitfield won reelection in that region's congressional districts, too. In Louisville, Republican Anne Northup, a McConnell protégé, ousted one-term Democratic incumbent Mike Ward, giving the GOP an unprecedented five of Kentucky's six House seats.

McConnell savored his first landslide. "I think there isn't any question that after the '96 election I began to be treated with a lot more respect," he says. "There is nothing people like more than success. My detractors at the big newspapers simply could not explain away this margin. After every other election I had endured these postelection analyses arguing that I had somehow not beaten anybody very good, or it hadn't been much of a margin, or this or that, or luck. There was simply no way to explain this in any other way than that it was a first-class ass-kicking and against a guy who was a credible person."

All his critics could say was what they always said—that he spent more money than his opponent. But, as McConnell explained, "All that does is help balance out all the advantages Democrats have. With party registration two to one, the AFL-CIO in big-time, the KEA [Kentucky Education Association] in big-time, the two big newspapers not only killing you on the editorial page, but trying to kill you on the news pages as well, a spending edge is the only thing that gives a Republican a chance to compete. But I have been treated since the 1996 election with a great deal more deference, even by my enemies in the state, and it's been nice."

To make his victory even sweeter, McConnell finally won unopposed election as chairman of the NRSC. His broad and sustained electoral successes and his deft handling of difficult issues no doubt paved the way to a post that he had sought twice before. Nor did it hurt his chances to have the solid support of his friends in high places, like majority leader Lott.

An exhilarating year was over. McConnell now headed back to the Capitol, where Democrat Bill Clinton still presided over a divided government. Historic events were on the horizon.

14

Going National
1997

Not wanting to be in Washington for the Clinton inaugural, McConnell joined a "CoDel," or congressional delegation, for a January trip to the Middle East and Bosnia. Upon returning, he immersed himself in opposition to the McCain-Feingold campaign finance reform bill that its sponsors had reintroduced the day after the inauguration. Resisting it would dominate his year.

It is widely accepted that, in the words of one scholar, "During the 1996 election, the most serious campaign finance violations since Watergate took place."[1] There was bipartisan consensus that the fundraising excesses of the Clinton-Gore campaign and the Democratic National Committee (DNC) cried out for some kind of congressional response. The closely coordinated Clinton-Gore/DNC campaign had accepted (and ultimately had to return) almost $3 million in illegal foreign contributions, solicited funds on federal property, and essentially sold access to decision makers and White House perks.[2]

Senate majority leader Trent Lott faced what McConnell called "a Hobson's choice" in assigning a Senate committee to investigate the Clinton campaign's fundraising irregularities. Lott could give it either to the Commerce Committee, chaired by the righteous reformer John McCain, or to the Governmental Affairs Committee, where Tennessee's Fred Thompson wielded the gavel. Both men had a fondness for the cameras, harbored presidential aspirations, and could easily succumb to popular and media pressures to change campaign finance law in ways McConnell thought both unconstitutional and politically dangerous for Republicans. Lott went with the lackadaisical Thompson, the marginally lesser of two evils on the issue.

Throughout the year, McConnell would work feverishly behind the scenes both to develop a palatable Republican alternative to McCain-Feingold and to keep Thompson's hearings focused on past violations of existing law instead of formulating new legislation. Citing his record of almost a decade, *National Journal* called McConnell "the most tenacious and boldest opponent of crusaders who seek to stem the rising tides of cash that increasingly influence the conduct of elections."[3]

In this session's incarnation, the McCain-Feingold bill would limit soft-money contributions to parties, crack down on political action committee contributions to candidates, and encourage overall campaign spending limits. McConnell was not opposed to all reform. He backed better disclosure of campaign contributions, a ban on foreign contributions, limits on the ability of labor unions to use mandatory dues for political purposes, and raising individual contribution limits. But he believed McCain-Feingold was an unconstitutional abridgment of free speech that would also hurt the political parties.

McConnell acknowledged that he had become "an abominable 'no' man" to many. McConnell built his opposition to McCain-Feingold on the foundation of *Buckley v. Valeo,*[4] a 1976 Supreme Court decision that struck down some post-Watergate campaign finance laws on First Amendment grounds. *Buckley* essentially held that political campaign spending was a form of constitutionally protected speech. According to the *Buckley* court: "The First Amendment denies government the power to determine that spending to promote one's political views is wasteful, excessive, or unwise. In the free society ordained by our Constitution it is not the government but the people—individually as citizens and candidates and collectively as associations and political committees—who must retain control over the quantity and range of debate on public issues in a political campaign."

McConnell strongly agreed.[5] And in the process, he became much better known on a national basis. "People had some interest in me," he recalls, "because they wondered who would be dumb enough to stand up against this worthy idea." So he worked to build a broad coalition of groups opposed to McCain-Feingold's restrictive reforms. In March, an ideologically diverse array of representatives from the American Civil Liberties Union, the National Education Association, the National Rifle Association, Right to Life, the Christian Coalition, and several other organizations joined him for a well-publicized press conference on the issue.

While the Thompson hearings predictably failed to live up to expectations, McConnell still had to counter many conservatives' understandable belief that campaign finance reform presented an opportunity to embarrass Clinton. That was a worthy objective, he believed, but not at the price of passing bad laws that would surrender "more power to our enemies" by enhancing the communication power of elites in academia, the media, and Hollywood, none of which would be subject to McCain-Feingold limitations.[6]

As liberal columnist E. J. Dionne noted in September, Republicans had to choose between McCain, whom almost all Senate Democrats supported, and McConnell. McCain claimed that the current campaign finance system was "corrupt." McConnell repeatedly called on him to substantiate such claims with names and denied that enough money was being spent on federal elections to produce much corruption. "Federal campaign spending," he said, "amounted to $3.89 per eligible voter, about the price of a McDonald's value meal."[7] He added, "McCain-Feingold is to democracy what the Clinton health care plan was to medicine, and I am going to do my level best to ensure that it meets the same fate."[8]

McConnell sought, and received, support from some of the most influential figures in the conservative media. To educate the Republican rank and file on the issue, he enlisted the considerable help of talk radio megastar Rush Limbaugh, whom McConnell considered "the most important voice in America to some grassroots conservatives."

He also found conservative columnist George Will to be "rock solid" and "a tower of strength" on the topic.

In the end, only seven GOP senators sided with McCain. That was too few to break McConnell's filibuster, and the campaign finance reform measure failed in an October cloture vote, 53–47. The debate was mercifully over for another year. McCain's post-vote comments on the Senate floor paid a backhanded tribute to McConnell: "He very forthrightly proclaimed that he would proudly cast a vote against any bill that sought to reduce the amount of money that currently soaks our federal election system. I commend him for his candor, and for having the courage of his convictions. . . . I wish all opponents of campaign finance reform were so forthright."

McConnell countered, "This is a war about who gets to speak in this country, who is going to have influence, what kind of country we're going to have, and it's a war between two sides that see it totally differently. It's all about the First Amendment, whether it's a national bill or whether it's a local ordinance." To fight that war whenever and wherever battle flared around the country, McConnell helped found the James Madison Center for Free Speech, a Washington-based public interest law center with the "sole mission" of "defending political speech."[9]

Although the campaign finance issue overshadowed all others this year for McConnell, he nonetheless found time to pursue some of his other favorite causes. He pushed for a tougher U.S. policy toward Burma, visited Ukraine to assist in its continued democratic development, proposed cutting Egypt's considerable foreign aid to encourage a more constructive attitude toward regional peace, and broke ranks with many Republicans to support a chemical weapons treaty. He also tried to pass tort reform that would give drivers reduced rates on automobile insurance if they would limit their rights to pain and suffering damages in lawsuits, sponsored legislation to protect black bears and civic volunteers, took a position of "studied neutrality" on Indiana senator Dick Lugar's tobacco buyout proposal, and helped block the confirmation of Bill Lann Lee as head of the Civil Rights Division of the Justice Department. McConnell considered Lee a "quota king," but could not stop President Clinton from using a recess appointment to make him the division's acting director anyway.

When this latest round of the campaign finance debate began, a *Baltimore Sun* profile had accurately observed, "Few outside his home state of Kentucky know the name Mitch McConnell."[10] That had changed over the course of the year. After what he called "struggling around in semi-obscurity" for more than a decade, McConnell raised his public profile considerably with his principled and skillful opposition to McCain's pet legislation.

McConnell had made his first appearance on NBC's *Meet the Press* in February. In June he made *National Journal*'s "Washington 100" list of the capital city's most powerful people.[11] Later that month, *National Review* ran an article he authored about campaign finance reform.[12] In August, Paul Gigot dedicated his influential "Potomac Watch" column in the *Wall Street Journal* to McConnell's ideas about the Republican agenda, crediting him for touting conservative ideas—such as tax reform that cuts taxes, legal reform, and an end to racial preferences—that would "unify Republicans" and allow them to "go where most Democrats are not able to follow."[13]

He was also the subject of a plethora of mostly favorable profiles. In September, the *Washington Post* ran one on the front page calling McConnell "the father of the modern-day Republican Party in Kentucky" and contrasting his modest lifestyle with his love of raising and spending campaign money. "McConnell's success," it added, "is usually credited to his intense, aggressive style, his prodigious fund-raising ability and almost unerring political instincts. He has a knack for homing in on an opponent's weakness and exploiting it relentlessly."[14]

Later that month, other generally positive pieces followed in *The Economist*[15] and *National Review*.[16] With characteristic condescension toward most things American, the British "newspaper" humorously described the "irresistibly villainous" McConnell's opposition to campaign finance reform as "refreshing," especially in contrast to the brazen hypocrisy displayed by Clinton and Gore on the issue. William F.

Buckley's pioneering conservative periodical described McConnell as "a slight man with an owlish, tight-lipped public demeanor reminiscent of George Will" in the course of comprehensively chronicling his political rise.

It was truly a breakthrough year in terms of McConnell's public image and reputation. *Courier-Journal* columnist Robert T. Garrett referred to the phenomenon as "the long-awaited third phase of McConnell's political career: He's going national." According to Garrett, becoming county judge and senator constituted McConnell's first phase, and his reelection and the GOP advance in Kentucky was the second.[17]

"It's a very competitive situation," said McConnell, reflecting on his rise. "You are in the midst of a hundred of the sharper politicians in America, and it is not easy to break out of the pack. . . . If you don't come in being a war hero or from a well-known family, you've got to make it on wit and guile. I must say, it took me longer than I thought it was going to."

On November 8, 1997, the twentieth anniversary of his election as Jefferson County judge, McConnell staged a reunion for those who had been with him in the beginning. He made clear to all that the gathering "was not a retirement party, but maybe a halftime celebration." A baseball analogy might have been more apt, because in 1998 McConnell would go to bat politically for a Hall of Famer from the national pastime.

15

Campaign Kingpin
1998

MCCONNELL HAD NEVER HELD a more important partisan position than chairman of the NRSC. The NRSC chair has some responsibility for developing and implementing campaign strategy and tactics, but the primary role is to raise money and decide where and how to spend it. More importantly, the post is an important rung on the ladder of Senate leadership, potentially leading to more prominent positions like whip or Republican leader.

With ferocious fundraising, McConnell had dug the NRSC out of a financial hole during 1997. Having done much of that hard work himself, McConnell told his colleagues that he "wasn't going to joust with any windmills" and "wasn't going to finance any landslides." The 1998 cycle would be an expensive one, with races in California, Illinois, New York, Ohio, and Pennsylvania. The NRSC began it with the goal of gaining five seats.[1] Privately, McConnell thought that defeating enough Democratic incumbents to do this would be extremely difficult. The GOP had not done that well since gaining a net dozen seats on Democrats in 1980. In 1986, 1990, and 1996, they had beaten no Democratic incumbents; in 1992 and 1994 they had ousted only two; and in 1984 and 1988, only one. Republican gains had consistently come from capturing open seats.

But Republican hopes nonetheless ran high. President Clinton was in deepening political trouble and a president's party tended to lose seats in the sixth year of a two-term presidency. This may have made for a certain lack of intensity, perhaps even overconfidence, on the part of GOP leaders Gingrich in the House and Lott in the Senate.

Closer to home, McConnell now had what he saw as "an historic opportunity to run the table and not leave a single Democrat left in the Kentucky congressional delegation." He "didn't want to wake up the day after the election in 1998 and say, 'Well, I was too timid. I didn't try.' I had to try." So he immersed himself in his own state's Senate race and the contest for the only Kentucky House seat the Democrats still held.

Recruited by McConnell, Republican congressman Jim Bunning had decided to run for the Senate. The prospect of a hard race against him convinced Wendell Ford, then seventy-two, that it was time to retire. McConnell recognized that Bunning had some weaknesses as a candidate. "He's a kind of hard-nosed guy," McConnell observed. "He's not a natural politician." On the other hand, the highly competitive Bunning, then sixty-six, still enjoyed star quality from being a seven-time baseball all-star pitcher. Significantly, he was a member of the House's powerful Ways and Means Committee and already had almost half a million dollars in the bank.

In a hard-fought Democratic primary, Scotty Baesler, the fifty-six-year-old Sixth District congressman, beat millionaire Charlie Owen, who spent a record $6 million, and the sitting lieutenant governor, Steve Henry. A former University of Kentucky basketball player and mayor of Lexington, Baesler enjoyed as much statewide name recognition as Bunning, or perhaps more. He characterized himself as a conservative "Blue Dog" Democrat and had voted against both Bill Clinton's record tax increase and his bureaucratic health-care plan. A tobacco farmer himself, he had also opposed the Clinton anti-tobacco crusade. Baesler would be tough for Bunning to beat.

In mid-May, in a move he knew would be controversial, McConnell abandoned Ford's tobacco bill, which he had cosponsored, and threw his support behind the buyout bill advocated by Indiana's Dick

Lugar. Ford's bill called for a fund financed from a $368 billion settlement between the tobacco companies and state attorneys general to pay farmers for their lost tobacco quotas. But Clinton and his most prominent Republican ally, John McCain, combined to push what McConnell described as "a $700 to 800 billion tax-and-spend bill" that would "enrich plaintiffs lawyers" while providing the tobacco industry with virtually no protection from legal liability.[2]

McConnell ardently opposed the Clinton-McCain approach, preferring to "stay with the current program that has served tobacco growers well over the years."[3] When it appeared that the offensive measure might become law however, he saw Lugar's Tobacco Transition Act as a palatable and possible alternative. Lugar's bill provided a buyout of tobacco quotas over three years at a fixed price, ended the quota program as of the 1999 crop, and phased out the price support program during the 1999–2001 crop years.

While he was catching considerable heat for supposedly "selling out" tobacco by considering either of the proposals under consideration, McConnell advised Bunning not to follow his lead, but instead to "stay in the same place as Baesler" on the issue. In June, after a four-week filibuster, the Senate finally killed the Clinton-McCain bill, barely beating back a cloture motion, 57–42. Ford was one of only two Democrats to join McConnell in opposition to that measure.

McConnell was relieved to have defeated what he considered as an ill-conceived bill based on regulation and litigation. "Had this bill passed," McConnell said, "I don't think there is any question that the alcohol industry would have been next, and then probably the gaming industry, which would certainly have affected Churchill Downs and Keeneland," Kentucky's premier horseracing tracks. "The plaintiff lawyers are licking their chops using this model for the next attack, industry by industry."[4] Despite a summer full of sound and fury, however, the tobacco issue ultimately had little effect on the Kentucky Senate campaign.

By mid-summer, Bunning had not raised as much money as anyone had hoped. McConnell soon realized that Bunning's staff lacked the experience and know-how to run the campaign on their own, and with Bunning's blessing dispatched his trusted chief of staff, Kyle Simmons, to run the campaign. Simmons was not enthusiastic, but appreciated what his boss thought to be a chance to "beat Wendell [Ford] and beat the *Courier-Journal* and beat the *Herald-Leader* and beat the whole Democratic establishment." Simmons started with Bunning's campaign on August 1, just before the yearly Fancy Farm political picnic. The event that would prove to be a turning point in the campaign.

McConnell recalls that he had already addressed the rowdy rural crowd when Baesler took to the stage and "acted as if he were crazed. He was moving around the podium like he was guarding somebody in basketball. He was misusing English . . . in a strangest sort of way." He came across as "some kind of fundamentalist preacher or something." McConnell had arranged for the day's proceedings to be videotaped, and as he was leaving the stage he told Simmons, "Kyle, I think we may have something here. This could be really significant." They did, and it was.

The Bunning campaign later produced an ad showing Baesler's manic Fancy Farm rant set to the musical background of Richard Wagner's *Ride of the Valkyries*. The effect made Baesler come across like Adolf Hitler addressing the Nuremburg rally of the Nazi Party. Democrats and liberal media cried foul, but the spot had the kind of powerful political effect that McConnell and Simmons had hoped for.

More substantively, the NRSC's first ads in Kentucky promoted Bunning as a major player on Social Security, an issue then characterized as "the third rail of American politics" because of the potential electoral danger to anyone who dared discuss it. The spots sought to show that Bunning had the coveted quality of "gravitas" and was an expert on a key issue to Kentucky's considerable contingent of senior citizens. From then on, the campaign quickly turned into an all-out television war, and Republicans were winning. According to a CNN consultant, "from August through September, Bunning's ads ran 868 times" in three major television markets "compared to Baesler's 435. There were also 1,580 Republican Party ads for Bunning," but only "475 Democratic Party ads" for Baesler.[5]

The Republicans began nightly tracking polls about a month out from Election Day. They showed Bunning with a slight lead of 3 or 4 points well into October. While Baesler was not competing in Bunning's home Fourth District in northern Kentucky, in part because of the expense of Cincinnati's media market, Bunning was bringing the battle into Baesler's home Sixth District, where Lexington television was less expensive.

About ten days before the balloting, however, Bunning had fallen behind Baesler by about 4 points. This tightening seemed to be due to an effective Democratic ad showing farmer Baesler on a tractor claiming that Bunning had voted for tax breaks for millionaires while opposing any increase in the minimum wage. McConnell called a distraught Bunning at his home to buck up his spirits and assure him that the race was not over. It could still be won, McConnell said, but how Bunning behaved on an upcoming statewide bus tour would be crucial.

Bunning ran a new ad rebutting Baesler's. Nightly tracking polls over the campaign's final week showed the Republican recovering some lost ground. The campaign's last weekend featured frenetic and extremely expensive advertising by both the NRSC and its Democratic counterpart. McConnell raised a staggering $800,000 for the NRSC in a single day, a good bit of which found its way into the red hot Kentucky race.

When the ballots were tallied, Bunning eked out a win of 569,817 to 563,051—a margin of a mere 6,766 votes. He lost Louisville by about 20,000 votes, but carried his own Fourth District by almost twice as much as Baesler carried his home Sixth District. The candidates broke about even in western Kentucky, the former Democratic stronghold, with Bunning winning the Second District by roughly the same number of votes as he lost the westernmost First District. Bunning won big in the strongly Republican Fifth District of eastern Kentucky.

It was the first time in twenty-six years that both Kentucky's senators were Republican. It was also the first statewide Republican victory in Kentucky by anyone other than McConnell in thirty years. Making things even better for the Bluegrass GOP, a little-known state legislator named Ernie Fletcher captured the House seat that Baesler had vacated, winning a relatively comfortable spread of 53 percent to 47 percent. A doctor, Baptist lay minister, and former fighter pilot, Fletcher had an almost irresistible résumé in patriotic, religious, and authority-respecting Kentucky.

Baesler had beaten Fletcher by 25,000 votes in 1996, when McConnell had been too busy trying to get himself reelected to get involved. Fletcher's first congressional campaign "had been strictly amateur hour," McConnell recalls. Fletcher was "a quality guy" and "a first-class candidate" who could win the seat the second time around, except that he "had no earthly idea what to do." So McConnell had summoned him for a postelection meeting in December 1996. He told Fletcher, "Ernie, I think you can be the congressman," and asked him, "Would you like to do it right?" Fletcher agreed and "ended up being a very willing student and an excellent candidate."

Fletcher also got a political gift of sorts when Ernesto Scorsone, a state senator and undoubtedly "the most liberal Democrat" in a crowded primary field, captured that party's nomination. Among other things, Scorsone had voted against a bill banning gay marriage, supported several tax increases, and been heavily involved in some misguided state efforts at health-care reform. As a public defender, he had represented a defendant charged with raping a woman, shooting her twice, and leaving her for dead. In what was perhaps the most memorable move in the race, Fletcher ran a spot that featured the woman talking about the case. The *Lexington Herald-Leader* "went berserk," McConnell recalls. The president of the Kentucky Bar Association also blasted the ad. But the political needle moved in Fletcher's direction.

McConnell defended the ad as "legitimate" because "it told you something about Scorsone philosophically—that he wanted to practice that kind of law. We all make a conscious decision if you are a lawyer. What kind of lawyer do you want to be? To be comfortable practicing that kind of law you've got to believe that these kinds of people ought to get light sentences because you argue it all the time. I mean, I think you make a conscious decision in picking your clientele."

The Democrats played political hardball, too, by trying to stigmatize Fletcher "as some kind of religious nut, which he isn't," said McConnell at the time. "He is a religious guy. He's pretty devout. But in this day and age if you go to church on Sundays you are portrayed by the press as some kind of nut case. I think he's a solid, kind of right-of-center guy. . . . He's pro-life, but he's not on a mission. He's not trying to be a zealot."

McConnell stayed out of the race to fill Bunning's seat. Bunning backed an assistant, who lost the primary to Gex Williams, a far-right firebrand. McConnell sat down with Williams once, but realized there was nothing he could do for him that would produce a victory in the fall. He "was not credible, so I had no further dealings in the Fourth District and, regretfully, we lost the seat." Conservative Democrat Ken Lucas carried the district, 53 percent to 47 percent.

But Republicans now held seven of eight seats in Kentucky's congressional delegation. McConnell calls his "orchestration and involvement in turning [Kentucky] into a two-party state" one of the most gratifying parts of his public career. He had been heavily involved in most of the campaigns, and had learned that every race was different. Each campaign required its own strategy and had to be "custom-crafted" when it came to tactics. Refighting the last election and relying on national themes were, he believed, recipes for disaster.

Results were not nearly as good across the nation as they were in Kentucky. Republicans lost six seats in the House, a governorship, and seats in state legislatures. In the Senate, the GOP lost two seats that it had held (by two of the more colorfully named senators, Lauch Faircloth in North Carolina and Alfonse D'Amato in New York), but with Bunning in Kentucky and Peter Fitzgerald in Illinois, it had won two seats from Democrats. The Senate thus stayed 55–45 in favor of the Republicans.

The GOP did not take several seats it had hoped to secure. Liberal Democrat Barbara Boxer in California had been vulnerable, but managed to hold off challenger Matt Fong. McConnell concluded that Fong did not understand that ousting an incumbent with high negatives like Boxer required keeping the focus always on her. In neighboring Nevada, Republican John Ensign stuck to the NRSC strategy, but still lost to Democrat Harry Reid by a bare 400 votes.

Democrat Russell Feingold of Wisconsin misleadingly portrayed himself as a moderate to squeeze out a 2 percent victory over Congressman Mark Neumann, whom McConnell characterized as "very rigid on the abortion issue." Neumann had strong beliefs against partial-birth abortion and insisted on airing an ad about it. McConnell doubted that abortion was "a good television issue," whatever the candidate's position, and warned him that it would be hard to keep the debate from moving onto the broader issue of abortion generally. He believed this decision may have cost Neumann the closely contested election.

Congressman Bob Inglis lost to longtime Democratic incumbent Fritz Hollings in South Carolina. That race was over, McConnell now believes, as soon as the Republican governor Carroll Campbell decided not to run.

Of his first experience at the helm of the NRSC, McConnell concluded, "One of the clear lessons is the candidate does make a difference. You can only run so good of a campaign on behalf of a flawed candidate and expect to win. . . . It is pretty hard to elect a turkey."

After all was said and done, McConnell concluded that 1998 was essentially "a confirming election" in which voters were "extraordinarily content." The Monica Lewinsky scandal in which President Clinton was mired either did not matter or actually helped the Democrats. Impeachment ads run on behalf of House candidates in the last days of campaign seemed to backfire badly, especially with blacks. African-American turnout was high, and labor efforts on behalf of Democrats seemed effective. At a postelection press conference, McConnell conceded that Democrats were "clearly more motivated" and professed admiration for "the effort they made."[6]

On the day after the election, Senator Chuck Hagel of Nebraska said that he might challenge McConnell for the NRSC chairmanship. An independent-minded Vietnam vet, Hagel was a media favorite and had been increasingly critical of McConnell's sponsor for the campaign post, majority leader Trent Lott.

As House Republicans set about deposing the once-formidable Newt Gingrich as Speaker, McConnell got on the phone and spent about three "miserable" weeks calling people. He was relieved to learn that most did not seem to be blaming him for the party's election performance. Hagel nonetheless announced his NRSC candidacy on the day after Thanksgiving and began a highly public campaign for the post, featuring frequent media appearances.

In a *Roll Call* article, Hagel said that he thought he had fifteen, and later eighteen votes. McConnell was confident of forty-two firm votes based on his hard and fast rule of never counting a vote as being in his column until the person told him "eye to eye and point blank, 'I'm for you.'" With the help of Lott, against whom Hagel's campaign was indirectly aimed, McConnell won another tour at the top of the NRSC, 39–13, with three of his supporters out of the country on travel and therefore not voting.

It was a sizeable victory as Republican Senate leadership elections go, and very gratifying to McConnell. The 1998 results had been somewhat disappointing, and he looked forward to trying his hand at the task one more time. Before doing so, however, he had to cast what would perhaps be his most historic votes as a senator.

16

New Beginnings at Millennium's End
1999–2000

T HE YEAR 1999 MARKED McConnell's fifteenth in the Senate. It was also his most important yet.

In December 1998, with the Republicans' disappointment in the midterm elections still lingering, the lame duck House had voted out two articles of impeachment against President Clinton. One charged him with giving perjured grand jury testimony and the other alleged obstruction of justice. Two others failed. For the impeachment trial in the Senate, some Republicans favored a full-blown spectacle featuring live witnesses in the dock, but as the new chairman of the Senate Rules Committee, McConnell quickly decided that the country and his party would be better off if the Senate concluded the process as quickly as possible consistent with its constitutional duty.

"I wanted to get the damn thing over with because I knew we were not going to win," he later explained. Moreover, the prospect of intern Monica Lewinsky sharing the details of her illicit liaisons with Clinton from the Senate well simply appalled the straight-laced McConnell. Privately, he pushed two procedural priorities—minimizing the number of witnesses and conducting deliberations in private—that he hoped would both speed the trial and reduce the public perception of partisanship. Both prevailed. Publicly, he ridiculed the hypocrisy of Democrats who had urged public testimony in the Packwood matter, but resisted it now that one of their own was involved in a similarly sordid scandal.

Chief Justice William Rehnquist administered the oath to the one hundred senators on January 7, 1999. McConnell recalls it as "an incredible thing to be sitting there at the desk of Henry Clay,[1] looking up, and seeing the chief justice of the United States in the presiding chair and every senator sitting at their seat. . . . For two weeks everybody was there every day, sitting in their own seats and not talking." In an experience McConnell recalls as "surreal," Clinton delivered his State of the Union address to a joint session of Congress during the course of the impeachment trial.

On February 13, McConnell voted to convict on both articles, but with all the Senate's Democrats supporting Clinton, neither charge approached the two-thirds majority necessary for conviction. The perjury article failed 45–55; the obstruction article, 50–50. Explaining the acquittal of a president who had, among other offenses, lied under oath about an affair with a subordinate, McConnell noted, "Public opinion is not irrelevant in the Congress of the United States." America had learned "a very bad lesson" from the experience, he said. "If you're important in this country, you can lie under oath and obstruct justice and get away with it."

Along with his NRSC chairmanship, the impeachment proceedings turned McConnell into a television regular. He appeared on thirty-four national news and talk shows between December 19 and January 30, and was on the major Sunday morning political talk shows twenty-two times during the year. The *Courier-Journal's* Washington correspondent James Carroll wrote that "All Monica All the Time" had been replaced by "All Mitch All the Time." Tim Russert, the much respected host of NBC's *Meet the Press*, said of McConnell, "He's very smart, very focused, and very prepared."[2] The publicity was nice, but McConnell, then fifty-seven, fully expected to "go back to obscurity" afterward. That was not to be.

Seeking to further solidify his reputation in international affairs, he published an op-ed piece in the *Washington Post* advocating an aggressive policy for achieving the independence of Kosovo, an Albanian Muslim region of the former Yugoslavia.[3] Among other things, he called for arming the controversial Kosovo Liberation Army (KLA) to resist aggression and atrocities being perpetrated by the ruling Serbs. After the piece appeared, Serbian strongman Slobodan Milosevic denied McConnell a visa to visit Kosovo. McConnell was more supportive than many Republicans when President Clinton finally took military action in the region, but still could not convince the administration to fund the KLA. He had to settle for using his subcommittee chairmanship to advocate, and attempt to fund, a high-profile role for the United States in peacekeeping and reconstruction.

McConnell also took a leading role in the bipartisan opposition to renewal of the independent counsel statute, which was set to expire at the end of June. In addition to the just-completed impeachment ordeal, he had seen firsthand how an out-of-control independent counsel could turn an innocent person's life into a living hell. His former aide Janet Mullins, who had served as an assistant secretary of state under George H. W. Bush, had gotten caught up in an investigation of whether the Bush administration had improperly searched passport files for information about the young Bill Clinton's antiwar activities overseas. Mullins was eventually exonerated,[4] but not before suffering through incredible agony, expense, and damage to her professional reputation.

McConnell also garnered some meager attention by conducting a Rules Committee hearing on the politically correct, and occasionally outright anti-American, bias of certain exhibits at the Smithsonian Institution.

Campaign finance reform was, of course, a centerpiece of the incipient presidential campaign of Senator John McCain, then a media darling. McConnell once again led the battle to block the McCain-Feingold bill, which continued to evolve, but basically would have banned soft money and put restrictions on issue ads. During debate on the Senate floor, McConnell once again called upon McCain to back up his accusations of corruption and influence buying by saying "which specific Senators he believes have been engaged in corruption." McCain responded, "I refuse to, and would not in any way, say that any individual or person is guilty of corruption in a specific way, nor identify them." The self-proclaimed straight-talker instead read lengthy excerpts from a book by columnist Elizabeth Drew (who would later pen a fawning portrait of "Citizen McCain"[5]).

The testy exchange ended as follows:

McCONNELL: The Senator agrees "corruption" may not be appropriate. If there is no individual he can name who is corrupt, then "corruption" may not be the appropriate word; would the senator agree?

McCAIN: I would not, I say to the senator from Kentucky. He is entitled to his views, his opinions, and his conclusions. I am entitled to mine.

McConnell's high-profile role in the debate made him a favorite target of pro-reform pundits and reporters. Drew compared him to Darth Vader. *Time* magazine's Margaret Carlson called him a "thug." Maureen Dowd of the *New York Times* deemed him the "head man at the bordello."

Even former president Gerald R. Ford got into the act, telling columnist David Broder, "I don't understand why that fellow is so adamant." McConnell responded with an op-ed in the *Washington Post* explaining that "government restrictions on your ability to pay to project your speech impinge upon your freedom of speech," and that "'the static contribution limits" Ford had signed into law made "candidates, groups and parties . . . work a lot harder to reach the American people."[6]

Echoing Ronald Reagan's inaugural admonition about government, McConnell declared, "Regulation is the problem, not the answer." Instead of more restrictions, he supported stronger enforcement of current laws, indexing Watergate-era contribution limits for inflation, which would have more than tripled $1,000 contribution caps to $3,300, and frequent public disclosure of all contributions.

"Everybody ought to be free to speak and it's absolutely clear you have to have money to have effective speech," McConnell wrote. The issue boiled down, he suggested, to who gets to speak, how much they get to speak, and when they get to speak. "Is it just the press? Is it just the unions? Or do candidates and parties get to speak, too, without government micro-management?" Democrats were on the other side of the issue "because they believe it is to their advantage to have the newspapers, academia, and Hollywood having a disproportionate share of the public discussion."

McConnell got some good press, too. Writing in the *Wall Street Journal* in September, columnist Paul Gigot included McConnell with Ronald Reagan and Newt Gingrich as conservatives the liberal media loved to demonize. *Congressional Quarterly* named him one of fifty influential "drivers" of congressional debate, while John F. Kennedy Jr.'s trendy *George* magazine put him among its "Washington Power 50."

And, despite their virulent opposition to most of McConnell's positions, both the *New York Times* and *Washington Post* ran relatively positive profiles.[7] Although the latter called him "the gray man with the bloodless lips," it added a more flattering political description: "master strategist, champion fund-raiser, proud obstructionist." The *Post* posed the critical question of whether, as he made "one of his periodic goal-line stands against the cheery do-gooders in the campaign finance reform movement," McConnell was "a principled libertarian fighting for a pure right to speech, or a crafty pragmatist scrambling to secure his sources of succor." Its implicit conclusion was that he had somehow managed to be both and to achieve respect and senatorial stature in the process.

Despite his ever increasing activity and visibility in the nation's capital, McConnell never forgot where he came from or who sent him to Washington every six years. For example, although Kentucky was far from the frontlines of the Cold War, it suffered some serious consequences from its role in arming America for that long twilight struggle.

In the latter half of 1999 McConnell began a long-running Washington-style bureaucratic battle on behalf of affected Kentuckians.

In August, the *Washington Post* ran a front-page story revealing that "thousands of uranium workers were unwittingly exposed to plutonium and other highly radioactive metals" at a federally funded uranium enrichment plant near Paducah, Kentucky, that had been making material for nuclear weapons since 1952.[8] McConnell sprang into action immediately to put the Paducah plant at the front of the line for funding of cleanup and worker health assessments. He also fought to force the Pentagon to consider alternatives to on-site incineration as a way of disposing of the chemical weapons stockpiled at the Bluegrass Army Depot near Richmond, Kentucky. Both of these battles would rage on for years, however.

Although McConnell had never wanted to succeed to Wendell Ford's title of "Mr. Tobacco," 1999 was nonetheless a good year for him on the subject so important to his state. First, he played a prominent role in barring federal claims against amounts that states recovered in litigation with tobacco companies. Next, he managed to get tobacco included in a disaster relief bill to the tune of $125 million for Kentucky burley growers. Finally, he made it easier for farmers to hire migrant workers, an area that would continue to inform his views on immigration legislation.

Using his post on the Appropriations Committee to maximum benefit, he continued steering as many federal dollars as possible to Kentucky. By the end of 1999, McConnell had brought home almost a half-billion dollars in projects during his Senate career. He paid particular attention to helping his alma mater, the University of Louisville, get the federal grants it needed to upgrade its research status and to aiding the University of Kentucky's College of Agriculture.

In response to questions about how he squares such "pork barrel projects" with his professed conservatism, McConnell quips, "My definition of pork is a project in Indiana." More seriously, he explains, "I feel like once we establish how much we are going to spend in a given year, that it is my responsibility to try steer as much of it as I can to our state. And I think I have been reasonably good at that." He openly advocates for legislative earmarks on grounds that a state's elected representatives know a lot more about its local needs than do executive branch bureaucrats who would otherwise decide how and where to spend appropriated federal funds.

McConnell also excelled in raising private money for his pet projects. After Kentucky created a "Bucks for Brains" program in which state government would match private money to endow professorships at state universities, McConnell rustled up a million dollars to finance what would become the Mitch McConnell Chair in Leadership at the University of Louisville. The occupant of that faculty seat would also serve as a full-time director at the McConnell Center for Political Leadership. Gary L. Gregg II, Ph.D., a distinguished young conservative academic, was selected. Predictably, liberals in the university faculty and state legislature howled in protest, confirming in McConnell's mind that their demands for diversity on college campuses did not extend beyond skin color or gender to the realm of ideas or political perspectives.

The year was a mixed bag for McConnell and the GOP in Kentucky state politics. Governor Paul Patton, a Democrat, won reelection without serious Republican opposition, but a pair of party switches gave Republicans a majority in the Kentucky state Senate for the first time in history. After a midsummer meeting at McConnell's home in Louisville, a Democratic state senator from Louisville's working-class South End changed his registration to Republican, and another from far western Kentucky soon followed. A 20–18 Democratic majority had suddenly and unexpectedly become an unprecedented 20–18 Republican majority. The stunning consequences of this shift were confirmed when both the party switchers were reelected as Republicans when they next faced voters in 2002.

Before the General Assembly convened, McConnell went to Frankfort with some words of advice for members of the new Republican majority: stay together and do not raise taxes. Over the next several years state Senate president and key McConnell ally David Williams would prove extremely effective in making sure his caucus heeded

McConnell's counsel. As a result, an era of unprecedented GOP influence in Frankfort followed.

Even David Hawpe, editorial director of the *Courier-Journal* and caustic critic of McConnell on just about everything except campaign finance reform, had to concede that his nemesis had "a remarkable year" in 1999. "Precisely because he is direct and analytical in dealing with people of influence, he himself has become enormously influential in the nation's capital, not to mention a regular presence on the TV blatherfests that originate there," Hawpe wrote. "He's become our most powerful man in Washington since Alben Barkley," the former Senate majority leader and vice president under Harry Truman.[9] *Courier-Journal* political writer Al Cross agreed, deeming McConnell "the key player of the decade in Kentucky politics," who had "eclipsed" the Democrat Ford and "may leave an even greater political legacy."[10]

McConnell had at long last earned the respect, albeit sometimes acerbic and always grudging, of even his most hostile antagonists in both the Senate and the media. Under similar circumstances, many senators cannot resist seeing themselves as potential presidents. McConnell promptly and prudently disclaimed any such ambitions. "My career is here in the Senate," he said. "I have no desire to spend my weekends in New Hampshire or Iowa. . . . I feel like I'm at the top of my game, and I want to continue to do this as long as the people of Kentucky think I'm effective."[11]

Of the senators and several other Republicans who did dream of the White House in 2000, both McConnell and Chao became "committed and deeply involved" in the campaign of Texas governor George W. Bush, son of former president George H. W. Bush, of whom they remained fond. McConnell served as chairman of Bush's Kentucky campaign, Chao as chair of the fundraising-oriented Kentucky Victory Campaign, which staged an event that raised $1.7 million, about $1 million of which remained in Kentucky while the rest went to the Republican National Committee.

For the fourth time, McConnell, as Kentucky's senior Republican elected official, chaired the commonwealth's delegation to the national convention, this time in Philadelphia. "The strategy at the convention was to keep the number of middle-aged white guys on the podium to a minimum," he recalls. Accordingly, while his wife addressed the partisan throng in prime time, McConnell was relegated to an almost invisible Monday afternoon slot. He spent most of his time at a series of fundraising events for the NRSC that left him exhausted. The convention gave Bush a little bounce in the polls, but Democratic nominee Al Gore would quickly recapture that lost ground after his party's conclave.

Kentucky started the campaign as a key battleground state. Bush visited it ten times over the course of the campaign. McConnell hit Gore hard every chance he got, describing the vice president as having "the personality of a cardboard box." He also hammered him on key issues where Gore stood against Kentucky's interests, such as tobacco, coal, and emissions standards for automobiles, which Kentucky manufactured in abundance. At the annual Fancy Farm political picnic, McConnell had young Republicans dress as Buddhist monks to ridicule a controversial Gore fundraising event at a Buddhist temple. Although Gore hailed from the neighboring state of Tennessee, he abandoned hope of winning Kentucky soon after a Labor Day visit and ultimately lost it by a staggering 16 points.

McConnell spent election night in Washington at the NRSC. Republicans again faced a number of tough Senate races around the country and suffered a net loss of five seats.

Deaths played a pivotal role in two of them. Georgia Republican Paul Coverdale passed away in the summer and was replaced by conservative Democrat Zell Miller. In Missouri, Democratic challenger Mel Carnahan died in an autumn airplane crash, but his name remained on the ballot. Missouri's governor announced that he would appoint Carnahan's widow to the seat if her husband won. The dead man did, ousting Republican incumbent John Ashcroft, who quipped, "I always said no man alive could beat me."

Washington's Slade Gorton, one of McConnell's best friends in the Senate, fell as well, as did William Roth of Delaware, Spencer Abraham of Michigan, and Rod Grams of Minnesota. In addition, Democrats captured an open seat in Florida. This stinging setback left the Senate in what would prove to be a short-lived 50–50 tie, the first time since the 1880s that the chamber was split down the middle.

"It was the first arguably not very successful election I had been involved in," McConnell acknowledged. Others considered it his second consecutive subpar performance as NRSC chairman. He feared that these back-to-back disappointments would hurt his chances of ascending further in Republican Senate leadership, but fortunately for him the presidential election occupied the attention of both the public and his party.

Gore won the popular vote, but lost in the Electoral College by a narrow margin provided by Florida's decisive twenty-five votes. The balloting in the state was incredibly close, and Democrats advanced several controversial claims of irregularity. Putting self before country, Gore took the matter to the courts, where the campaign continued for thirty-six days. The controversy left McConnell "distraught," "miserable," and "riding an emotional roller coaster" as he watched the farcical court-ordered partial recounts. He advanced the Bush cause as best he could, sometimes calling Gore the "Tonya Harding of American politics" in reference to the thuggish figure skater who had conspired to injure a competitor who had beaten her for an Olympic berth.

As Rules Committee chairman, McConnell would preside over the presidential inauguration. The thought of introducing Gore as president was, he said, "enough to make me want to call in sick." But he had to plan for that unpleasant contingency nonetheless. Relief came on December 12, 2000, when the U.S. Supreme Court reversed the Florida Supreme Court, which had ordered a full statewide hand recount of so-called undervotes. The decision effectively ratified the determination of Florida election officials that Bush had won the state by a few hundred votes out of more than six million cast.[12]

"I don't think I have ever felt better, including my own election victories, than the night of the Supreme Court decision," McConnell recalls. "I felt so deeply that Al Gore was a horrible person and was wrong for the country and ought not to be president of the United States."

Bush's victory capped a year in which McConnell had achieved some major successes in the Senate and in Kentucky state politics. For the second straight time, he had helped get tobacco included in disaster relief legislation. He had also reduced growers' fees by getting rid of a poor "pool," or storage stock of tobacco. Together, these measures meant about $700 million for Kentucky's tobacco farmers, many of whom called his accomplishment the "McConnell Miracle."

Although the issue of an anti-flag-burning amendment to the Constitution had flared up yet again, McConnell was able to put it out without getting singed politically. Seeing the issue more than ever before as one of political speech, he urged the *Courier-Journal's* Hawpe to help drum up liberal editorial pressure on Senator Robert Byrd of West Virginia to change his position and oppose the amendment. Byrd did, announcing his switch in a speech to the Veterans of Foreign Wars. This gave opponents thirty-six votes, two more than needed to defeat the amendment. Only two other Republicans joined McConnell in voting "no," thus demonstrating his willingness to stand against his party on matters of principle.

The uranium-enrichment plant in Paducah, now privately owned, also occupied much of his attention in 2000. The plant still required extensive federal involvement for environmental cleanup and health-care monitoring for past employees. McConnell viewed the workers as "soldiers in the Cold War," a perspective that helped him justify his support for a new federal entitlement for them along the lines of workers compensation at the state level.

Closer to home, Louisville and Jefferson County voters finally approved a merger of the two local governments. McConnell had been working for this result since the commencement of his first term as county judge. He had gotten involved again in the late 1990s, when he once more urged putting the measure on the ballot in a presidential election year, when turnout would be high. His advice at long last heeded, the merger passed by a 54 percent to 46 percent margin. He considered it the long overdue conclusion of a matter unfinished when he left local government for the Senate. Making things even better, and to his surprise, Republicans won a respectable eleven of twenty-six seats on the initial Metro Louisville legislative council.

As a new millennium loomed, McConnell made preparation for his next appearance on the national stage and for an even more prominent role in Republican Senate leadership.

17

Everything Changes
2001

F OR THE FIRST TIME in his Senate tenure, which now encompassed four presidential elections, Mitch McConnell attended the counting of the electoral votes in the House of Representatives in December 2000. The historic ceremony, in which George W. Bush was finally and officially elected president by the bare margin of 271 electoral votes to Al Gore's 266, was marked by an irony: Gore himself, in his capacity as vice president of the United States and president of the Senate, presided over the session.

Because Bush had won the presidency despite losing the popular vote, both McConnell and Gary Gregg, director of the McConnell Center at the University of Louisville, anticipated that there would be a big push to abolish the Electoral College. To head off any radical change to one of the Constitution's most significant antidemocratic protections, McConnell wrote the introduction for, and Gregg edited, a book of articles, essays, and speeches in defense of the Electoral College.

In his introduction to *Securing Democracy: Why We Have an Electoral College*, McConnell argued that despite its "complexities and inefficiencies," the Electoral College is "the linchpin of American political prosperity [that] has formed our political parties, moderated our more extreme elements, and forged the presidential campaigns that have given direction to our ship of state."[1] To the surprise of many conservatives, however, there was no real groundswell of support for any such reform, and McConnell doubts that states with relatively small populations would ever let it happen anyway.

As soon as the Supreme Court decision sealed Bush's win, McConnell had begun assisting his wife, Elaine, in landing a spot in the new president's cabinet. Late in 2000, she interviewed for the post of secretary of transportation, but Democrat Norman Mineta seemed to have an edge. After Linda Chavez withdrew her name for secretary of labor, McConnell lobbied Vice President Dick Cheney hard, arguing that Chao would offer the administration everything it would have gotten with Chavez—an intellectual woman of proven ability and ties to an important ethnic community—but without the baggage. Chao also knew a lot of union leaders already from her work with the United Way. On January 11, Bush asked her to serve as secretary of labor. McConnell proudly introduced his spouse at her Senate confirmation hearing, which went smoothly and led to her prompt approval on a voice vote.

McConnell—who had rotated out as chairman of the NRSC—continued to be concerned about how much blame he would bear for being chairman when Republicans lost five seats. To his great relief, the repercussions were less than he feared. He concluded that he could still be a viable candidate for the position of whip, the number two position in the party's leadership. Don Nickles of Oklahoma, who had held the position for three two-year stints, could not run again under a Republican conference rule adopted in 1996. McConnell continued his characteristically intense but low-key campaign for the post.

Inauguration day dawned cold and rainy. McConnell rode in the car with President Bill Clinton and George W. Bush as they traveled up Pennsylvania Avenue from the White House to the Capitol. "Clinton did most of the talking," but was "yawning a lot." McConnell jokingly suggested to Bush that Clinton had been up all night partying, but they both would later learn that he had been up all night pardoning instead. It soon came to light that Clinton had issued several controversial clemencies almost literally on his way out of the executive mansion's door.

As chairman of the inaugural ceremonies, McConnell arranged for music from two of his alma maters, the Manual High School choir and the University of Louisville chorus. He considered it a great and enjoyable honor to introduce Bush as president for the first time. In yet another exercise of parochial privilege, he made sure that Korbel Champagne, a product of Louisville's Brown Forman company, was served at the postinaugural lunch, where he sat next to the new first lady, Laura Bush.

The ceremonies over, Congress returned to work. John McCain soon started making noises about once again offering the McCain-Feingold campaign finance reform measure. In its latest iteration, the bill not only banned soft money as before, but also prevented certain groups such as corporations and labor unions from advertising within sixty days of a general election and restricted some ads from mentioning candidate's names. The "one good thing" McConnell saw in the bill was an increase in the "hard money" contribution limit from $1,000 to $2,000 per election, to be indexed for inflation going forward.

With Republican ranks depleted, McConnell worried that there would not be enough votes to fight off cloture and prevent a vote on the bill. He hoped that President Bush would follow through on his threat to veto this kind of campaign finance reform if it passed, but to his dismay soon discovered otherwise. Unable to stop McCain from moving the measure and not willing to risk bottling up the new president's entire legislative agenda while trying, Senate majority leader Trent Lott agreed to schedule a debate and a vote on McCain-Feingold.

Senators offered several amendments, including measures to replace the ban on soft money with a cap, to institute outright federal funding of elections, and to loosen limits on candidates who faced extremely wealthy opponents. Most were defeated, and the bill at long last moved toward a final vote.

On the day before the roll call the *New York Times* published an op-ed by McConnell entitled "In Defense of Soft Money."[2] Presciently predicting the rise of the shadowy outside groups that would gain attention in the 2004 presidential campaign, McConnell warned of the dangers that ill-conceived reform posed to the political parties and put the blame for the bad legislation on Bill Clinton as much as anyone else. "One result of McCain-Feingold is certain: America loses," he argued. "The parties are vital institutions in our democracy, smoothing ideological edges and promoting citizen participation. The two major parties are the big tents where multitudes of individuals and groups with narrow agendas converge to promote candidates and broad philosophies about the role of government in our society." He continued:

> If special interests cannot give to parties as they have, they will use their money to influence elections in other ways: placing unlimited, unregulated, and undisclosed issue advertisements; mounting their own get-out-the-vote efforts; forming their own action groups. Unrestrained by the balancing effect of parties, which bring multiple interests together, America's politics are likely to fragment. "Virtual" parties will be able to proliferate—shadowy groups with innocuous-sounding names like the Group in Favor of Republican Majorities or the Citizens for Democrats in 2012 that will hold potentially enormous sway in a post-McCain-Feingold world where the parties are diminished for lack of money.

McConnell predicted that under McCain-Feingold, "the power of special interests will not be deterred or diminished. Their speech, political activity and right to 'petition the government for a redress of grievances' (that is, to lobby) are protected by the First Amendment." He closed with a call not to weaken the two-party system "in favor of greater power for wealthy candidates and single-issue groups." McCain-Feingold, he wrote, "will not take any money out of politics. It just takes the parties out of politics."

On the Senate floor the following day, April 2, 2001, McConnell again emphasized the adverse effects the reform would have on the political parties and the advantages it would give the wealthy and the media.

This new world won't take a penny out of politics, not a penny. It will all be spent. It just won't be spent by the parties. It will be spent by the Jerome Kohlbergs [a billionaire reformer] of the world and all of the interest groups out there. . . . Welcome to the brave new world where the voices of parties are quieted, the voices of billionaires are enhanced, the voices of newspapers are enhanced, and the one entity out there in America, the core of the two-party system, that influence is dramatically reduced.[3]

Shortly before the final vote, McCain paid soldierly tribute to McConnell, saying, "There are few things more daunting in politics than the determined opposition of McConnell, and I hope to avoid the experience more often in the future."[4] The Senate then passed the bill, 59–41, and sent it to the Republican-controlled House, where it would await action for months. In the meantime, McConnell started assembling a legal team for the court challenge he thought would soon be necessary.

Although the liberal media lambasted McConnell for resisting the reforms, his work won plaudits on influential conservative pages. In his farewell column, the *Wall Street Journal*'s Paul Gigot praised McConnell as one who "opposed terrible legislation when no one else would."[5] Fred Barnes of the *Weekly Standard* praised McConnell as "unashamedly conservative and fearless in taking unpopular positions."[6]

Financing elections was one thing, but reforming their administration was on almost everyone's political agenda after the controversial and problem-plagued presidential contest of the preceding year. Democrats gave highest priority to helping local governments pay for more modern election equipment, Republicans on tougher anti-fraud provisions. McConnell thought that "motor voter" legislation, the legislative legacy of his former Kentucky Senate colleague Wendell Ford, was a big part of the problem and readily agreed to take the GOP point position on election reform. He pushed for statewide voting lists and stronger voter identification requirements, two elements that managed to survive what was to be a long and tortuous path to passage of a bill.

Shortly after President Bush's budget and tax cut package passed the Senate, Vermont's James Jeffords bolted the GOP to become a nominal independent. This gave Democrats a working Senate majority and with it came control of committee chairmanships, floor action, and conferences with the House. McConnell decided to move back to the Judiciary Committee for a single session. There, newly dominant Democrats blocked some of Bush's judicial nominations. Before long, and in a break with precedent that utterly dismayed McConnell, they would go even further and filibuster judicial nominees so as to deny them an "up or down" vote on confirmation. The issue would simmer for some time before eventually boiling over.

McConnell blasted Democrats for changing the substantive and procedural ground rules that governed Senate consideration of judicial nominees. He accused them of adopting an abortion-based litmus test, abandoning American Bar Association ratings when conservative judges got good ones, and using circuit-wide holds in which a single senator insisting on certain nominees from his or her home state would block all nominees from any state to that appellate court. He urged his Democratic colleagues to return "to traditional standards and practices in the confirmation process." He added, "I fear that if we don't—if we don't resist this game of victory at any cost—the damage will be greater than those who perpetrate it can imagine."[7]

In an April 23 cover story, the *New Republic* ran an inflammatory article by John B. Judis about Chao and McConnell entitled "Sullied Heritage: The Decline of Principled Conservative Hostility to China." The venerable liberal monthly cast the piece as a case study of how two conservative stalwarts—the Heritage Foundation and McConnell— had sold their respective political souls by moderating their formerly hawkish views for the sake of Chinese money that the Chao family had steered their way. Elaine's father, a shipping magnate, had supposedly cultivated, and benefited from, a relationship with his former classmate Jiang Zemin, who rose to become China's leader. The piece made several serious suggestions of impropriety, but provided little factual support or outright accusations of any wrongdoing.

In a letter to the magazine, Steven J. Law, then serving as Chao's chief of staff at the Department of Labor, accused Judis of "picking through the intellectual dumpsters of reactionary websites and peddling their neo-racist conspiracy theories as his own."[8] Citing Judis's multiple "equivocations," Law noted, "When you blow away the flimsy accusations propped up by these disclaimers, all that's left is xenophobic hysteria."

McConnell considered the Judis article to be an outrageous fabrication that tried to depict a family that had fled the communists as mercenary sympathizers. He dismissed it as "vitriolic and absurd," "scurrilous," "outlandish," "baseless," "made-up," "utter nonsense," "xenophobic," and "quite possibly the most bizarre experience" of his public career.

Then, when Al Cross reported on the article in Louisville's *Courier-Journal*, McConnell really got mad. In an op-ed response, he accused Cross, at that time the president-elect of the Society of Professional Journalists, of "regurgitating unsubstantiated gossip" that failed "even the most basic standards of journalistic integrity."[9] Judis was "a political assassin of the left" who was "breathlessly connecting rumor to hearsay with innuendo to imply that my positions on U.S.-China policy have been bought by Chinese sympathizers and the Chinese government." McConnell asked, "If you're going to insinuate that a United States senator is a Communist sympathizer, should you at least be required to show a scintilla of evidence and name a few sources?" Turning to the substance of Judis's journalistic jihad, he declared that "my fundamental position toward China remains unchanged," explaining that his record is one of "condemning China when they violate human rights" while at the same "working to allow Kentucky businesses to profit from Chinese markets. . . . I have never been reluctant to stand up for democratic values even in the face of strident Chinese opposition." The fallout from the Judis article was minimal and, like other such teapot tempests, was forgotten altogether in the wake of truly epochal events to come.

On the morning of September 11, 2001, McConnell was at his Washington home. He delayed his departure for work after hearing reports of a plane hitting one of the World Trade Center towers in New

York. He was watching television and saw a second plane hit the other tower. Elaine, who was at work at the Labor Department, brought some staffers home with her. Later that day, after a third hijacked plane had struck the Pentagon, and a fourth crashed in Pennsylvania, McConnell attended a meeting of senators at a Washington police station. That night he went to the Capitol with many other senators and representatives who sang "God Bless America." Not long after, anthrax-laced envelopes sent to the Capitol disrupted operations for several days.

It seemed that things would never be the same. President Bush's decision to dislodge the Taliban and pursue al Qaeda in Afghanistan had broad support, but the bipartisan comity was short-lived. The business of government slowly returned to the *status quo ante*, complete with plenty of partisan recrimination.

An October survey showed McConnell with a 77 percent approval rating in Kentucky. Nonetheless, the name of Lois Combs Weinberg had surfaced as a potential Democratic candidate in the next year's election. She was the daughter of former Kentucky governor Bert Combs, a Democratic icon, but McConnell preferred her as an opponent to the wealthy Charlie Owen, who was once again rumored to be contemplating the race.

At the Fancy Farm picnic in August, popular Democratic governor Paul Patton surprisingly endorsed Weinberg. The governor's blessing angered Owen, but pretty much sealed the nomination for Weinberg. Patton was thinking about challenging Jim Bunning for the Senate in 2004, and there was widespread speculation that he announced support for Weinberg as the result of a deal with McConnell in which McConnell promised not to meddle in the Democratic Senate primary. Others speculated that McConnell had pledged to assist in a free-speech defense that two former Patton aides were advancing in litigation that arose from the 1995 gubernatorial election. Although both theories fit the facts and the McConnell *modus operandi*, he denies having anything to do with Patton's pulling the rug out from under Owen.[10]

As military action was under way in Afghanistan, McConnell accompanied President and Mrs. Bush to Fort Campbell, Kentucky,

155

home of the 101st Airborne, for Thanksgiving Dinner. He concluded that Bush had "an A+ personality," which was an important political asset. The year to come would provide McConnell with ample opportunities to show that he had some pretty considerable political assets of his own.

18

Record-Breaking Republican
2002

B Y JANUARY 2002, LOIS Combs Weinberg had raised a million dollars for her effort to unseat McConnell. Lacking support from the
Democratic establishment, Charlie Owen opted against the race. "Anybody who had that kind of deep pocket could be a serious problem,"
observed McConnell, once again glad to have gotten the opponent he
preferred.

In March, a Bluegrass Poll put McConnell's approval rating at a
quite respectable 62 percent. The stratospheric numbers that he and
other incumbents had enjoyed in the immediate aftermath of the September 11, 2001, terrorist attacks had come down, as they inevitably
had to. But he began his preparation to fight another tough campaign
from a firm political foundation.

In the first big legislative event of the year, the House of Representatives passed its version of McCain-Feingold, called Shays-Meehan,
and sent it to the Senate. This time, not even McConnell could beat
back the bill. Senator Phil Gramm of Texas, who had announced that
he would retire when his term expired at the end of that Congress,
took to the floor in eloquent opposition. At the end of his remarks, he
paid an emotional tribute to McConnell:

It is awfully easy to stand up and defend things that are popular. It is very difficult to defend ideas that are unpopular, to be attacked every day in the media because of the position you take. There are not many people who are tough enough to do that. There are probably only three or four—five people in the Senate, and I am being generous. . . . I don't know whether they will ever build a monument to the senator from Kentucky, but he is already memorialized in my heart. I will never forget the fight he has made on this bill. I thank him.[1]

McConnell, too, made a floor speech before the vote on final passage of the legislation he had fought so long and hard against. He ranks it at or near the top of his Senate orations, and as one of the most comprehensive expressions of his reasons for opposing this kind of campaign finance reform, it merits an extended excerpt here:

Madam President, I begin by citing the ultimate campaign reform: The first amendment to our Constitution. It says Congress shall make no law—no law—abridging freedom of speech or of the press. I refer to freedom of the press because it is the robust exercise of that freedom which has brought us today to assault the freedom of speech. Over the past five years, the *New York Times* and the *Washington Post* have joined forces to publish an editorial an average of every five and a half days on campaign finance reform.

To buy that editorial space in the *New York Times* or the *Washington Post*, it would cost $36,000 and $8,000, respectively, for each editorial. Multiply that amount by the number of editorials of each paper, and it equals a total value of $8 million in unregulated soft money advertising that frequently mentions federal candidates. Of course, that type of corporate, big-media, soft-money expenditure will not be regulated in this new law.

Why is the press, the institution that has unlimited free speech, so interested in restricting the speech of everyone else?

Let's take a closer look. The unconstitutional issue ad restrictions in this bill purport to limit advertising within proximity to an election. However, it does not, interestingly enough, apply to newspaper ads. So the already powerful corporations that control the news—and, in many instances, the public policy—in America will get more power and more money under this new law.

One has to wonder why that blatant conflict of interest has not been more thoroughly discussed in a debate about the appearance of such conflicts. . . . With no basis in fact or reality, the media consistently and repeatedly alleges that our every decision can be traced back to money given to support a political party. I trust that every Member in the Chamber recognizes how completely absurd, false, and insulting these charges are. We have been derelict in refuting these baseless allegations. I doubt we will ever see a headline that says 99 percent of Congress has never been under an ethics cloud. That is a headline we simply will not see.

Each Member is elected to represent our constituents. We act in what we believe is the best interest of the country and, obviously, of our home states. Does representing the interests of our state and our constituents lead to corruption or the appearance of corruption? These allegations are not an attack on us, they are an attack on representative democracy.

What we are talking about today is speech: the government telling people how, when, and how much speech they are allowed. This wholesale regulation of every action of every American anytime there is a federal election is truly unprecedented. . . .

Today is a sad day for our Constitution, a sad day for our democracy, and for our political parties. We are all now complicit in a dramatic transfer of power from challenger-friendly, citizen-action groups known as political parties to outside special-interest groups, wealthy individuals, and corporations that own newspapers.

After a decade of making my constitutional arguments to this body, I am eager to become the lead plaintiff in this case and take my argument to the branch of government charged with the critical task of interpreting our Constitution.

Today is not a moment of great courage for the legislative branch. We have allowed a few powerful editorial pages to prod us into infringing the First Amendment rights of everybody but them. Fortunately, this is the very moment for which the Bill of Rights was enacted. The Constitution is most powerful when our courage is most lacking.

Madam President, I congratulate Senator McCain and Senator Feingold for their long quest on behalf of this legislation and also Congressmen Shays and Meehan.[2]

The debate over, the bill at long last passed, 60–40. Breaking his campaign promise to veto the measure and offering no explanation for his change of heart, President Bush signed it into law without fanfare.

This epic battle behind them, McConnell noted that he and McCain "kind of warmed up to each other after having been involved in some pretty heated disputes at various times over the years." McCain once again paid tribute to McConnell on the Senate floor. "I won't miss our annual contests on this issue. No one in his right mind would want to continue against so formidable a foe. I can only hope, however, that should I ever find myself again in a pitched legislative battle—shy as I am of entering into them—that my opponent is as principled as Senator Mitch McConnell."[3]

For his part, McConnell moved aggressively to be the lead plaintiff in what he believed would be a successful legal challenge to the constitutionality of McCain-Feingold. Although plenty of powerful interest groups, ranging from the California state Democratic Party to the National Rifle Association, also arrayed themselves against the legislation, he succeeded in having the suit styled as *McConnell v. Federal Election Commission.* The litigation went to a three-judge panel of the U.S. District Court for the District of Columbia.

Turning his attention back to his own ongoing reelection campaign, McConnell took pleasure in the fact that former one-term Democratic congressman Tom Barlow mounted a primary challenge to Weinberg. With a disdain as understandable as it was unwise, Weinberg dismissed Barlow as "token" opposition. As it turned out, she survived the primary by less than a thousand votes, 231,013 to 230,055, or 50.1 percent to 49.9 percent. The surprisingly tight primary struggle devastated her general election prospects. National Democratic money promptly dried up. McConnell would eventually raise almost $6 million for his campaign, Weinberg only $2.2 million.

"At that point," McConnell says, "it crossed my mind that we might have a chance of winning big." In 1966, John Sherman Cooper had garnered 64.5 percent of the vote. That mark stood as the biggest percentage for any Republican Senate candidate in Kentucky history. McConnell doubted he could top it, but believed he might be able to come close.

To the dismay of many of her leftish and civil libertarian supporters, Weinberg went after McConnell for opposing a constitutional amendment against flag desecration. Having encountered this line of attack many times before, McConnell was ready to meet it. He pulled from the shelf film that had been made for a 1996 ad featuring a D-Day veteran and ran it in a powerful ad portraying freedom of speech as one of the main things for which Americans had fought and died. Weinberg went nowhere with the issue.

McConnell also hit back hard. Opposition research revealed that Weinberg and her husband had been engaged in a long-running dispute with a woman over rights to a natural gas well in eastern Kentucky. At one point, Weinberg agents apparently went onto the woman's property with a bulldozer. At the same time, however, the Weinbergs owned a house in the Virgin Islands. Reprising a tactic from his previous two campaigns, McConnell juxtaposed these two facts in ads portraying Weinberg as a wealthy elitist instead of the populist she pretended to be.

In September, Governor Paul Patton first lied about, then tearfully admitted, a tawdry extramarital affair. His consort not only ran a state-regulated nursing home business, but had been his appointee to the state lottery board. This scandal added yet another nail to the already airtight coffin of fellow Democrat Weinberg's campaign and also doomed Patton's planned challenge to Jim Bunning for the Senate in 2004. Moreover, it offered Kentucky Republicans a golden opportunity to finally wrest the governorship from Democratic hands.

On October 11, in the midst of the campaign, McConnell voted for a resolution authorizing President Bush to use military force in Iraq, where dictator Saddam Hussein had repeatedly refused international demands to disclose and dispose of his supposed stocks of weapons of mass destruction. Popular support for an invasion was so high that Weinberg did not even attempt to take political advantage of the issue. McConnell would go on to become one of the most consistent and eloquent advocates for Bush's controversial decision to act on the congressional authorization and launch a preemptive war in Iraq.

By the time the campaign ended, even the liberal *Courier-Journal* would endorse McConnell, who had begun his meeting with the paper's editorial board by asking, "Who has the unfortunate task of writing the endorsement of my opponent?"[4] Even McConnell's most ardent critics could not make a credible case for Weinberg's election.

Pre-election tracking polls put McConnell at 58 percent the week before the election. An energetic and well-funded turnout effort targeted registered Republicans who had voted in 1998, but not 2000, as well as those who had registered since 2000. The late push paid off with a McConnell landslide. Carrying 113 of Kentucky's 120 counties, McConnell garnered 731,679 votes to Weinberg's 399,634. By winning 64.7 percent of the vote, he eclipsed Cooper's record for the largest share of a Senate ballot ever earned by a Republican in Kentucky. Running a race that he colorfully characterized as "stronger than mule piss,"[5] the former intern had finally surpassed his political hero, at least in an electoral respect.

Nationally, Republicans gained two seats and retook the Senate, the first time since Theodore Roosevelt that a party had done this during the first midterm election of a new presidency. Then popular, President Bush had barnstormed hard with obvious benefits. In Minnesota,

Norm Coleman beat former vice president Walter Mondale, and in Missouri, Republican congressman Jim Talent defeated the accidental senator Jean Carnahan. "The Democrats were pretty dispirited over it all," McConnell observed with satisfaction.

Despite running for reelection on his own, McConnell and his staff were also "deeply involved" in helping Kentucky Republicans win election victories that consolidated control of the state Senate. As a result, the commonwealth's GOP increased its majority to 21–17 in that body. Soon thereafter, a Republican also won a special election brought about by a skillful redistricting maneuver by state Senate president David Williams. In just a couple of years, the party had gone from seemingly perpetual minority status to firm control of the upper chamber.

A week after these election victories, McConnell's Republican colleagues elected him as majority whip, the party's second highest Senate leadership position.[6] He had been quietly campaigning and securing commitments for months. Bowing to reality, his only potential opponent, Idaho's Larry Craig, opted against the race a week before the balloting.

As whip, McConnell would be responsible for knowing how the GOP senators would vote on an issue, making sure they were present for meetings and votes, and assisting majority leader Trent Lott with strategy and tactics. "I've always said the Senate is a hundred people with the biggest egos and the sharpest elbows in America," McConnell commented. "Every single one of them would like to be in charge of the other ninety-nine." To succeed in any Senate leadership position, he said, "You have to convince the others who might like to lead themselves to let you do that."

He promised to help President Bush push his agenda through the Republican-controlled Senate, but also to work with Democrats. He initially planned to spend most of his time on the floor while the Senate was in session so he could "be in the middle of every single piece of legislation." But he would quickly discover the inefficiencies associated with that practice and find more effective ways to influence and monitor legislation.

Robert Bennett of Utah, McConnell's campaign manager for the post, called him "a man of absolute principle," a "great political mind," and a strategist who "understands what's doable and what's not, so he won't tilt at any windmills." Charlie Cook, the savvy editor of the *Cook Political Report*, said that McConnell was "as good a strategist and tactician as one can find on Capitol Hill."[7]

These talents would be put to the test sooner than even McConnell could have imagined. In early December, at a one-hundredth birthday party for Strom Thurmond, the South Carolina senator and 1948 presidential candidate on the segregationist Dixiecrat ticket, Lott said, "I want to say this about my state. When Strom Thurmond ran for president, we voted for him. We're proud of it. And if the rest of the country had followed our lead, we wouldn't have had all these problems over the years, either."

At the outset, McConnell strongly defended his longtime friend, but not his controversial comment, and suggested that the proud Mississippian might resign from the Senate if ousted from leadership. This would deprive Republicans of their working majority if a Democrat succeeded to the seat. McConnell also threatened to seek censure of certain Democrats for some of their embarrassing public comments if they attempted sanctions against Lott for his ill-chosen words. But on December 20, with disenchantment rising within both the Republican establishment and the conservative base (especially after Lott cynically endorsed vigorous affirmative action programs in an apologetic television appearance on Black Entertainment Television), McConnell told Lott he needed to "step down as soon as possible."[8]

Lott reluctantly did so. McConnell made no effort to succeed to the majority leader position. Three days later the GOP caucus chose Bill Frist, just elected to his second term as senator from Tennessee. A fifty-year-old Princeton- and Harvard-educated heart surgeon and heir to a fortune from the world's largest hospital company, Frist had a lot of political assets but lacked institutional experience and parliamentary expertise. He would have to rely heavily on McConnell's mastery of Senate procedure.

After celebrating what had been a successful year despite its unpleasant end, McConnell, sixty, scheduled his annual year-end physical examination with the Capitol physician. He passed with flying colors, but the doctor said that he should take a stress test simply because of his age. McConnell had no symptoms, but still felt a vague "sense of foreboding." Ever the prudent and realistic planner, he jotted down a few thoughts about funeral arrangements just in case.

19

Surgery and Successes
2003

O N JANUARY 7, 2003, Vice President Dick Cheney administered the oath with which McConnell began his fourth Senate term. Back in control, the Republican majority promptly passed eleven appropriations bills that their Democratic predecessors had left unfinished.

Four days later, on the eve of the State of the Union address, McConnell took that stress test the Capitol physician had recommended. He failed, "which was," he admitted, "pretty scary." After undergoing a cardiac catheterization, McConnell got the news that he needed triple-bypass surgery right away. He consulted with Frist and spent an anxious weekend before undergoing a successful operation the following Monday morning, February 3.

McConnell returned to his office only three weeks later, but became so exhausted that he could not accomplish much. After five weeks, he was working a few hours a day and made it back to the Senate floor for much of the mid-March "vote-a-rama" associated with the budget resolution. Votes often came at ten-minute intervals, and he would lie down in his nearby "hideaway" office in between them.

By midyear, McConnell was back at work full speed. As whip, he spent much more time at the Capitol building than he had before. He now managed two staffs, a "regular" one at his office in the Russell

Building to deal mainly with Kentucky issues, and a whip staff at the Capitol to address federal issues and count votes among his Republican colleagues. He discovered that his responsibilities as whip allowed him almost no down time, since he had to work constantly to get the needed number of votes on a myriad of issues.

Although being number two carried with it some inevitable frustrations, McConnell liked Frist, whom he admired as something of a Renaissance man. The working relationship between them quickly developed into an effective and harmonious one, and their first session as a leadership team proved productive. He was especially proud that the Senate passed the third largest tax cut in history, with Vice President Cheney casting a tie-breaking vote.

Back home, Kentucky had not been governed by a Republican since Louie Nunn left office in 1971. McConnell was determined to see that a GOP candidate won the governorship in 2003. He had begun the preceding year by turning state GOP attention to campaign finance. Kentucky's partial public financing law and relatively low $1.9 million spending limit would continue to handicap Republicans in overcoming Democratic advantages in registration and media support. So the law had to go.

Having twice failed to convince courts to strike down the law, McConnell turned for help to state Senate president David Williams, whom he regarded as "a very, very intelligent, very skillful political operator." Williams and his Republican caucus insisted on defunding the public financing system as a condition of passing a state budget. They held firm, even after Governor Patton called a special session, and Kentucky went without a budget for the fiscal year that began on July 1, 2002. Then, in disregard of the state constitution, but without any real opposition from Republicans afraid of being blamed for shutting down the government, Patton proceeded to pay out state funds as if a budget had passed.

Rallying around a battle cry of "No welfare for politicians," Republicans had run against the public financing system in the state Senate elections of 2002. Opposition to taxpayer-funded campaigns proved to be powerful and popular. After Republicans gained Senate seats in the November elections, House Democrats bowed to reality and surrendered. The General Assembly finally passed a budget in early 2003, but it did not appropriate any money for public financing of that year's campaign for governor. This set the stage for a well-funded and highly competitive gubernatorial race. Now all the GOP needed was a candidate.

In early 2002, McConnell had met in his Capitol office with congressman Ernie Fletcher, from Lexington, telling him, "I think you'd be a hell of a candidate."[1] Two other well-respected Republicans were interested in the contest, but McConnell put his support behind Fletcher, believing he had by far the best chance to win in the fall. McConnell supported Fletcher privately at first, but more and more publicly as the primary campaign progressed, although he never made an actual endorsement.

McConnell explained, "Ernie was articulate. He was intelligent. He had been through some tough races, and he had the least seniority to give up" of any of Kentucky's representatives. "For all of those reasons, it seemed to me he was a logical candidate for governor. . . . And he ended up being an excellent candidate"—except for one near-fatal mistake.

McConnell staffer Hunter Bates harbored political aspirations of his own, and his boss had boldly endorsed him as the Republican candidate for the Fourth District congressional seat for 2004. It was the state's only congressional seat still occupied by a Democrat. Nonetheless, the endorsement "was greeted rather rudely," McConnell says, "as being sort of heavy-handed on my part." Northern Kentucky was Jim Bunning's home turf, and he did not take kindly to having a McConnell loyalist forced on him and his region.

The matter resolved itself within a month or so, however, when Fletcher offered Bates the lieutenant governor spot on his ticket. The office of lieutenant governor was essentially powerless, but McConnell "had wholeheartedly advocated" the choice for several reasons, including that Bates had just managed McConnell's record-breaking statewide race and knew how to run one.

Everything was proceeding according to plan until Steve Nunn, the son of the last GOP governor and now seeking to follow in his father's gubernatorial footsteps, filed a lawsuit alleging that Bates did not meet the state constitution's six-year residency requirement. Kentucky law required candidates for governor and lieutenant governor to file together, so the lawsuit against Bates was effectively an attempt to disqualify Fletcher, too. Bates lost the first legal round when a local court ruled that the time he had spent living in the Washington, D.C., area while working for McConnell had interrupted his Kentucky residency despite the fact that he had maintained significant contacts with the commonwealth. Bates saw that a prompt resolution was required and formally resigned from the ticket without appealing.

Fletcher selected Steve Pence, the U.S. attorney for the western half of the state, to succeed Bates. But this did not stop Nunn or his running mate, state representative Bob Heleringer, who pressed to have Fletcher banished from the gubernatorial ballot. They put Fletcher in the witness box during a second suit, but the court ruled that Fletcher was a bona fide candidate and entitled to replace Bates on the ticket. In an appeal decided shortly before the May primary, the state Supreme Court ruled unanimously for Fletcher in what it acknowledged to be "a close case on the law."[2]

Despite these difficulties, Fletcher won the primary in a landslide, getting almost five times as many votes as Nunn. Summer surveys showed Fletcher comfortably ahead of Democratic nominee Ben Chandler, the state attorney general and grandson of A. B. "Happy" Chandler, the legendary former Kentucky governor, U.S. senator, and major league baseball commissioner. Chandler had prevailed in the Democratic primary by a narrower-than-expected margin (143,150 to 132,627) over state Speaker of the House Jody Richards, but only after a hard-hitting Chandler ad had driven a millionaire nursing home magnate named Bruce Lunsford from the field.

Although Chandler had often been at odds with the Democratic establishment and Governor Patton, he campaigned under the dark cloud that Patton's adultery and public disgrace had cast over the entire party. Fletcher held his lead throughout the campaign, largely by heeding McConnell's counsel to run the race on the single issue of "cleaning up the mess in Frankfort." McConnell and Billy Piper, the chief of his Senate staff, were frequently involved in conference calls with Fletcher and his team to discuss strategy and tactics.[3]

The contest was light on discussion of other issues. Fletcher promised not to raise taxes, vowed to move beyond "the good ole boy politics of a bygone era," and said he could cure Kentucky's budget ills by eliminating "waste, fraud, and abuse." Chandler, desperate to divert attention from Patton and the condition of Kentucky after decades of Democratic dominance, tried to make hay from job losses and the "Bush economy." McConnell dismissed this Democratic tactic as "rather foolish" given Bush's 60 percent approval rating in Kentucky.

Late in the race Chandler finally started arguing that he could reform Frankfort more effectively than Fletcher could. This was the approach McConnell would have urged on the Democrat from the outset, since "it was clear from the surveys" that it was the only issue that really resonated with voters. McConnell observed, "Chandler had enough facts to demonstrate that he had fought against the mess in Frankfort, but that dawned on them too late. The Democrats finally tried to do that in the last two weeks, but by that time we had already laid the groundwork that he was part of the whole morass over there."

Fletcher rolled to victory in November, amassing 596,284 votes to Chandler's 487,159 in a rare display of strength down the ballot. Republicans also captured the offices of secretary of state and agriculture commissioner. McConnell was elated, and Fletcher's December 9 inauguration was almost as much a celebration of McConnell's role as architect of his party's ascendancy in Kentucky as it was of Fletcher's win.

This victory and the many that preceded it were gratifying for McConnell, not only because "winning is fun," he said, but also "because it has a huge impact on public policy. It makes a difference who wins elections. If you don't win, you don't make public policy. So one of my great satisfactions here is that I played a great role in turning this into, at the very least, a two-party state and potentially a Republican state."

By focusing "on winnable races that were worth being involved in," McConnell had made Democrats a minority party in Kentucky in terms of influence, if not in numbers. He encouraged Republicans to figuratively "shoot the wounded" and finish off the remaining Democrats. Practicing what he preached, he quickly turned his attention to the special election that would fill Fletcher's now-vacant congressional seat in February of the following year.

In the meantime, the *McConnell v. Federal Election Commission* case, challenging the constitutionality of the McCain-Feingold campaign finance reform law, had made its way to the U.S. Supreme Court. The previous May, almost six months after hearing arguments in the case, the three-judge panel of the U.S. District Court for the District of Columbia issued an incomprehensible 774-page opinion that upheld some portions of the law but struck down others.[4] Dissatisfied with anything less than outright victory, McConnell bypassed the Court of Appeals as provided by statute and immediately filed a petition for Supreme Court review signed by former solicitor general and Clinton-Whitewater independent counsel Kenneth Starr. The fact that he had gone forward without consulting any of the co-plaintiffs irked some of them.[5]

The Supreme Court heard an unusually generous four hours of oral argument on September 8. McConnell was cautiously optimistic that a favorable decision would be forthcoming. He was wrong.

On December 10, a fragmented court issued a 5–4 decision upholding most of McCain-Feingold.[6] In the most significant parts of the opinion, a bare majority of justices held that (1) political parties and candidates could be banned from using unregulated "soft money" for federal election activities; (2) the ban on party donations to tax-exempt entities was generally valid; (3) "soft money" could not be used for issue ads that clearly identified a candidate; (4) the cost of third-party issue ads coordinated with federal candidates' campaigns could validly be considered as contributions to those campaigns; (5) a pro-incumbent "blackout" period, forbidding the use of federally regulated funds to mention a candidate's name in an ad within sixty days of the election, passed muster; and (6) labor unions and corporations were generally required to pay for issue ads from separately segregated funds. Chief Justice William Rehnquist and Justices Anthony Kennedy, Antonin Scalia, and Clarence Thomas filed vigorous dissents.

Surprised and disappointed, McConnell called the decision the Supreme Court's worst since *Dred Scott.* He thought it hurt the political parties, especially by regulating formerly nonfederal funds they used in state races. McConnell regretted that the law would redirect campaign finance dollars to organizations much less accountable than the parties, and would burden political speech that ought to be free, but he had also concluded that it would be largely ineffective in reducing the amount of money in political campaigns as its proponents hoped. He called McCain the day after the decision and "congratulated him on his great victory."

"The Supreme Court has spoken," McConnell said publicly. "They are the last word." But even as he acknowledged this lamentable reality, he added, "The issue is never over. You are talking about the ability of people to speak in a free society, and political speech, which is at the core of the First Amendment. People want to have their say." He continued, "There won't be any less speech or money spent. Dramatically more will be spent, just in a different way."[7] About this he was correct.

In the meantime, McConnell had immersed himself in the business of a busy Senate. After leading a group of five senators to Iraq, Afghanistan, Pakistan, and Turkey, he returned home and worked hard to make sure that the $20 billion of rebuilding funds for Iraq contained in an $87 billion supplemental spending measure took the form of a grant, not a loan, as some Republicans sought.

Also that fall, the Senate fell two votes short of passing the conference report on the energy bill and barely overcame procedural hurdles to adopt the conference report on the pricey Medicare prescription drug benefit. McConnell saw the huge entitlement expansion as politically essential, so his party could boast that "a Republican president and a Republican Congress enacted the first significant Medicare bill since the system started in the '60s." Many conservatives were not impressed.

To McConnell's disappointment, and despite his best efforts, President Bush did not seek full funding of the antifraud portions of the election reform bill that had passed the year before. Contrary to form, McConnell moved to violate the budget act to "get all the money out and maximize the chances of having a more honest election in '04," which he thought would be "substantially to the advantage of the Republicans." His goal in attempting to circumvent standard procedure was to provide funding to states and localities for election improvements that would "make it easier to vote, but harder to cheat."

In a year-end assessment, the *New York Times*, the unofficial organ of the speech regulators, admitted that McConnell's much-admired performance as captain of the losing campaign finance crusade could still "pay dividends" for him politically. Calling him "smart and not shy about letting it show," the *Times* said he was "considered by many colleagues to be among the savviest tacticians in the Senate and a relentless opponent." Said one senior Senate source, "He is very good at working behind the scenes to help members." On full display over a panoply of issues for the first time, this combination of characteristics put him first in line among the probable successors to Frist as Republican leader.[8]

For once, McConnell agreed with the *Times*. He continued carefully to position himself for advancement and used his ever-increasing power to gain even more.

20

Buyout, Bunning, and Bush
2004

I N HIS FIRST MAJOR address to his party after its long-awaited return
to the Kentucky Governor's Mansion in late 2003, McConnell had
sounded a cautionary note. "It is important not to be seized with hubris.
You are only as good as the next election. And just as soon as you
start delivering bad results you will have the experience that is one of
my favorite sayings in politics. 'You meet the same people on the way
down that you did on the way up.' So I try not to allow myself to get
too high or too low."

He spoke from experience. When McConnell was in his twen-
ties, Kentucky had a Republican governor, two Republican senators,
and three of the state's seven U.S. representatives. By the time he
was elected county judge in 1977 "we were down to nothing," largely
because of intraparty jealousies and squabbles.

The year that was about to unfold would prove McConnell a
prophet. It began with a February special election to fill Ernie Fletcher's former congressional seat. After polling showed Ben Chandler, the
just-defeated Democratic gubernatorial nominee, to be far and away
the favorite, the National Democratic Congressional Committee pursued him hard. McConnell tried to bluff Chandler out of the race by
publicly warning that the day he announced his candidacy would be

the best day of his campaign. But Chandler enjoyed high name recognition, and his loss in the governor's race was more of a referendum on the disgraced Patton than any kind of verdict on him.

In making the race, Chandler was conceivably risking his political career. But he needed a job, knew that a win would erase any negativity from the governor's race, and rightly reckoned that he remained popular with Kentucky voters, especially on his home district's turf. A win against the Republican godfather would confirm his status as the state's top Democrat.

Turning on a dime, Chandler signed the Americans for Tax Reform "no new tax" pledge that he had refused to sign in the governor's race. In an attempt to seem strong on defense, he endorsed retired general Wesley Clark's hopeless candidacy for the Democratic presidential nomination. He quickly concluded that he could not "out-defense" Bush and the Republicans, however, and shifted his focus to protecting military veterans. It worked.

Republicans nominated state senator Alice Forgy Kerr, sister of the serial GOP gubernatorial aspirant Larry Forgy. She seemed to be the only hopeful prepared to do everything necessary to win, including raise a lot of money fast. McConnell publicly endorsed her for the nomination and, after she got it, helped fund her campaign via his leadership political action committee, the Bluegrass Committee. He also dispatched a trio of trusted staffers to direct the effort.

Chandler nevertheless cruised to victory by a comfortable and somewhat surprising 12 percent margin. With big wins so rare in the recent Democratic past, this one propelled him to titular party leadership. Never in Kentucky history had anyone who lost a race for governor recovered more quickly or completely.

Undeterred, McConnell turned his attention to recruiting candidates for the Kentucky state legislative elections that fall. Republicans were seeking to take the majority in the lower chamber, where Democrats held a sixty-three to thirty-six edge with all seats up for grabs, and hold it in the upper, where Republicans had a twenty-two to sixteen advantage with nine of the eighteen seats up for election.

The Kentucky GOP "used to have to beg people to run," McConnell observed, "but now they are coming to us." In state races, McConnell looked for people who were "reasonably attractive and articulate and can put some time into it." With the help of longtime party stalwart Bob Gable, he found more such people than almost anyone expected.

Fletcher, however, was faltering fast. His first six months featured a series of missteps and embarrassments, ranging from misbegotten personnel moves to failure to pass either a state budget or his tax reform plan in his first legislative session. To make matters worse, the transponder of his state plane malfunctioned as he flew to Washington in June to attend Ronald Reagan's funeral. Panic ensued on Capitol Hill as dignitaries and mourners were sent scrambling because of fears that the unidentified flying object was a terrorist attack. Oblivious to the havoc his plane had caused, Fletcher then inserted himself into a position of grossly undue prominence next to Secretary of State Colin Powell at the service.

Kentucky Republicans lost another special election, this one for a state Senate seat in the heavily Democratic Henderson area in near western Kentucky. McConnell had advised Fletcher to call the election for November, when Republicans would be going to the polls in large numbers, but the governor instead called it for July, virtually assuring low turnout and defeat.

This second special election loss sobered state Republicans. Still, the party was confident about its biggest race upcoming in the fall, Senator Jim Bunning's reelection bid. No well-known Democrat had filed against him, and he held a huge advantage in name recognition and financial resources over his eventual Democratic foe, an obscure state senator, Dr. Daniel Mongiardo.

As the cherry blossoms colored Washington that spring, the National Commission on Terrorist Attacks Upon the United States, better known as the 9/11 Commission, was becoming mired in partisanship. Fearing that the panel would fail to produce an actionable report, McConnell made a strong statement on the Senate floor:

There is no question the terrorists are at war with us. Unfortunately, it is becoming increasingly apparent in Washington we are at war with each other. . . . Sadly, the Commission's public hearings have allowed those with political axes to grind, such as Richard Clarke, to play shamelessly to the partisan gallery of liberal special interests seeking to bring down the President. These special interest groups have undeniably exploited the Commission for political gain.[1]

The Commission soon pulled itself together and issued a respectable, but far from perfect, bipartisan product.

On other issues, however, Democrats seemed internally conflicted over whether to cooperate with Republicans to get things done, thus risking political benefit to President Bush, or to simply obstruct. They opted for the latter, and little else of significance happened legislatively as the presidential campaign raged.

However, McConnell and other tobacco-state legislators kept pushing for a buyout of the production quotas that producers owned as part of the federal price support program, which was collapsing under the weight of foreign competition and health concerns. McConnell was determined that any legislative end to it would be on terms favorable to his agricultural constituency. But the tobacco situation was so dire that in 2003 McConnell had come close to telling the Kentucky Farm Bureau that there would be no buyout.

Indeed, there were several obstacles to pulling it off. One was capturing the revenue to fund it. Paying for the buyout required something eerily similar to a tax increase, even if it was called something else and paid for by smokers in the form of higher prices passed through to them by the tobacco companies. It was also a problem that the benefits accrued mainly to a few states, with Kentucky prominent among them.

Because of the revenue component, buyout legislation had to originate in the House, where a measure that Fletcher had originally coauthored during his days as a congressman was tweaked and revived. Its backers attached the measure to a "must pass" piece of international tax legislation. In June, the House passed a $9.6 billion buyout proposal that did not provide for federal regulation of tobacco by the Food and Drug Administration, a provision several liberal senators strongly supported. The Senate then passed its own $11 billion buyout measure that did include federal regulation.

Both McConnell and Bunning got themselves appointed to the conference committee. House Appropriations Committee chairman Bill Thomas of Florida chaired the conference committee and was extremely receptive to input from McConnell's legislative assistant for agriculture, in crafting the "chairman's mark" that would provide the basis for negotiation. That mark omitted the federal regulation component, so the Senate conferees moved to add it by amendment, knowing that the House conferees would not accept the change. The conference report ultimately provided for a $10.1 billion buyout to be paid for by the tobacco companies over ten years based on their respective market shares, but not for federal regulation.

Both chambers passed the compromise and President Bush signed it into law in late October. McConnell, who had endured considerable criticism when he first contemplated a buyout back in 1998, felt vindicated. He noted that growers had been close to "getting nothing at all," adding that getting any buyout "is a legislative miracle." In Kentucky, the nation's leading burley tobacco producer, more than 100,000 people would share about $2.5 billion.[2]

Responding to later criticism, he defended his work on behalf of Kentucky's tobacco industry:

I secured $328 million in Tobacco Loan Assistance Payments for growers in 1999—the first such payments for tobacco growers in history. I secured $340 million more in 2000, $129 million in 2001, and $53 million in 2002. I personally led the effort to forgive losses on 1999 crop price support loan stocks, saving tobacco farmers $625 million. And I secured the $10 billion buyout, ensuring tobacco farmers economic security even as many choose to retire from tobacco farming. I'm proud of my record and I stand by it.[3]

Given Frist's intention to leave the Senate when his term ended in 2006, McConnell had started making confidential contacts with his colleagues about succeeding him as the chamber's top Republican. He employed the same vote-counting criterion he had always used, counting only those senators who looked him in the eye and made an unconditional commitment to vote for him. As usual, McConnell made no public statements and did not talk to the press about his leadership aspirations. He simply worked hard at winning as much support as possible.

Pennsylvania's Rick Santorum, a movement conservative widely regarded as a rising star, was also interested. According to *Roll Call*, McConnell's decision to try to lock in votes early gave him an edge. "I am not as laser-beamed as Senator McConnell," Santorum said as he shifted his focus to being elected Republican whip. This left McConnell as the clear frontrunner, if not the only credible contender, for Republican leader.[4]

McConnell was trying hard to ensure that Republicans would maintain their Senate majority. Under McCain-Feingold, the NRSC had only about half the net dollars to spend in the 2004 election cycle as previously. McConnell and other senators in or aspiring to leadership positions used a variety of techniques to help Republican candidates, and especially challengers running against Democratic incumbents.

One such tactic was so-called leadership PACs, but these were limited to $10,000 per primary and general-election cycles. Senators also contributed money to the NRSC from their own campaign committees. McConnell gave around $350,000 from his 2008 treasury. Perhaps the most significant new technique was "routing." A highly successful example of routing was the Louisville fundraiser McConnell held for Richard Burr, Jim DeMint, and John Thune, candidates in North Carolina, South Carolina, and South Dakota, respectively. The event produced more than $50,000 for each of their campaigns, not to mention grateful supporters for McConnell's leadership bid. All three won, as the GOP sent seven new Republicans to the Senate while losing only one seat that it had held.

Of all the races that year, Bunning's hard-fought reelection victory was naturally the most gratifying for McConnell, though this time Bunning had wanted to do things himself and his way. McConnell counseled him to ignore his Democratic opponent, the little-known senator and doctor, Dan Mongiardo altogether and never mention Mongiardo's name. But the gaffe-prone Bunning ignored this advice and quickly caught media hell for saying that his opponent looked like the wicked sons of Saddam Hussein. The remark earned Mongiardo, a son of first-generation immigrants and the first in his eastern Kentucky family to go to college, both attention and sympathy.

Although Bunning surpassed McConnell's fundraising record for a Kentucky Senate contest, amassing more than $6 million, he seemed to blunder almost every time he opened his mouth. In August, he alleged that Mongiardo operatives had assaulted his wife at the Fancy Farm picnic. He claimed that the police escort he employed at routine campaign stops was necessary to protect him from terrorist threats. Then it emerged that he had read from a teleprompter during his only debate with Mongiardo, in which he had participated from a Washington television studio while Mongiardo was in Kentucky. These serial mistakes played into Mongiardo's campaign theme that Bunning was too old and out of touch.

National media came to Kentucky as the race tightened, and many outlets were there when Bunning committed his crowning gaffe. At a large luncheon meeting of the Louisville Rotary Club, he responded to a reporter's question by admitting that he knew nothing about a highly publicized national news story in which some Kentucky reservists serving in Iraq had allegedly refused to perform a mission because it was too dangerous. He volunteered that he had not read a newspaper or watched television news in several weeks and said he got all his information from Fox News. Within twenty-four hours, the Democratic Senatorial Campaign Committee had turned this into a devastating ad.

Stories about Bunning's age and mental competence started showing up all over state and national media. A poll published in the *Courier-Journal* ten days before the election showed Bunning ahead by a mere 6 points, 49 percent to 43 percent. Democratic and Republican tracking polls showed his formerly enormous lead practically disappearing.[5]

Eight days before the election, Bunning began a statewide bus tour intended to present him in a secure environment, yet most of the publicity centered around an insult. State Senate president David Williams was part of the caravan, and rashly called Mongiardo "limp-wristed" and a "switch-hitter." Another GOP state senator, Elizabeth Tori, then questioned whether one could rightly call Mongiardo a "man."

These slurs were clearly signals to the social conservatives who were expected to turn out in large numbers to support a Kentucky constitutional amendment banning gay marriage. McConnell says the statements were "very harmful" and "not premeditated," but advised Bunning against rebuffing his own key supporters in the final days of a close campaign.[6] So Bunning did not distance himself from the controversial comments, and Mongiardo once again looked like a victim. The press made the epithets the big issue of the race's last few days.

Concluding that it was too late to rehabilitate Bunning's image, McConnell urged an all-out attack on Mongiardo. He knew Bunning would lose unless he gave voters a reason to be against Mongiardo, whose negatives were polling very low. McConnell called for 100 percent attack ads until election day. Bunning gave the okay.

With President Bush running strongly in Kentucky, McConnell moved fast to "federalize" the race by linking Mongiardo with the Democratic presidential candidate, liberal Massachusetts senator John Kerry, and in a way that pandered to the commonwealth's considerable anti-gay marriage contingent. Mongiardo and Kerry agreed that there was no need to amend the federal Constitution to protect traditional marriage, so McConnell conceived an ad pairing the two on this issue and urging voters to remember the Democrats' position when voting on the state amendment.

In a rare move of addressing two issues in one commercial, the same ad hit Mongiardo for taking campaign money from trial lawyers while opposing limits on lawsuits against doctors. It was a powerful one-two punch.

Going into the final weekend, McConnell believed that Bunning was going to lose. Many campaigns quit using tracking polls on the Thursday before the vote because it takes three days to establish a credible track. Bunning's did not, however, and a Sunday night tracking poll showed him rebounding to a 49 percent-40 percent lead. McConnell concluded that the ads had stopped Bunning's collapse, but he still forecast a cliff-hanger in which undecided voters would break for Mongiardo.

On election night, Bunning gained strength as the tally moved westward. He won his home congressional district in northern Kentucky by around 50,000 votes and then carried the First and Second Districts of western Kentucky by about 30,000 each. His margin was 873,507 to 850,855, or 50.7 percent to 49.3 percent, actually a significant improvement over his 1998 performance. Looking back at a race he described as "painful" because of the nature of the Democratic attacks, Bunning choked up before a postelection GOP audience. He profusely thanked McConnell for his support. "I hope everybody here understands how much he stuck his neck out for me through thick and thin during that race last year," Bunning said.

McConnell also helped design the strategy and tactics that helped Republicans turn in an unexpectedly strong showing in state legislative contests. The party planned on Fletcher's being a positive force in the fight for control of the state House and Senate. But McConnell recognized that the governor's "poll numbers were in the tank" and advised him to lie low until after the election. Fletcher complied.

Instead of running on Kentucky issues, McConnell wanted to federalize these state races, too. He helped plan a direct-mail and radio blitz connecting Kentucky Democrats to Kerry. It worked. With considerable assistance from Bush at the top of the ticket and from the gay marriage amendment at the bottom, Republicans picked up a state Senate seat and went up from thirty-six to forty-three in the House.

Commenting on the outlook for Kentucky Republicans after Fletcher's victory in 2003, McConnell had observed that "the test of how long we are going to be able to stay on top will depend upon whether Fletcher and McConnell get along and Fletcher and Bunning get along and all of us make a conscious effort to minimize jealousies and differences." He was proven right in 2004, a remarkable year in Kentucky politics. Kentucky's GOP big three had worked together well, and the state party apparatus had proved itself once again.

Earlier in the year, the Kentucky Republican Party had completed a $600,000 renovation of its headquarters in Frankfort. In a fitting tribute, the party named the modernized house for McConnell, who had raised most of the money to pay off the building's debt. As the Kentucky GOP stood at its historic high tide of success in the state, there was no doubt or denying that McConnell had been both the strategic architect and master builder.

President Bush's reelection victory was also meaningful for McConnell, who reprised his role as state campaign chairman. McConnell had suffered from a bad "sense of foreboding" throughout the presidential campaign. Little had gone right for Bush from the capture of Saddam Hussein in late 2003 through the end of the Democratic convention the following summer.

McConnell's name came up in one of the presidential debates. Responding to a question about the minimum wage, Bush said that he supported a plan proposed by McConnell. The problem was that McConnell had no real plan, only an idea about coupling the wage hike with tax and regulatory relief for small businesses. Luckily for both men, the media made nothing of the presidential overstatement.

Although the weapons of mass destruction that had been Bush's rationale for the Iraq war did not exist, McConnell still called the administration's policy "gutsy" and "right" and mounted a powerful defense of it on the Senate floor. He strongly believed that the liberation of 25 million people and the institution of free government in Iraq opened the door to democracy throughout the Middle East. So McConnell, who was one of the staunchest supporters of the president's policy in Iraq, breathed a significant sigh of relief when Bush ran up an especially impressive 20 percent margin in Kentucky.

Late in the year, McConnell traveled to the Middle East to accept an honorary degree from Israel's Weizman Institute. On the day after the funeral for longtime Palestinian leader Yassir Arafat, McConnell met with Israeli prime minister Ariel Sharon and former prime ministers Benjamin Netanyahu and Shimon Peres. He also inspected Israel's controversial security fence and concluded that it would reduce violence and thus enhance the chances of peace.

2004 had been a tough year, but it had ended well. Republicans reelected a president, kept control of the Senate, and reelected the unopposed McConnell as their whip. His resulting satisfaction would be extremely short-lived.

21

An In-Between Year
2005

THE POLITICAL PICTURE LOOKED promising to McConnell as the new Congress convened in January. President Bush and Senator Bunning had been reelected, the former as the first president since Franklin Roosevelt to win reelection with increased majorities in both congressional chambers. Governor Ernie Fletcher was beginning a session of the Kentucky General Assembly comprised of a Republican state Senate and seven more Republican state representatives than when the legislature had last gathered. Republicans in Kentucky and around the country felt confident that their party was everywhere on the ascent.

Newsweek's Howard Fineman penned a flattering profile of McConnell, calling him "the take-no-prisoners ruler of the Bluegrass" and "the master of all of the Kentucky he surveys." Noting the statue of Henry Clay in the county courthouse, Fineman quoted Louisville's Democratic mayor, Jerry Abramson, as saying, "We may have to take Clay down and put Mitch up there instead."[1]

Characteristically cautious, however, McConnell once again warned his state's GOP against overconfidence, and privately worried about the Fletcher administration's "excessive exuberance." Paraphrasing President Nixon, he observed, "Your greatest mistakes are typically right after your greatest triumphs."

Sure enough, Fletcher soon found himself mired in an investigation by state attorney general Greg Stumbo, an aggressive Democratic partisan who had become the state's top prosecutor after Kentucky Republicans inexplicably nominated a scandal-plagued former Democrat with no chance of winning. Stumbo soon stumbled on a perfect pretext for a politically motivated quest to destroy the state's first Republican governor in three decades. A disgruntled bureaucrat alleged that Fletcher's administration had violated the state's merit system law by improperly firing, transferring, and passing over Democrats in order to hire more Republicans. Kentucky's Democrats had ruthlessly done the same thing to Republicans for decades, but they did not create a permanent record of their misdeeds by using Blackberries and e-mail as Fletcher's young go-getters did.

Stumbo could have handled the matter administratively or civilly, but instead a batch of unprecedented grand jury indictments were issued throughout the summer as the investigation drew steadily closer to Fletcher. At a surreal pep rally in the state Capitol rotunda on August 29, the governor announced a blanket pardon covering everyone except himself. The next day, he invoked his Fifth Amendment right against self-incrimination and refused to testify before the grand jury. A few weeks later, he fired several employees, including four he had pardoned. The Democrats who had helped elect Fletcher deserted him in droves, and more than a few Republicans, disgusted by what seemed to be yet another state government scandal, joined them.

The state Republican Party chairman, former Fletcher administration official Darrell Brock, was among those indicted. McConnell initially considered it untenable to have the state party leader under indictment, but Fletcher feared that removing Brock would look like an admission of wrongdoing. Reluctantly, McConnell acquiesced in keeping Brock, but began to quietly reassert control over the party operation, primarily through its budget committee. Fletcher then reversed course and called for Brock's resignation, but by then McConnell had become comfortable with Brock's remaining in the post and blocked his ouster. By year's end, Fletcher exercised almost no authority over the GOP, and McConnell was growing ever more frustrated with him.

The Republican situation in Kentucky had become highly problematic. Although McConnell regarded the Fletcher matter as not worthy of much attention, the Kentucky media focused on the case relentlessly. The situation "was not by any objective standard a serious scandal," says McConnell. "These are people who were allegedly trying to hire their friends in politics, which strikes me as kind of a small-time indiscretion if there is any." But, he adds, it "was treated by the two major newspapers as a serious credible scandal."

As the media never tired of noting, McConnell did not publicly comment on the situation. He had nothing to do with the patronage mess and could only make matters worse by talking about it. So he just kept quiet. Privately, however, he blamed Fletcher for the bungling and incompetence that gave "Stumbo the gun to shoot them with."

McConnell still did what he could to strengthen the party's position. He worked with congressman Ed Whitfield to secure another party switch that gave Republicans forty-four seats in the state House, the most it had held since 1944. He hoped this change was a sign that Republican allegiance in Kentucky had grown to a point where the party could withstand the governor's growing unpopularity, though he feared that Democrats would be able to tar all GOP candidates by association with Fletcher. In the meantime, he counseled state Senate president David Williams, whom he praised as "the smartest guy down in Frankfort," to fill the power vacuum "in a highly responsible way."

Back in Washington, McConnell was making more headway. He considered 2005 to be "the most successful legislative year for Republicans" since he had been serving there. The accomplishments included passage of all thirteen appropriations bills and measures on class-action reform, bankruptcy reform, energy, and highways, deficit reduction for the first time in eight years, and confirmation of a new chief justice of the United States. McConnell also helped put a statue of recently deceased civil rights icon Rosa Parks in the U.S. Capitol.

Still, he lamented what he saw as the reluctance of Democrats to move beyond an outdated New Deal mindset to creatively address big problems that cried out for immediate attention. Social Security, facing a crisis from impending Baby Boomer retirements, was one subject needing creative answers. President Bush barnstormed the country trying to goad Congress into tackling the politically difficult topic. McConnell urged GOP senators who had good relationships across the aisle to find *any* Democrat who would publicly support *any* reform legislation, but Democrats determined to deny Bush such a big success simply would not do business on the issue. The president ultimately expended considerable political capital to no effect, and he ended the quest looking weaker than when he began.

Senate Republicans faced several other challenges, and sometimes McConnell's leadership position forced his hand or limited his options in responding to them. For example, he privately thought that President Bush's nomination of White House counsel Harriet Miers to the Supreme Court was a "huge mistake." "By any objective standard, she was not ready for today's Supreme Court," he now concedes. But at the time he swallowed hard and praised the nominee from the Senate floor, declaring her "well qualified to join the nation's highest court" and "an excellent nomination."[2] Miers encountered immediate trouble, however. Eventually McConnell suggested to majority leader Bill Frist that he had to tell Bush, "Mr. President, this nomination is not going to fly." Frist did so, and soon thereafter, Miers asked the president to withdraw her nomination. Bush quickly followed with a much better nominee, U.S. Court of Appeals Judge Samuel A. Alito Jr.

Partisan wrangling over judicial nominations occupied much of the legislative year. Although the Senate had always voted on the confirmation of judicial nominees who enjoyed majority support, in the previous Congress the Democrats had routinely threatened to filibuster nominees to the federal appellate bench—and occasionally did just that. When they continued their obstructionism into 2005, Republicans contemplated changing the Senate rules, which they could have done with a simple majority vote, to ban filibusters of judicial nominations.

To head off such a confrontation, commonly referred to as the "nuclear option," seven senators from each party formed a "Gang of Fourteen" and disavowed the filibuster except in unspecified "extraordinary circumstances." McConnell had two "spies" in the Gang of Fourteen—Lindsey Graham of South Carolina and Mike DeWine of Ohio—who informed him about deliberations and developments within the group.

The advent of the Gang of Fourteen allowed a deal that cleared all but one of the nominations then being filibustered, including the three that were most controversial—William Pryor, Priscilla Owen, and Janice Rogers Brown. Despite conservative criticism of the Republican "gangsters," and of Frist for caving in to them, McConnell thought the resolution "a 100 percent win" and "one of the great success stories of 2005." If not for the deal and the "filibuster-averse" environment that followed it, the Alito nomination "would not have had a chance." He credits Frist for keeping the nuclear option alive.

McConnell recognized and respected the pivotal role that moderate to liberal Republican senators, mainly from the Northeast, could play in such situations. He had long ago accepted such ideological diversity as inevitable in a truly national party. Explaining his efforts to reelect Rhode Island's Lincoln Chafee, perhaps the Senate's most liberal Republican, he said, "My view is that we are better off to have a Republican who once and a while votes for us from Rhode Island than a Democrat who never votes for us from Rhode Island."

The moderates' impact was again on display in December. Five of them defected on the fiscal 2006 budget reconciliation conference report, which *National Journal* described as "the first serious attempt since 1997 to curb spending on entitlement programs." GOP leadership saw the measure as important "to reassure restive core supporters about the party's commitment to fiscal restraint."[3] McConnell had to call Vice President Dick Cheney back from Afghanistan so he could, in his role as the Senate's presiding officer, cast the deciding vote if it was needed. It was. The measure passed 51–50, with Cheney breaking the tie. Said McConnell at the time, "We couldn't have the Vice President on the other side of the world and lose the only genuine reduction in the deficit since 1997. . . . So I made the call. I wasn't uncomfortable about it. I'm not afraid to make such a call when necessary."[4]

McConnell bemoaned the fact that the Republicans were getting so little credit for the booming economy. He felt the same way about what he saw as demonstrable progress in Iraq, which he visited twice. Three successful elections had taken place there with higher turnout rates than in many American votes. But victory in Iraq was becoming increasingly difficult to define, much less achieve, and public restlessness was growing. "Iraq is now the central battlefield in the War on Terror," McConnell declared in an Independence Day newspaper column. "If we leave before the fight is through, Iraq could fall prey to men like Osama bin Laden, and become a factory of hatred. But if we stay and help the Iraqis as they train their own security forces, write a constitution that guarantees a voice for all, and form a new government, Iraq has the potential to help lead the entire Middle East towards democracy and peace."[5]

After Iraq's successful legislative elections, McConnell elaborated his argument in a floor speech, asserting "that it is squarely in our national security interest to help the Iraqis build a thriving and healthy democracy. Democracy is the ultimate antidote to terrorism." The United States must defeat the terrorists in Iraq "so that country can become a hinge of freedom in the greater Middle East. We know the terrorists cannot defeat us on the battlefield; our military might is absolutely unmatched. We know they cannot defeat our ideas, because when people are given a choice, they will choose liberty and democracy over terror and tyranny every time. So this debate turns on just one simple question: do we have the will to win in Iraq?"

By then, however, inept handling of Hurricane Katrina in late August had left the Bush administration looking incompetent. The combination of Iraq and Katrina produced what McConnell called a "toxic brew" that pushed the president's approval ratings down into the low 30 percent range. He believed that Bush needed to get his numbers back into the low fifties or he would be a big drag on the prospects for retaining Republican congressional majorities in 2006.

Over the course of the year, McConnell met with Bush privately and in small groups on several occasions. He always found the president impressive and upbeat. "I never walk away from him not feeling like the country is in good hands and not being amazed by his toughness, his resilience, and his ability to take a punch." Events would soon severely test this positive appraisal.

On the campaign finance front, McConnell filed an amicus brief in a Supreme Court case testing the constitutionality of the McCain-Feingold law's blackout period on "electioneering communications" as applied to television advertisements devoted exclusively to urging voters to contact elected officials about pending governmental matters.[6] He considered this a blatant and especially egregious abridgment of First Amendment freedom of political speech.

But he teamed with McCain in June to pen an op-ed piece in the *Wall Street Journal* honoring the sixtieth birthday of Aung San Suu Kyi, the Nobel laureate and "courageous leader of Burma's democratic opposition."[7] The pair successfully pushed for renewal of U.S. sanctions and increased international efforts "to address the threat that the Burmese regime poses to its people and the region." McConnell, long the Senate's leader on the issue, could now refer to an unofficial bipartisan Burma Caucus comprised of Senators McCain, Dianne Feinstein, Pat Leahy, Sam Brownback, and a Senate newcomer, Barack Obama of Illinois.

Bucking a brewing conservative sentiment against earmarks, McConnell continued bringing projects back to Kentucky, particularly money for the University of Kentucky, the University of Louisville, and Western Kentucky University, riverfront projects in several cities, and Louisville's Twenty-first Century Parks Project. Needled for securing $199,000 for Kentucky "beaver control," he defended his earmarking by saying that he knew better than any bureaucrat how to spend money in his state and noting that such projects amounted only to 1 percent of the $2.6 trillion federal budget. "You could wipe them all out and it would be like dropping a pebble in the ocean."[8]

Amid all this action, McConnell became the longest serving Kentucky Republican in the Senate, eclipsing John Sherman Cooper's 7,479 days of Senate service on June 27, 2005. Delivering the inaugural Cooper lecture at the Somerset Community College later that summer, he was asked what Cooper, who famously became a dove on Vietnam, would have thought about the Iraq war. McConnell said that it was impossible to know, but doubted that Cooper could have charted his independent course had he become the Senate's Republican leader in 1959. He added that after leaving the Senate, Cooper had concluded that he may have erred in supporting so much of President Lyndon Johnson's Great Society. He chalked up Cooper's moderate voting record to having come of age during the Depression and attributed Cooper's later doubts about the Democratic program to Ronald Reagan's influence and political success, which had moved more than one moderate Republican, including himself, rightward.

Having achieved one major milestone in Kentucky political history, McConnell continued to position himself for what he hoped would be another. Alben Barkley, a Democrat, was the only Kentuckian ever to be elected a party leader in the Senate. McConnell wanted to become Kentucky's first Republican to serve as Senate majority leader, but was becoming increasingly apprehensive about his party's prospects for retaining control of the chamber the following year.

Complicating his plans, Trent Lott sometimes made noises about regaining the position. While in Lexington, Lott introduced McConnell as the man who *probably* would be and should be the next majority leader, but continued making opaque public comments about returning to leadership. So McConnell kept a wary eye on his colleague, with whom he was tied as "the most effective Senate Republican" in a poll of Republican Senators published by *National Journal* in May.[9]

Another Capitol Hill paper, *Roll Call*, named McConnell one of the "top partisan street-fighters in Congress over the past 50 years."[10] He was, the respected journal said, "Arguably one of the Senate's most conservative members," but "has carved out a niche as a Republican stalwart in both policy and politics. He is often assigned to be the GOP's point man in leading the charge for his party and criticizing those on the other side of the aisle. . . . The Kentucky Senator has been quoted as saying: 'I'm proud of my enemies. I wouldn't trade them for anything.'"

The Hill, yet another newspaper for and about Congress, called him "as fastidious in appearance and command of legislative details as he is in accumulating political capital," and added, "His willingness to delve into arcane subjects and his understanding of Senate folkways appear to make up for a less-than-dynamic public persona." Senate allies described McConnell as "careful—not cautious," while his aides said he ends up "splitting his arguments between political and practical."[11]

Determined not to become "the Tom Daschle of 2008," McConnell raised $2.3 million toward his 2008 reelection campaign, including $1.7 million in Kentucky alone.[12] He figured himself to be the most likely target if Democrats tried to even the score for the 2004 ouster of the South Dakota Democrat who had been his party's Senate leader. They would, with vigor.

22

Republican Leader
2006

MCCONNELL BEGAN 2006 HOPING, indeed even expecting, to end it as Senate majority leader. But the year quickly became a bad one for Republicans at almost every level.

Things actually opened on a high note for McConnell. He assumed the presidency of the prestigious Alfalfa Club, described by the *Washington Post* as "an exclusive fold of about 200 rich and influential people." At the club's annual dinner originally held in honor of the birthday of Robert E. Lee,[1] McConnell made humorous remarks in front of a crowd including the president, the vice president, cabinet secretaries, the chief justice, congressional elites, business leaders, and celebrities. He would have little else to laugh about in 2006, however.

Although bipartisan in nature, congressional corruption hurt Republicans more than Democrats. In January, lobbyist Jack Abramoff, once the poster child of the Republican "K Street Project" to integrate corporate lobbyists into legislative processes, pled guilty to federal fraud, corruption, and tax charges. McConnell had neither met nor accepted any campaign contributions from Abramoff, but nonetheless donated to charity the $19,000 he had received from Indian tribes whom the felon had represented. A Texas grand jury indicted the

House majority leader, Tom DeLay, for conspiracy to violate campaign finance laws. Making matters worse, two of "The Hammer's" former aides were convicted in Abramoff-related fallout. DeLay had to step down from his post and, eventually, leave Congress altogether.

Despite such damage done to the congressional image, there were some legislative successes. By a 58–42 vote, the Senate confirmed Samuel Alito to replace Sandra Day O'Connor as a Supreme Court justice. McConnell hoped this might portend more favorable rulings on campaign finance cases. One such case challenged Vermont's limits on both campaign spending and contributions. His hopes were realized in June when the new justice concurred in a 6–3 decision striking down the law as a violation of the First Amendment.[2]

In May, President Bush asked for an emergency supplemental spending bill providing $92.2 billion for military operations in Afghanistan and Iraq and for hurricane recovery efforts, with an additional $2.3 billion for bird flu pandemic preparations. The Senate passed a $109 billion measure bloated with special-interest spending. Not wanting publicly to oppose essential and popular items, McConnell voted for the bill, but put together a letter from thirty-five senators stating their willingness to sustain a presidential veto. This helped Bush issue a credible veto threat, which produced the bill he had initially requested.

McConnell also supported legislation extending Bush's tax cuts on stock dividends and capital gains and mitigating the unintended impact of the voracious alternative minimum tax. As the Senate moved to the next year's budget, the *Wall Street Journal* described McConnell as "a growing force in shaping this year's 'endgame' strategy for Senate Republicans."[3]

The Senate also dealt with several hot-button issues important to the party's conservative base, but McConnell's votes did not always please the right wing. With his support, the Senate passed an immigration reform law that established a path to citizenship for illegals, created a guest-worker program, and enhanced border security a bit. Explaining his view of "this extraordinarily complex problem,"[4] McConnell later said that "you can't round everybody up and send them back. But you certainly, in terms of the issue of citizenship, should not reward somebody for illegal entry. If they want to become a citizen, there's a process for doing that and they ought to get at the back of the line in whatever country you came from and wait your turn like everybody else."[5]

Many conservatives criticized the bill as "amnesty," but having voted for amendments to toughen the bill and expecting more such steps in a Republican-controlled House-Senate conference that never occurred, McConnell noted, "More work needs to be done to improve the bill as Congress considers it further. However, this is a necessary first step to balancing our tradition as a nation of immigrants, but also a nation of laws." He went on to take a second step by supporting a successful bill to build fencing on the Mexican border.

Conservatives were considerably happier with McConnell for backing a constitutional amendment banning gay marriage and a bill abolishing the estate tax, although neither passed. He voted "no" on legislation permitting more stem cell lines for federally funded embryonic research, which the Senate approved, 63–37, but President Bush vetoed. He also backed a bill that passed the Senate, 65–34, to make it a federal crime to transport an underage girl across state lines to have an abortion and avoid state parental notification laws.

The flag-protection constitutional amendment returned to the Senate yet again. In an op-ed McConnell wrote, "No act of speech is so obnoxious that it merits tampering with our First Amendment. Our Constitution and our country are stronger than that."[6] His position put him at odds with all but two Republicans, and as one of thirty-four "nays" on a measure needing a two-thirds majority to pass, his vote provided the margin of the measure's defeat.

Though definitely not a doctrinaire conservative, and despite frequently feeling compelled by his leadership position to support the president despite any personal misgivings, McConnell earned an 84 rating from the American Conservative Union.[7] *National Journal* gave him a score of 84.3, making him the twelfth most conservative senator that year.[8] Americans for Democratic Action assigned him a "liberal quotient" of 5 percent.[9] The AFL-CIO said McConnell voted right a mere 13 percent of the time.[10]

Throughout 2006 the issue of Iraq inexorably overshadowed everything else on the congressional, and national, agenda. Events there spiraled seemingly out of control and public support for the American military mission steadily shrank. That summer the Senate beat back one effort calling for troop withdrawal within a year (86–13) and another calling for troops to begin coming out by year's end (60–39).

Speaking about the war while in Kentucky during the August recess, McConnell admitted that "in some ways it hasn't gone as well as we would like." He said he was "optimistic" that the Republicans would remain a majority in the Senate after the upcoming election, in which Democrats needed a gain of six seats to take control, but added that "it would be awfully helpful if the president had a better approval rating and the [political] environment were better."[11]

McConnell reacted quickly when a 5–3 Supreme Court contorted the Geneva Conventions to hold against the Bush administration's attempt to try terrorists in military tribunals established without congressional authorization.[12] He sponsored the Military Commissions Act of 2006, which let the president establish military commissions to try alien enemy combatants. It passed Congress and became law in mid-October.

Against this backdrop, McConnell continued his behind-the-scenes campaign to become majority leader. In June, a *National Journal* profile described him as "the consummate inside player." He was, said the piece, "intense, tenacious, and determined to win ... a hard worker, a keen strategist, a tough in-fighter, and a student of the Senate. Republicans praised him for not showboating and for allowing others to soak up time before the cameras."[13] John McCain complimented McConnell's "very brilliant political mind," while Chuck Hagel called him "the smartest political thinker we have in our conference. He understands the world politically better than anyone else." Joan Claybrook, president of the liberal lobby Public Citizen, was less charitable: "He is all politics all the time. He doesn't have a principled position on anything."[14]

Early in the year, McConnell meticulously rechecked his commitments in light of Lott's continued rumblings about trying to return to the majority leader post "if Republicans lose so many seats in November that the caucus demands leadership changes and resists promoting McConnell."[15] He found his support to be solid, a fact that Lott was finally forced to acknowledge.

That hurdle overcome, McConnell soon faced another. In mid-October the *Herald-Leader* ran a four-part series of highly critical articles that, said its editorial board, "showcased McConnell's finely tuned ability to play the interconnected interests of colleagues desperate for campaign donations and lobbyists pushing legislation."[16] The *Washington Post* described the series, which claimed that McConnell had raised nearly $220 million during his Senate career, as "portraying the senator as an insatiable solicitor of political money from interest groups—including tobacco companies, car makers, and pharmaceutical firms—with whom he is cozy."[17]

The writer, John Cheves, had been a regular *Herald-Leader* reporter, but this series was written with a $37,500 grant from the Center for Investigative Reporting. The Center's original source for that money was a grant from the Deer Creek Foundation, which had funded several left-wing organizations, including the Brennan Center for Justice, a group that had litigated against McConnell on campaign finance issues. While Cheves was working on the series, the Knight-Ridder chain sold the *Herald-Leader* to the McClatchy Company. In belated recognition of the funding arrangement's questionable appearance, the new owner decided to repay the grant, but proceeded to publish the series anyway.

Unaware of the writer's agenda and funding, McConnell had given Cheves two extended interviews, but precious little from them appeared in the series; nor did the newspaper post the complete transcript on its website as it easily could have. The paper also ignored or simply refused to correct multiple inaccuracies and misleading impressions in the series alleged by McConnell's staff.

In the first and second installments, citing contributions from the tobacco, security, corporate finance, gambling, automobile, accounting, insurance, and pharmaceutical industries, Cheves described a sinister "nexus between [McConnell's] actions and his donor's agendas."[18] He also attacked McConnell for using his position as chairman of the Senate Appropriations Subcommittee for Foreign Operations to direct foreign aid to Israel, Armenia, and Ukraine "while their lobbying groups donated heavily to him." McConnell explained that such donors support him because they like his pro-business, conservative philosophy, and added, "building up your finances so you can amplify your voice is critical to any successful political activity. It's a central part of the process."

In the third installment, Cheves implied an improper linkage between coal industry contributions to McConnell and federal mining regulation under Chao, the senator's wife. The article also charged McConnell with being a Chinese stooge for the sake of campaign money and the Chao family's business interests.[19] Finally, in the fourth piece of the series, Cheves suggested that McConnell did special favors for lobbying clients of his former chief of staff, Hunter Bates, in exchange for campaign contributions. Most of the examples involved issues like litigation reform, national security, and child safety that had long been McConnell priorities.[20]

The series failed in its apparent purpose of derailing McConnell's drive to leadership. Nothing in the stories constituted either an ethical or legal violation. "The bottom line," McConnell noted, "is that the *Herald-Leader* was paid by my political opponents to spend six months researching my record. Their conclusion: There is no 'evidence of improper personal benefit.' Ironically, the only thing that an objective, nonpartisan source found that required sanction was the special-interest funding of the *Herald-Leader*'s own research."

In November, however, public disgust with congressional corruption, despair over Iraq, and disenchantment with Bush would cost Republicans their majorities in both houses of Congress. Democrats picked up twenty-seven seats to take a 230–205 majority in the House.

In the Senate, they gained six seats to secure a 51–49 majority. Republicans failed to win any Senate seat held by a Democrat, while Democrats knocked off six Republican incumbents.

McConnell recognized the election as a referendum on President Bush and the Iraq war. Bush's failure to change course in Iraq badly hurt his party's candidates, and so Republicans, including McConnell, were surprised and upset when Secretary of Defense Donald Rumsfeld announced his resignation on the day *after* the electoral debacle. Back in August, McConnell had called Joshua Bolten, the president's chief of staff, to advise him, "*If* you are thinking about changing direction, do it in time for the voters to take it into account." To drive home his point, he faxed Bolten a newspaper article about Lyndon Johnson halting the bombing of Vietnam just before the 1968 election, which helped Hubert Humphrey almost attain a come-from-behind victory over Richard Nixon.

"We had on our hands an awful lot of angry, defeated Republican candidates, and frankly with good reason," McConnell observed. "The Rumsfeld resignation might have signaled to independent voters that change was coming." In McConnell's opinion, Bush's failure to remove Rumsfeld earlier was a rare "blown call" by an otherwise talented White House political operation. Later, Bush would boast of refusing to change policy to bail out his party.

McConnell's point was powerfully illustrated in his home congressional district, Kentucky's Third. Since winning the seat a decade earlier, Anne Northup had held it against all Democratic comers. In 2006, she ran what McConnell called "her usual perfect campaign" but still lost to a liberal Democrat, John Yarmuth. (Northup's loss was especially galling to McConnell because Yarmuth was a former Republican who had succeeded him on Marlow Cook's Senate staff and run for county commissioner when McConnell was county judge.) The election had hinged on the single issue of Iraq. The two other House Republicans in Kentucky who faced serious challenges, Ron Lewis and Geoff Davis, had held their congressional seats, and overall McConnell thought the party had dodged a major bullet.

But the Senate defeats dashed McConnell's long and carefully cultivated dream of becoming majority leader. Now he had another concern: Would Republican senators seek a new leader? GOP senators seemed satisfied to take out their frustrations on Bush, the departing Bill Frist, or the NRSC, headed by North Carolina's Elizabeth Dole, who, McConnell thought, "did a fine job under extremely difficult conditions, probably the toughest election environment for Republicans since 1974."[21] In November, and to his great pleasure and relief, the Republican minority elected McConnell their leader without opposition. Lott had to settle for the whip's job, a position opened by Rick Santorum's loss, and he beat Tennessee's Lamar Alexander by a single vote in a race in which McConnell avoided any involvement.

Upon assuming his new post (which senators have not referred to as "minority leader" since Democrat Robert Byrd sought to banish that nomenclature when it applied to him), McConnell reminded his colleagues of the minority's significant power under the Senate's rules. The day after his elevation, he told radio host Hugh Hewitt, "It takes sixty votes to do just about everything in the Senate. Forty-nine is a robust minority. Nothing will leave the Senate that doesn't have our imprint. We'll either stop it if we think it's bad for America, or shape it, hopefully right of center."[22]

Given the Democrats' miniscule majority, their leader, Harry Reid of Nevada, would need Republican support. Throughout the previous year, he had led a Democratic strategy that McConnell characterized as "block and blame." Now he had what McConnell called "the hardest job in town . . . in trying to move the ball in this fractious place, with its rules."[23] The new Republican leader promptly challenged Reid and the Democrats to take on big issues like Social Security and immigration reform, both of which would require bipartisan cooperation.

McConnell and Reid shared common characteristics. Each was "a consummate dealmaker whose top priority is legislative achievement," a *Washington Post* reporter wrote. Both "rose through the Senate ranks by mastering the rules and building strong relationships with colleagues. Both are combative lawyer-politicians who . . . are veteran practitioners of the Senate's opaque, clubby brand of politics, with no apparent desire to become president or grab television time to espouse their parties' goals."[24]

McConnell quickly made clear that although he was a friend of President Bush, "I was elected by the Senate Republicans and they are the ones to whom I am responsible."[25] According to the *New York Times*:

> Mr. McConnell is in a pivotal spot. Not only will he be the nexus between his party and Senate Democrats, and between Senate and House Republicans, he will also be a main conduit between Congressional Republicans and President Bush, making him responsible for managing a relationship that has been altered and complicated by the election.
>
> After working in near lockstep with the White House for six years, some Senate Republicans are unhappy with the administration, attributing much of the blame for their party's defeat to the president and his political strategists. In addition, Mr. Bush will not face the voters again, while Republicans will be trying to regain their majority in two years, making those on Capitol Hill more inclined to protect their own interests.[26]

So, at the end of twelve tumultuous months, McConnell had to settle for leading a minority that would use aggressive tactics in service of a defensive strategy. Carrying this off would require him to make more floor speeches and have "media availabilities" than before, so he promptly ramped up his press operation. Donald Stewart, who was, as *Roll Call* noted, "one of the most aggressive GOP press aides in the Senate,"[27] would head his leadership communications team.

The year 2006 turned into a tough one for Republicans in Kentucky, too. In May, a special grand jury empanelled in heavily Democratic Frankfort indicted Governor Ernie Fletcher on three misdemeanor counts of conspiracy, official misconduct, and political discrimination. Three months later, a judge ruled that Fletcher could not be tried while in office. Attorney General Stumbo, who wanted to run for governor himself but was barred by an ethics opinion from doing so as long as he was prosecuting Fletcher, expediently dropped the charges. Fletcher admitted that "evidence strongly indicates wrongdoing" by his administration and that the investigation and prosecution were "necessary and proper exercises of his [Stumbo's] constitutional duty." Stumbo agreed that the actions of Fletcher's administration "were without malice."

Kentucky's GOP lost six seats in the state House, but managed to maintain control of the state Senate. McConnell concluded that Fletcher's chances of a second term were "virtually nil" and thought the governor should announce that he would not seek reelection. Instead, Fletcher pushed on, deriding the investigation as a "witch hunt" despite his legal admission to the contrary.

Although McConnell considered the investigation and prosecution of Fletcher little short of an outrage, he could neither endorse the administration's obvious political incompetence nor make matters better for Fletcher or himself by commenting. In August, Fletcher again challenged McConnell's control of the state party organization by trying to install his ally and habitual McConnell critic Larry Forgy on the state party's executive committee. McConnell blocked the move.

On a happier note, the McConnell Center opened and dedicated magnificent new facilities in the University of Louisville's library building. The additions included an Elaine Chao Auditorium, faculty offices, historical exhibits, and modern classrooms. Senator Edward Kennedy visited the center in April, giving what McConnell called "a presidential-quality" speech. Conservative intellectuals Victor Davis Hanson and Charles Murray also paid calls.

Looking back on a year made difficult for Republicans by the president's unpopularity, McConnell stood by his statement that Bush was "one of the great presidents in the history of the United States,"[28] although he later admitted that if the Iraq war "doesn't come to a better conclusion it is not going to be the view of many other people, short term. Whether in the long term people will have a different view or not, I don't know."

He explained his reasoning this way: "The fundamental decision of this president to go on offense in the war on terror is the reason we haven't been attacked again here at home. I think the way you measure success in the war on terror is, 'Have you been attacked again here at home?' The answer is, we haven't been. But war is not clean and it raises the question of whether any president can sustain any kind of military action for any period of time in an era of instant news."

Bush's decision "to be proactive in the wake of the 9/11 attack, to go on offense," was, McConnell believed, "as monumental a decision as the containment policy of Truman or the Marshall Plan in terms of a sort of mega-tactic, a big strategy to deal with a big impending conflict that is likely to go on for a long time." McConnell remained loyal to Bush without regard to his own reelection prospects.

Although he had given $1.4 million from his reelection fund to the NRSC over the previous two congressional campaign cycles, McConnell still ended 2006 with around $2.6 million on hand and a presidential fundraising visit expected in February. He would then stop raising money in Kentucky in deference to the gubernatorial race, but focus instead on national efforts.

For some years, the senior senator from Kentucky had occupied Henry Clay's desk in the Senate chamber. McConnell reluctantly surrendered it to assume another prestigious perch, the Republican leader's desk first used by Charles McNary of Oregon in 1937. Having carved his name in his new desk in keeping with Senate tradition, he set about trying to use his leadership post to carve his name in American history.

23

The Defensive Coordinator
2007

MCCONNELL AT LEAST SHOWED a sense of humor about the hard situation he and his party faced as 2007 began. At sixty-four, he had hoped to be Senate majority leader, but found himself minority leader instead. He was also outgoing president of the Alfalfa Club. In his farewell speech to that organization's star-studded annual January dinner, he deadpanned, "I really thought the story in the Senate this year was going to be about a long-time loyal deputy . . . a mild-mannered statesman . . . but tough as nails behind closed doors . . . rising to the position of majority leader. And it was. It just wasn't *my* story. It was Harry Reid's."[1]

Kidding aside, he immediately set about crafting a strategy designed to serve both the nation's and the Republican Party's interests. It began with repeated bows toward bipartisanship. Before the 110th Congress commenced, the Senate convened informally and behind closed doors in what McConnell considered an extraordinary meeting at which Democrats and Republicans "talked about how friendships can be stronger than party affiliations, and how those friendships can help get things done."[2]

By year's end, however, conservative columnist George Will would conclude, to his considerable satisfaction, that "nothing important happened" in Congress. What did get done was indeed the product of bipartisanship, but not the amicable kind envisioned at the pre-session meeting. Instead, Democrats had tried to impose their will, but, relying on the Senate rule requiring sixty votes to bring most measures to a final vote, the GOP managed to block bad legislation and shape other bills into something both sides could accept. "The Senate is built for defense; the House is built for offense," McConnell explained. "There are two things you can do with forty-one or more dissenters. One is to block, and the other is to shape."

Iraq was once again the dominant political issue. In January, President Bush called for a troop "surge" that would add around thirty thousand American forces. The Senate unanimously confirmed General David Petraeus, America's foremost counterinsurgency expert, to lead it. "If it can't be done under General Petraeus, then it cannot be done at all," said McConnell.[3]

Nonetheless, a bipartisan Senate majority opposed the surge from the outset.[4] McConnell described himself as "the strongest supporter of the president you could find in the Senate on this effort,"[5] but even he acknowledged that the surge would have only six to nine months to show success or "we'll have to go in a different direction."[6]

Republican John Warner of Virginia, ranking member of the Armed Services Committee, offered a resolution expressing opposition to the surge. Majority leader Reid tried to impose Warner's as the only Republican resolution upon which the Senate would vote. McConnell convinced his conference to resist, and Republicans offered to allow a vote on Warner's resolution only if Reid would also permit votes on two Republican alternatives that were much more supportive of the president. Reid refused, but then fell eleven votes short of the sixty he needed to end debate on the Democratic companion measure he had hoped to pair with Warner's. Only two Republicans broke ranks on this pivotal roll call.

It was a procedural victory with considerable substantive consequences. "Our goal was not to kill the Iraq resolutions," said McConnell. "Our goal was to have the debate, but in a manner that was fair to both sides."[7] Even conservative columnist Robert Novak, who fretted that Senate Republicans had taken a public relations hit by blocking the debate, had to admit that they had "prevented Harry Reid from ordering the parameters of that debate."[8]

By doing so, the Republicans set an important precedent that would keep them relevant and powerful for the rest of the year. Calling McConnell "fearless, tactical, and loyal to the White House—meaning everything is filibusterable," ABC News recognized the far-reaching effect of the early session skirmish. "All of American politics in 2007 (and, of course, 2008) will be determined by the fallout from Democratic efforts on Capitol Hill to force President Bush to change course in Iraq."[9]

Writing in *Time*, William Kristol said, "Mitch McConnell's performance as Senate Republican leader has also—for the first time in a long time—given Republicans a congressional leader worth rooting for as he outmaneuvers the Democrats in their efforts to put Congress on record against Bush's Iraq policy."[10]

It may have been the most noteworthy, but the Iraq debate was not the only time Republicans would refuse to be railroaded in the early days of the young Congress. Unabashed McConnell fan Fred Barnes of the *Weekly Standard* cited some others:

> They weren't railroaded when a bill boosting the federal minimum wage to $7.25 an hour reached the Senate floor in January. Democrats wanted a "clean" bill with only the wage hike. Republicans wanted tax cuts for small businesses that would be affected by the higher wage. Reid tried twice to halt debate and failed. So tax relief was added to the minimum wage bill. Republicans also used the filibuster to have a say on congressional ethics reform. McConnell mustered 46 votes to block the shutoff of the ethics debate.[11]

Roll Call reported that McConnell had "privately urged Senators to trust him—and accept the political risks—by voting to block movement" on these bills unless they included GOP-backed provisions. With each such success came the increased credibility so very critical to effective Senate leadership.

McConnell realized that he had to strike a delicate balance with his blocking strategy. In his view, the GOP's minority status was not its biggest concern. The public's negative perception of the party was even more dangerous. "Exit polls show that we still have a loyal base of supporters, but they also show that the intensity of that base is fading," he told the winter meeting of the Republican National Committee. "This is serious business. But it makes our political strategy looking forward pretty easy to deduce. From this day on, Republicans in the House and Senate, and everywhere else, should have one goal in mind, and that's to recapture the party's rightful mantle as the party of reform."[12]

Fundraising followed close behind on the priority list, however. In early March, President Bush headlined an event for McConnell and the NRSC in Louisville that netted $2.1 million. Organizers called it the largest fundraiser in state history.[13] Responding to editorial criticism from the *Courier-Journal* that he put "cash over conscience,"[14] McConnell hit back at this "low blow to impugn my motives for standing with the president to be some 'fealty to the moneyed interests.'" The president "is right to protect America by taking the fight to the terrorists. Under his policies, there hasn't been a single terrorist attack on American soil since 9/11—something very few of us thought possible in the aftermath of that horrific event. When I support the president, I do so to defend our country from further attack."[15]

An antiwar group launched a $200,000 ad campaign in Kentucky taking McConnell to task for his support for Bush and the administration's Iraq policy. The spots interspersed clips of McConnell making positive statements about Iraq with negative footage and statistics.[16] Citing the presence of Fort Knox, Fort Campbell, and a large number of military retirees in Kentucky, McConnell said, "It's not exactly Berkeley that they chose to try to kick off an antiwar campaign. I don't think it works in the Bluegrass State."[17]

Kentucky was now preoccupied with its gubernatorial primaries. Incumbent governor Ernie Fletcher was being challenged by two opponents in the Republican primary, one of whom was former U.S. representative Anne Northup. While McConnell doubted that Fletcher could win in the fall, with his own campaign looming he could not afford to take sides. He stayed neutral in public and passive behind the scenes. *Courier-Journal* columnist Al Cross opined that McConnell might have uncharacteristically "managed to alienate two elements of his own party"—Fletcher friends and foes—"just as he was starting what he has said will be his toughest campaign for reelection."[18]

Fletcher prevailed in the primary, but with only 50.1 percent of the vote. Saying he had "never met a finer man," McConnell quickly endorsed the governor and called for Republican unity. But the primary had left wounds. Larry Forgy bluffed that he might challenge McConnell in 2008 to punish him for not doing enough to help the embattled Fletcher.

Back in Washington, May brought the culmination of a bitter, months-long battle over funding for the Iraq war. President Bush had vetoed the initial bill because it contained a timetable for troop withdrawals, or a "surrender date" as McConnell called it, and the House failed to override. The measure that passed provided $95 billion for operations in Iraq and Afghanistan through September 30, but also billions more for domestic projects.

With the success of the troop surge still uncertain, McConnell publicly predicted a change in administration policy by autumn. "I think that the handwriting is on the wall that we are going in a different direction in the fall, and I expect the president to lead it." He added, "We've given the Iraqi government an opportunity here to have a normal country. And so far, they've been a great disappointment."[19]

A rancorous immigration debate marked the beginning of the summer. As he had in the past, McConnell supported so-called comprehensive reform despite the political benefit to Democrats from regularizing the legal status of the estimated twelve million illegal immigrants. He backed, but hoped to toughen, a bill introduced by Reid but identified with John McCain. The Republican conference was almost equally divided. "As leader, I felt like I had an obligation to go through the process and see what it looked like," McConnell explained.[20] However, he recognized that Democrats would control the conference committee, making it considerably more difficult than it would have been in 2006 to improve any bad bill that made it out of the Senate.

The topic triggered much more public attention than in sessions past, and the prospect of any form of preferential treatment for illegals set off a firestorm in the national conservative base. The bill appeared dead after Reid forced, and lost, early efforts to end debate and unwisely ignored Republican demands for more time for amendments. McConnell pledged to whittle down the number of GOP amendments and urged Reid to return to the measure soon.[21]

Reid relented. A few weeks later, thirty-nine Democrats and twenty-four Republicans agreed to consider the bill.[22] McConnell, increasingly attuned to the growing disconnect between his position and Kentucky attitudes on the issue, took the hard line on most of the amendments. And when it became apparent that the bill would fail, he bowed to the popular will, voted "no," and more or less abandoned the floor during the decisive roll call that fell fourteen votes short of ending debate on the measure itself. "This isn't a day to celebrate," McConnell said after the vote.

"McConnell came under intense and somewhat unfavorable scrutiny earlier this year—both within his own party and elsewhere—for taking a near-absent role in the Senate's debate over immigration reform," according to a *Roll Call* postmortem.[23] Novak quoted an unnamed conservative Republican senator who said, "If this were a war, Sen. McConnell should be relieved of command for dereliction of duty." He continued, "Not only did the minority leader end up voting against an immigration bill that he said was better than the 2006 version he supported, he abandoned his post, staying off the floor during final stages of the debate."

The Senate's Republicans "drove another nail in George W. Bush's political coffin and undermined hopes for winning the growing, and winnable, Hispanic vote," Novak concluded. "Contending that the time 'wasn't now' for immigration, McConnell added: 'It wasn't the people's will. And they were heard.' He was blaming Republican failure on his fellow citizens, which seldom works in politics."[24]

Reflecting on the debate, McConnell said, "I heard from a lot of Kentuckians. . . . They didn't like the idea of someone being rewarded for a crime, or the impact that this would have on a society whose first rule is the Rule of Law. They didn't trust the government to suddenly get serious about border control after neglecting it for two decades. And I don't blame them. I worried about all that too. And to every one of them, I say today: 'Your voice was heard.'"[25]

He could, however, take some satisfaction in the fact that more voices would be heard after the Supreme Court agreed with the position he had advocated in his amicus brief in *Federal Election Commission v. Wisconsin Right to Life, Inc.*[26] By a 5–4 vote, the justices struck down McCain-Feingold's prohibition on electioneering communications that mentioned candidates within certain time periods before a federal election. With this "victory for free speech and confirmation that grassroots advocacy organizations have the same free speech rights as all Americans," McConnell said, "we can begin to undo the stranglehold that campaign finance legislation has placed on political debate."[27]

The Democratic Senatorial Campaign Committee and assorted antiwar groups started running television ads against McConnell, declaring, "It's time to start bringing our troops home" from Iraq.[28] Senate Democrats also staged a theatrical all-night "debate" on Iraq in mid-July. Reid asked Republicans to accept simple majority votes on Iraq-related legislation, but McConnell refused, reminding his counterpart that "the sixty-vote requirement had become a standard hurdle for controversial measures in a narrowly divided Senate, including in recent years when Democrats were the minority party."[29]

Despite a few defections, Republicans again blocked a proposal to withdraw troops. Reid then surprised senators by announcing that there would be no votes on several other proposals intended to force Bush to revisit his war plans. McConnell was blindsided. "It's certainly the lowest point I can recall in my twenty-some-odd years here," he said, "and I think it is an illustration of why this new majority [has] sunk to a 14 percent approval rating in the polls."[30] An uncharacteristically caustic McConnell complained, "We were elected to legislate, not strut across a stage. This isn't Hollywood. This is real life in the

Senate." He went on to rebuke Democrats for trying "to have it both ways on Iraq for too long. They voted to send General Petraeus to Iraq by unanimous vote, even as many of them undercut his mission and the morale of our troops by declaring it a failure."[31]

The bipartisan goodwill with which the session had begun was gone. "The Senate has been plunged into a procedural knife fight," reported the *New York Times*, "with Democrats forced to scramble to find 60 votes not just on contentious issues like an Iraq withdrawal plan, but on once-routine matters like motions to proceed to a spending bill." In the debate over a bill on higher education, "Republicans brought forward proposals intended to embarrass Democrats on terror detainees and union elections [and] Democrats countered with a resolution urging President Bush not to pardon I. Lewis Libby, Jr., a former top White House aide. Republicans struck back with a resolution deploring the pardons issued by President Bill Clinton,"[32] intended to embarrass New York senator and presidential hopeful Hillary Clinton.

The media began to speculate that McConnell might be vulnerable in his reelection bid the next year. Political analyst Stu Rothenberg, writing in the *Washington Post*, thought McConnell could face problems like those of Senator Tom Daschle, who narrowly lost reelection in 2004 because his "role as the leader of his party in Washington made it impossible for him to convince Republican and Republican-leaning voters back in South Dakota that he was one of them."[33] *LEO*, an "alternative" weekly in Louisville, ran a cover caricature of McConnell as *MAD* magazine's Alfred E. Neuman with a story entitled "What, Me Worry? Inside the growing movement to oust Sen. Mitch McConnell."[34]

McConnell readied himself for the most ferocious fight of his electoral career. He launched a website dedicated to "Kentucky Heroes." The first piece featured Alben Barkley, the Democrat who had served as Senate majority leader and Truman's vice president, and reminded readers of the relative rarity of truly national figures from their state.

David Hawpe, the *Courier-Journal*'s editorial page editor, responded by contending that McConnell was actually more like Earle Clements, the Kentuckian who served briefly as acting Senate majority leader in

1955 while Lyndon Johnson recuperated from a heart attack. Both had been county judges, were "cool, crafty and reserved," and "built the state machinery that has dominated their respective parties for significant periods of the modern era," but neither was "widely loved." Hawpe quoted from a *Courier-Journal* editorial about Clements that he claimed "could just as easily have been a reference to Mitch McConnell":

> It is this seeming coldness, plus a tendency toward political expediency, that accounts for the senator's enemies—and he has many of them.... His very charm, and his mastery of the political statement, curiously enough, have also created enemies.... [He has] a political intelligence [that] enables him to strip issues of their emotional surroundings and see them for their actual political worth [and] gives him the ability to think far beyond the more immediate goals of his fellow legislators.[35]

McConnell may have taken the intended criticism as a compliment.

Since the attacks of September 11, 2001, the need to intercept terrorist communications was critical, but also controversial, especially among Democrats. In early August, the Senate passed by a vote of 60–28 McConnell's Protect America Act of 2007, extending for six months the Foreign Intelligence Surveillance Act, which was set to expire. McConnell knew that the Democrats were desperate to leave on recess, but that they would look soft on national security if they departed without renewing the law. So he simply refused to compromise on key issues like intercepting terrorist communications outside the United States and legal immunity for cooperative communications companies. He advised Admiral Michael McConnell, the director of national intelligence (and no relation), to stop negotiating and take a hard line.

Democrats had little choice except to capitulate. As adjournment loomed, Reid was actually rounding up votes for the McConnell's measure. Republicans returned home to their respective states fresh from a significant legislative win on a subject central to keeping the homeland safe.

By summer's end, however, McConnell found himself dealing with a political squall. Senator Larry Craig of Idaho was arrested for soliciting sex in a Minneapolis airport's men's room and pled guilty to a misdemeanor. McConnell was determined to avoid the kind of politically damaging mistakes House Republicans had recently made in dealing with comparable cases. "This was potentially more about us than it was about Larry," McConnell explained.

The day after the story broke, he told Craig that the matter would go to the Ethics Committee for potentially embarrassing public hearings. The next day he told him to step down from his committee leadership positions. When Craig announced that he would resign at the end of his term the next year, McConnell called it "a difficult decision, but the right one."[36] Although Craig soon reneged, McConnell had accomplished his primary objective—proactively protecting the Senate Republicans.

Despite a drumbeat of hostile news and editorial coverage of McConnell in his state's mainstream media and left-wing blogs, most Kentuckians were still focused on the governor's race as autumn began. Fletcher faced the man McConnell beat for the Senate in 1996, Democrat Steve Beshear. The governor simply could not overcome the fallout from the merit system imbroglio and lost by 17.4 points. Republican candidates at least won two down-ticket races, leaving hope that the Republican brand was still viable. McConnell now faced the unpleasant prospect of running for reelection the next year with an old Democratic nemesis sitting in the governor's mansion.

Although they did not yet have a candidate, state Democrats were increasingly giddy about their chances of beating McConnell. To bring them back to reality about how hard any challenge would be, McConnell tapped his growing $9 million campaign war chest and took to airwaves early with new television ads emphasizing the big things he had done for Kentucky.[37] Fletcher's and other Republican endorsements quickly quashed any speculation about a divided GOP.

McConnell also enjoyed some positive earned media when pro-democracy protests broke out in Burma. The *New York Times* credited him with "putting and keeping [Burma] high on the agendas of the State Department and White House during times when it received little public attention." Noting that his interest in Burma did not help McConnell in Kentucky, the director of Human Rights Watch, Tom Malinowski, said, "The only reason to do what he's doing is because he cares about the issue."

When the world finally, if briefly, joined him in focusing on the issue, McConnell again condemned the Burmese junta and expressed hope that the protesters "would stay in the streets and overwhelm this regime with numbers." He acknowledged, however, that "it takes great courage, and it's easy for us to preach from over here, sitting safely in our offices."[38] McConnell privately wondered if this essentially passive and peaceful people would ever muster the kind of sustained movement needed to throw off the regime.

After General Petraeus reported to Congress that the troop surge was working, and American casualties dropped, the Iraq issue started to recede from the forefront of national debate. Congressional Democrats had to try a different political gambit. They settled on expanding children's health care to include older and wealthier participants.

McConnell had supported the so-called SCHIP, or State Children's Health Insurance Program, when it was created in 1997. He now offered a "Kids First" bill to expand it, but opposed a Democratic measure that he said would "raise taxes on working Kentuckians to pay for health care for well-to-do families in New York who could buy it themselves."[39] He warned of a slippery slope leading to "government-run health care for everyone."

The Democrats passed two bills, but the House twice upheld President Bush's vetoes. McConnell was understandably happy when SCHIP was finally continued on its current terms until after the next elections.

The year's last big legislative battle was over a $555 billion omnibus spending measure made necessary by the failure to pass regular appropriations bills. In late December, congressional Democrats abandoned their efforts to spend more than President Bush wanted while cutting his $70 billion request for war funds. According to the Associated Press, "Bush and his Senate GOP allies forced the Iraq money upon anti-war Democrats as the price for permitting the year-end budget deal to pass and be signed." It was "a bitter finish for majority Democrats who tried to force a change in President Bush's war policy."[40]

But McConnell took some hits from conservative media over the bill's 9,800 earmarks. After he said, "You can knock out all the earmarks, and it wouldn't save any money," the *Wall Street Journal* editorial page retorted, "Well, $7.4 billion is real money where we come from, and that misses the way in which earmarks have become opportunities for corruption and an incentive for overall spending."[41]

The ever-critical Novak argued that politics explained McConnell's apparent preference for pork over restoring the Republican reputation as a party of fiscal discipline: "Launching his 2008 campaign in Kentucky—he has warned this may be his most difficult reelection—McConnell in an ad stressed his performance as an appropriator delivering earmarks (highlighted by $280 million for his state's universities). His office regularly issues statements bragging about how much bacon he brings home to Kentucky in appropriations bills."[42]

Despite such criticism, McConnell still doggedly defends his position on earmarks. Once the budget's top line is set as low as possible, he will "fight like hell for Kentucky."[43] He does, however, support greater transparency to increase the chances that anyone doing anything corrupt will be caught.

By year's end, polling showed that more Kentuckians now considered the economy and health care, not Iraq, to be the top issue facing the next president.[44] Referring to the thirty-four votes Senate Democrats had held on the Iraq war in 2007, McConnell boasted that the GOP had prevailed "on every one that either attempted to substitute our judgment for the judgment of our commanders or cut off funds for our men and women in the field."

In his valedictory address at the end of the first session of the 110th Congress, McConnell claimed success in promoting the Republican priorities of "keeping Americans safe and secure, protecting their basic freedoms, protecting their wallets, and spending their money wisely." He said his party had ensured these priorities "by shaping worthy legislation or by blocking legislation that would undermine them," citing the examples of the minimum wage bill, the energy bill, judicial confirmations, and temporary relief from the alternative minimum tax.

With a reelection race ahead, McConnell returned home to tell Kentuckians that he and the Republican senators he led had stopped Democrats in Washington from raising taxes and utility bills, spending more, surrendering in Iraq, and putting the "rights" of noncitizen foreign terrorists ahead of American security. They had denied other Democratic dreams, too, including doing away with secret ballots in union elections, weakening union financial disclosures that let members see how bosses spend dues money, providing in-state tuition rates at public universities to illegal aliens, closing the terrorist detention facility at Guantanamo, Cuba, and giving the District of Columbia a congressional vote without amending the Constitution first.

McConnell lamented that the new Democratic majority did not want to "do anything significant." He explained that the session was largely unproductive because they had pursued partisan bills that would serve them as talking points instead of bills Republicans could accept that could actually become law.[45]

With polls giving Congress an approval rating even lower than President Bush's, national pundits pondered whether the McConnell strategy would prove politically effective.[46] Voters could blame Republicans for blocking progress, thank them for blocking bad ideas, or maybe neither. Perhaps the electorate just wanted change—an unsettling prospect for a Republican incumbent about to seek a fifth term in a terrible environment for his party.

24

The Most Consequential Republican
2008

I N 2008, MITCH McCONNELL would confirm his status as the foremost Republican politician in Kentucky history by winning a Ken-
tucky-record fifth U.S. Senate term. Overcoming an economic crisis, a
multimillionaire opponent, scurrilous attack ads, and a national Democratic landslide, he emerged as "Washington's most important Republican and second-most consequential elected official," in the words of
columnist George Will.[1]

McConnell credits his critics for motivating him. After antiwar
groups had run television ads against him and demonstrators descended
on his Louisville home in 2007, he realized that the campaign would
be both nationally significant and extraordinarily expensive. So he
started fundraising at a ferocious pace. As GOP Senate leader, McConnell wanted to completely fund his own campaign so the NRSC could
use its resources elsewhere.[2] He needed every nickel of the almost $20
million he ultimately raised or borrowed. Those seeking to unseat him
spent $14 million on TV alone, including $6 million in national Democratic Party ads.

McConnell's own initial ads had already informed Kentuckians
that he was only the state's second son to be elected a Senate party

leader, and other spots emphasized the federal funding he had procured for the commonwealth and the jobs it produced. But nonetheless he polled early in 2008 to determine whether voters considered his leadership position to be an asset despite his close association with President Bush. He learned that it was. Thus, the campaign's theme—"Clout vs. Change"—was set and would never really vary, even as an economic crisis arose during the race's homestretch.[3]

To deter any ambivalent Democrats from running against him, McConnell's campaign reported in early January that it had raised a daunting total of $10,889,516, including more than $6.6 million in 2007 alone. It had $7,317,138 of this as cash on hand, a sum exceeding the total spent by any previous U.S. Senate campaign in Kentucky. Campaign manager Justin Brasell warned potential foes that they "would need to raise more than $35,000 per day each and every day between now and the election to collect what we've raised to date."[4]

As is often the case in presidential election years, politics largely overshadowed legislative activity in Washington. McConnell began the second session of the 110th Congress by noting the nation's many challenges and stating, "There will be a strong temptation to politicize them or put them off as the current administration comes to a close and a new one prepares to take its place. This would be an irresponsible path, and it's one we should not take. We've had a presidential election in this country every four years since 1788. We won't use this one as an excuse to put off the people's business for another day."

He urged Democrats not to repeat their mistakes of the previous session. "I think we can agree, for instance, that we all worked best last year when we worked together," he said, giving several examples of partisan Democratic measures that passed only when Republican concerns were incorporated.[5]

Democrats evidently took his counsel to heart, and in the first half of the year the two parties worked together to pass expensive legislation. The first bill was a $152 billion stimulus package that passed in February with McConnell's support. The plan was to put $120 billion in borrowed money into taxpayers' hands by May in the hope that they would spend it and boost the faltering economy. They didn't. A second measure was a $307 billion farm bill that passed in May. McConnell voted to override President Bush's veto after getting key provisions of his Equine Equity Act, which liberalized the depreciation schedule for racehorses, inserted into the final bill. The measure was worth an estimated $126 million over ten years to an extremely important Kentucky constituency and gave him the cover he needed to vote for the farm bill despite its cost.

Parting company with the president on the farm bill also helped reduce McConnell's voting support for Bush administration policies from 92 percent over the preceding seven years to 74 percent in 2008.[6] But as the national debt soared beyond $10 trillion, some fiscal conservatives squirmed over the fact that he had supported some of Bush's most infamous expansions of the federal government, from the No Child Left Behind Act, to the Medicare prescription drug benefit, to 2005's earmark-laden $286 billion highway bill, to the stimulus package and farm bill.

When no top-tier Democratic challenger to McConnell emerged, Bruce Lunsford's limitless pocketbook proved irresistible to the head of the Democratic Senatorial Campaign Committee (DSCC), Chuck Schumer of New York. Lunsford, who had lost badly in the past two Democratic gubernatorial primaries, was well known in the state and could finance his campaign from his estimated $90 to $100 million fortune. He had built his wealth in the nursing home business until changes in Medicare reimbursement drove his company, Vencor, into bankruptcy. Lots of local Louisville shareholders lost lots of money. Lunsford's legacy also included a federal false claims case he settled for $104.5 million and bad publicity for evicting residents and providing poor care at his companies' facilities. Somehow he had emerged from all of this with his economic, if not his political, fortunes largely intact.

Lunsford won the Democratic primary over a political novice with 51.1 percent of the vote. Shortly thereafter, a Rasmussen Reports poll showed him with a lead over McConnell of 49 percent to 44 percent.[7] However, the McConnell campaign immediately released an internal poll showing the incumbent ahead by 50 percent to 39 percent, and putting his approval rating at a very respectable 57 percent, and quoting commentators from the *Rothenberg Political Report* and the *Cook Political Report* dismissing Rasmussen's methodology and results as "stupid" and "really flawed."[8]

The first phase of the general election campaign focused almost exclusively on energy policy. As gasoline prices soared to near $4 per gallon in Kentucky, McConnell chanted the mantra of "find more, use less" and offered a plan for doing just that. Designed to put both national Democrats and Lunsford in a bind by calling for things Kentuckians wanted but liberals abhorred, it included oil exploration in the Arctic National Wildlife Refuge, expanded drilling off U.S. coasts, and expanded support for coal. It quickly became apparent that the energy issue was a loser for Lunsford.

When Senate Democrats foolishly decided to debate California Democrat Barbara Boxer's so-called "cap-and-trade" climate change legislation in June, they let McConnell press an evasive Lunsford to take a position on that anti-coal bill. McConnell trumpeted his adamant opposition to the measure, which would have raised energy taxes just as consumers were feeling the pain from already high gas prices. CNBC commentator Larry Kudlow praised McConnell's "very impressive presentation of the conservative opposition to this crazy bill," and added, "If there's any tougher conservative in the Senate, I don't know who that is."[9]

McConnell skillfully used the bill debate to score two separate political points. First, he attempted to force Democrats into politically difficult votes on Republican amendments to Boxer's bill. Second, because Harry Reid could neither pass the climate bill nor muster the votes to close off debate, the majority leader simply had to take it off the floor and swallow the political cost of a highly publicized legislative failure. Moreover, Lunsford's fellow Democrats had left him looking bad with Kentucky's powerful coal industry.

To protest Senate inaction on judicial nominees, McConnell insisted that Senate clerks read an entire five-hundred-page amendment. This took more than ten hours, but called attention to Reid's failure to honor what Republicans considered a commitment from him to hold confirmation votes on fifteen appeals court nominees—the historical average in the final two years of recent presidencies—before the end of the Bush administration. "That commitment should be kept for the good of the institution," McConnell said, adding, "I think the adults on the other side of the aisle [know] this is a precedent that ought not to be set."[10]

A television station's poll published in mid-June showed McConnell ahead of Lunsford 50 percent to 46 percent. His internal polling revealed that more people viewed him favorably than unfavorably, and it narrowly stayed that way through election day. Not so with Lunsford, however, who began the race with high negatives that McConnell reinforced with attacks on the Democrat's lavish lifestyle, his homes in multiple states, and another business venture—Valor Healthcare—accused of providing shabby health care to veterans, many of whom were willing to appear in McConnell ads. This unremitting assault kept Lunsford's numbers "upside down" throughout the campaign.

McConnell reported another $3 million in contributions from April through June, bringing his total to $15 million, much of it admittedly from what critics would call "special interests." During the same period, Lunsford took in only $600,000 beyond the $2.5 million he contributed himself. "If I was a senator and it took me $15 million to get reelected, I would go ahead and quit the job," Lunsford said. McConnell's campaign manager countered, "Bruce Lunsford's biggest fan is Bruce Lunsford."[11]

Seeing the energy issue as a winner for both himself and Republicans nationally, McConnell launched ads sarcastically thanking Lunsford for his role in raising a state gas tax as part of Governor John Y. Brown Jr.'s administration almost thirty years earlier. McConnell also penned an op-ed piece for the *Wall Street Journal* touting the Gas Price Reduction Act of 2008.[12] That bill provided for deep-sea exploration more than fifty miles off the coast of states that wanted it, lifted a ban on developing oil shale deposits, increased incentives for electric vehicles, and strengthened U.S. futures markets to guard against financial speculation suspected of artificially inflating prices. He chided Democrats daily for failing to act or seeking to pass a "speculation only" bill that would address financial maneuvering to manipulate prices but do nothing to increase production.

Lunsford floundered. "Increasing drilling—to keep us addicted to oil—is probably not the long-term right thing to do," he said. He declined to say if he supported a proposal to drill in the Alaskan National Wildlife Refuge, and could only argue that McConnell's support for it was "propaganda."

In the meantime, Senate Republicans finally succeeded in their long fight to include legal immunity for telecom companies that cooperated with the government in the Foreign Intelligence Surveillance Act. Eventually even Barack Obama, by then the presumptive Democratic presidential nominee, reneged on his promise to oppose it.

In July, the Supreme Court, with McConnell's support, struck down the so-called Millionaire's Amendment to the McCain-Feingold law.[13] That amendment would have let McConnell, as the opponent of a wealthy, self-funding candidate, raise money in larger chunks than he otherwise could have. Without it, Lunsford could contribute as much of his fortune to his campaign as he wanted while McConnell was restrained by the existing contribution limits. McConnell was consistent in his First Amendment position even though in this instance the legislative infringement would have helped him.

At the month's end, the *Cook Political Report* changed its rating of the McConnell-Lunsford race from "solid Republican" to "likely Republican." The liberal website DailyKos released a poll that put McConnell comfortably ahead by 11 percent.

The Fancy Farm picnic in early August proved less eventful than in the past. Lunsford paraphrased Ronald Reagan's famous question from 1980, asking, "Are you better off today than you were six years ago?" and hit at McConnell for "selling the American dream to the highest bidder." A disdainful McConnell never mentioned Lunsford by name, criticized the failure of national Democrats to reduce high gas prices and ridiculed Obama. "Here is the Obama plan. Obama says pump up your tires and go to Jiffy Lube!" He added, "At least Bill Clinton could feel your pain. Obama wants to increase your pain."[14] Neither side's barbs affected the race, however, and the campaign settled into a short-lived stasis.

A few days later, Lunsford hired a new media consultant who had worked John Kerry's 2004 presidential campaign, and the DSCC tasked a former Schumer operative to invigorate Lunsford's moribund effort.[15] Survey USA gave McConnell a twelve-point lead over Lunsford in mid-August, but the Democrat's ads soon became harder-hitting and more effective.

None of three debates between McConnell and Lunsford was carried on statewide television or made much difference in the race. As usual, McConnell insisted on formats that minimized moderator or reporter involvement so he had to worry only about a single adversary instead of several. He knew he could win such encounters decisively, but also recognized that the press would not report it that way. Since newspapers would give each candidate the same quantity of column inches regardless of the quality of their respective performance, he was reluctant to accord Lunsford equal status on any platform.

The first debate took place at a meeting of the Kentucky Farm Bureau on August 20. McConnell answered a question about trade agreements by lambasting Lunsford's ties to organized labor: "He's not going to be for any of these trade agreements that would allow you to sell your products abroad because the AFL-CIO is not going to let him." McConnell emphasized his clout as the minority party leader, and refuted Lunsford's claim that he would have influence as a freshman senator in the majority party:

[A]n interesting study by the *National Journal*, which covers Congress, looking at freshman senators in this Congress . . . picked Bob Casey of Pennsylvania as the most effective freshman senator in terms of directed congressional funding to his state. He was able to get $16 million for the commonwealth of Pennsylvania. That's a

state that is three and half or four times as big as ours. Your senator, the guy you're looking at, *brought home $500 million last year for
the commonwealth as the leader of the minority party in the U.S. Senate.*

In early September, McConnell once again chaired Kentucky's
delegation to the Republican National Convention. His speech was
canceled along with other nonessential convention business, however,
when Hurricane Gustav hit Louisiana just before the meeting was to
begin. He praised Republican nominee John McCain's selection of
Alaska governor Sarah Palin as his running mate. "I think she was the
candidate that made the most sense," McConnell said.

"We all know this is going to be an election about change, and
the issue is what kind of change. What McCain wanted to do was to
underscore his reform credentials and to get somebody who was in a
position to reach out to women voters, somebody that large numbers
of Americans could identify with." He urged McCain and Palin to run
against the unpopular Democratic "do-nothing" Congress, which "is a
lot more relevant to the future than the outgoing president, which the
other side seems to want to run against."[16]

In his acceptance speech, McCain said, "We lost the trust of the
American people when some Republicans gave in to the temptations
of corruption." Lunsford quickly aired an ad using that passage to suggest that McCain had "singled out Mitch McConnell on corruption."
But the ad's small print did not cite McCain's convention speech, but
actually referenced the testy 2000 floor exchange between McConnell
and McCain over campaign finance reform. In that instance, McCain
criticized McConnell for supposedly telling senators that it was okay
not to vote for a tobacco bill because the tobacco companies would run
ads for them. In fact, McCain never leveled any charge of corruption
against McConnell.

To counter the Lunsford ad, McConnell's campaign rapidly
responded with McCain's comments at a June fundraiser in Louisville:
"Can I say again how much I appreciate the leadership and steadfast-
ness and courage and frankly the very tough job that Senator Mitch

McConnell has in Washington, D.C.? It's hard trying to do the Lord's work in the 'city of sin,' and Mitch does it, and he does it well. So thank you, Mitch, for everything."[17]

During their second debate, held without a moderator in mid-September, McConnell hit Lunsford with queries about the recent conflict between Georgia and Russia. After Lunsford focused on process instead of substance, McConnell said, "I think it's pretty obvious that Bruce doesn't even have an average newspaper knowledge of this issue." He then took a hard line in answering his own question, saying that the United States should offer financial aid to Georgia, stall Russia's membership in the World Trade Organization, and bring Georgia into NATO. "Because the best way to deal with the Russians, if they want to have an empire again, is to draw a line so it's very, very clear that you don't go across it."[18]

McConnell also asked Lunsford if he would have voted for the 2003 Medicare Modernization Act that created the prescription drug benefit. When Lunsford obfuscated, McConnell pounced. "Is that a 'yes' or a 'no'?" he asked, noting that as a senator, "You don't get a maybe in the end. You have to vote 'yes' or 'no.'" When Lunsford called him a "porkaholic," McConnell responded with examples of federal money he had brought to Kentucky and said that he assumed Lunsford would rather see that money go to Ohio or West Virginia.[19]

At this point, the bottom fell out of the American financial markets and it looked like the entire economic system could be in jeopardy. McConnell had been in Washington while the problems silently grew and, fairly or not, some citizens blamed him for it. After a first multi-billion dollar bailout measure failed to pass the House, he continued pushing for bipartisan action. He clearly set forth his position in a September 24 floor speech. Describing the financial worries of his constituents, and blaming the problem on "the bad decisions of those in the subprime housing market," he declared: "The only reason to support this action is to save ordinary Americans from an economic disaster that they had no hand in creating. . . . If we are to take action then it needs to put Main Street ahead of Wall Street. This isn't about bailing out investment bankers, this is about keeping the U.S. economy from entering a downward spiral. To that end, any action we take must include the following: limits on executive compensation, debt reduction, congressional oversight and transparency, and taxpayer protection."

On the matter of executive compensation, McConnell said, "If weak companies are seeking government assistance, the taxpayers should expect no less than a firm limit on what kind of executive compensation might be possible for those involved in these distressed companies." As for debt reduction, he noted, "Any proceeds that are earned from the government buying these assets and then selling them in the marketplace must be used to reduce the national debt. These revenues must not be used to pay for unrelated and unnecessary pet projects."

Congressional oversight and transparency meant that "we in Congress will watch where every dollar goes to ensure there is no waste and no funny business," thus ensuring the final point, "that they [taxpayers] are protected first."[20]

McConnell's response to the financial crisis and the bailout didn't help. His lead over Lunsford all but disappeared. A poll concluded the day after his speech gave him a lead of only 45 percent to 44 percent—effectively a tie—among likely voters.[21] One McConnell campaign insider worried, "This bailout and the mood may be too much to overcome."

But McConnell refused to accept defeat for a financial bailout plan. "I said, 'No action is not a plan.' We're going to get it done, and we're going to get it done this week." He worked with Reid to "put country first" despite the potential political consequences to his reelection.[22] "Failing to pass this economic rescue plan would be grossly irresponsible," he said. "The voters sent us to Washington to respond to crises, not to ignore them."[23]

The revised $700 billion bailout bill passed the Senate on October 1 by a 74–25 vote. Kentucky's junior senator, Jim Bunning, called it socialism, but McConnell supported it, as did both McCain and Obama. The bailout was, McConnell said, "necessary but not necessarily precedential." He saw it as "a one-time response to a once-in-a-century crisis and said it should be terminated 'as soon as possible' by government selling the assets it has acquired in order to recoup the money it has spent."[24]

Well aware that a McConnell loss could drop the GOP's Senate seat count below the all-important forty-one required to continue the successful blocking of Democratic bills by filibuster, the national media descended on the suddenly close race in Kentucky. So did Democratic surrogates, including both Bill and Hillary Clinton and former senator Max Cleland of Georgia. Millions of national Democratic dollars started pouring into Kentucky. Without a hint of irony, the DSCC's debut ad in the race attacked McConnell for backing 1999 banking deregulation that Schumer himself had then called vital to America's future.

McConnell played up the race's importance to the conservative cause. "There is nothing the far left would like better, besides winning the White House, than to take me out," he said. "People who didn't even know my name a few years ago wish me ill. Imagine that—a nice guy like me! So a lot of these nasty attack ads that you've seen on TV have been paid for by people from New York and San Francisco. And I'm confident that nobody from San Francisco is going to elect the next senator from Kentucky."[25]

Thanks to his early fundraising and $2 million in loans to the campaign,[26] McConnell had the resources required to fight back effectively. By mid-October he had raised a total of $17.8 million, spent $12.6 million, and still had $5.7 million on hand. Lunsford reported spending $5.8 million and having $1.24 million in the bank. Some $5.5 million of his funds had come from his own pocket. The race was already the most expensive in Kentucky history by far and the spending only intensified. McConnell lavished money on ads saying that Lunsford "got rich the Wall Street way." Lunsford continued attacking McConnell for "giving tax breaks to big oil companies and the wealthiest Americans."[27]

The state's big newspapers in Louisville and Lexington endorsed Lunsford and steadily hammered McConnell in their editorial and op-ed pages in an effort to counter his financial advantage. John Cheves of the *Lexington Herald-Leader* resumed his anti-McConnell crusade with hostile articles. One identified a "vulture investor" who saw the economic crisis as "the opportunity of a lifetime" as McConnell's third-largest campaign donor.[28] The state's ten other papers that made endorsements preferred McConnell unanimously, however.

No holds were barred. For example, Greg Stumbo raised McConnell's military record: "I'll tell you how sorry he is. He's sending young men and women to die in Iraq and Afghanistan, and he will not share with the people of Kentucky how he got out of military service—how in the height of the Vietnam War he was able to dodge military service."[29] To counter these attacks McConnell produced his military discharge form, which declared him medically unfit, and his honorable discharge certificate.[30]

McConnell continued pounding home the point that he was too valuable to Kentucky to replace with a rookie. That message still resonated with voters. His poll numbers started to recover and then stabilize. Two surveys near the end of October put McConnell ahead by 4 and 5 points, respectively.[31]

Although McConnell hailed from the state's biggest city, he had spent countless hours crisscrossing the commonwealth's backroads, especially in his early campaigns. Returning to these roots on a late campaign bus tour garnered him good publicity while bolstering both his vote totals and his spirits. State Senate president David Williams warmed up the crowds with his old-fashioned oratory before McConnell, who gave the same speech sixty-two times almost without variations, told audiences that he shared their rural values. After urging his listeners to help him not for his sake, but for theirs and their children's, he ended these pep rallies by exhorting the crowds to help him "pulverize" Lunsford or "beat him like a drum."

The campaign concluded with unprecedented media saturation. During the final week McConnell was airing 5,000 points' worth of ads on broadcast television in Louisville and Lexington and even more on cable, meaning that voters might see a McConnell ad fifty times in a week. Imitating McConnell's memorable 1984 commercials, Lunsford tried some bloodhound ads of his own. McConnell had an even better one on the air within twenty-four hours.

As the vote approached, McConnell, who had virtually quit reading newspapers or watching television, confidently told anyone who inquired, "I'm going to win." Inside the campaign, however, some with access to tracking poll data were still not so sure, right up until election day.

But the race turned out to be not nearly as tight as many had anticipated. McConnell tallied 953,816 votes, beating Lunsford by more than 106,000 votes. The 53 percent to 47 percent margin was actually the third largest of his five races. He received 214,000 more votes than in his landslide of 2002, and 221,000 more than in 1996. He lost the Louisville's Third Congressional District by 12 percent and the Lexington's Sixth by 1 percent, but easily won each of the state's other four districts by double digits. He won eighty-seven counties to Lunsford's thirty-three. Exit polls showed that McConnell won 11 percent of voters who said they also voted for Obama, which means that more than 82,000 voters split their tickets, or 80 percent of his margin of victory.

With the victory, McConnell became the first Kentuckian ever elected to five full Senate terms. His carefully crafted statewide GOP structure also emerged intact. Kentucky Republicans retained all their congressional and state Senate seats. And they did so without much help from McConnell, who was too busy tending to his own reelection. Given the awful environment for Republicans nationally, it was perhaps McConnell's most impressive electoral performance yet.

In the Senate, Democrats increased their majority to at least fifty-nine (Minnesota's race between Republican incumbent Norm Coleman and Democratic challenger Al Franken remained in doubt), defeating such incumbents as Elizabeth Dole in North Carolina and Gordon Smith in Oregon. McConnell would have significantly fewer Republicans to work with, with several compromise-seeking moderates among those remaining. A postmortem printed the following day on Politico.com put McConnell's position in perspective: "With his party in tatters, Mitch McConnell is now the most powerful Republican in the country—the lone GOP senator who can stand in the way of an unfettered liberal agenda in Washington, and a key go-to man to rehabilitate his party."[32]

In November 2008, Mitch McConnell's Republican Senate colleagues unanimously reelected him to serve as their leader. A few days after the election, McConnell had taken a cordial call from Barack Obama.[33] He described the president-elect as "an impressive individual" who was "easy to like, personally," and said that he intended to have a good relationship with the new president, whom he urged to govern from the center and tackle big issues.[34] McConnell knew, however, that if—or when—Obama did otherwise, as Republican leader he would be challenged to live up to the high expectations that had been created for him as a conservative bulwark and parliamentary master.

The man responsible for building a strong statewide GOP structure in Democratic Kentucky also indicated his focus on shoring up the Republican Party nationally. Just days after Obama's inauguration, McConnell issued a warning to his party at a meeting of the Republican National Committee. "We're all concerned about the fact that the very wealthy and the very poor, the most and least educated, and a majority of minority voters, seem to have more or less stopped paying attention to us," McConnell said. "And we should be concerned that, as a result of all this, the Republican Party seems to be slipping into a position of being more of a regional party than a national one." He added: "In politics, there's a name for a regional party: It's called a minority party. . . . As Republicans, we know that common-sense conservative principles aren't regional. But I think we have to admit that our sales job has been. And in my view, that needs to change."[35]

"The most powerful man in the Republican Party," as *The Economist* called McConnell, would face many challenges in the days, months, and years ahead.[36] There were, of course, big issues confronting the country, the deepening recession being the most pressing among them. The

Republican Party faced its own difficulties, as McConnell reminded his GOP colleagues. And as always, there would be many legislative and political battles to be fought.

The man whom *The Economist* described as "grey, owlish, bespectacled, and glum" always seemed a somewhat unlikely leader, and now he appeared particularly so in the age of the charismatic Obama. But Mitch McConnell, a politician of formidable talents and remarkable doggedness, had defied expectations and overcome stiff challenges throughout his long and successful political career.

Those who doubted McConnell's prospects of success going forward would do well to note this counsel from *The Economist*: "It would be a mistake to underestimate him."

Notes

Chapter 1: "Washington's Most Important Republican"

1. George F. Will, "Kentuckian in the Breach," *Washington Post,* November 13, 2008.

Chapter 2: Portrait of the Senator as a Young Man

1. Jill Lyttle Lewis, "Mothers Remember the Darndest Things . . . ," *Corbin Times-Tribune,* May 9–10, 1987.
2. Hilary Roxe, "McConnell Hails Vaccine, Recalls His Battle with Polio," *Lexington Herald-Leader,* April 13, 2005; *50th Anniversary of Polio Vaccine,* 109th Cong., 1st sess., *Congressional Record* 151, no. 42 daily e. (April 12, 2005): S 3448.
3. Kentucky gave eighteen-year-olds the vote in 1955, well in advance of passage of the Twenty-Sixth Amendment.
4. Senator Mitch McConnell, in discussion with the author, March 10, 2006.
5. *The Kentucky Encyclopedia,* ed. in chief John E. Kleber (Lexington: The University Press of Kentucky, 1992), s.v. "William O. Cowger."
6. Sherrill Redmon, in correspondence with the author, August 12, 2006.
7. Mitch McConnell, "Celebrating Dr. Martin Luther King Jr.," Louisville *Courier-Journal,* January 14, 2007
8. Bonnie Meyer and Mitch McConnell, "Constitution Should Meet Modern Needs," *University of Louisville Cardinal,* September 27, 1963.
9. *University of Louisville Thoroughbred* (Louisville, 1964) 31.
10. David Tachau, in discussions with the author, multiple occasions.
11. *Tribute to Senator Mitch McConnell, the Longest Serving Kentucky Republican Senator,* 109th Cong., 1st sess., *Congressional Record* 158 (June 28, 2005): S7493.

12. William Cooper in *The Kentucky Encyclopedia*, ed. Kleber, s. v. "John Sherman Cooper"; Billy Reed in *Famous Kentuckians* (Louisville: Data Courier, 1977), s. v. "John Sherman Cooper."

13. Robert Schulman, *John Sherman Cooper: The Global Kentuckian* (Lexington: The University Press of Kentucky, 1976), 7.

14. Albin Krebs, "John Sherman Cooper Dies at 89; Longtime Senator from Kentucky," *New York Times*, February 23, 1991.

15. *Tribute to Senator Mitch McConnell.*

16. McConnell, in discussion with the author, March 10, 2006.

17. "Sen. Mitch McConnell's Eulogy for Gene Snyder," *St. Matthews Voice-Tribune*, February 27, 2007.

18. Andrew Wolfson, "Ex-U.S. Rep. Gene Snyder, 79, Dies," Louisville *Courier-Journal*, February 18, 2007.

19. Senator Mitch McConnell, in discussion with the author, November 6, 2008.

Chapter 3: Lukewarm Lawyer, Passionate for Politics

1. Sherrill Redmon, in correspondence with the author, August 12, 2006.

2. Addison Mitchell McConnell Jr., *Haynsworth and Carswell: A New Senate Standard of Excellence*, 59 Kentucky L.J. 7, 20 (1970).

3. Ibid., 23–4.

4. Ibid., 28.

5. Ibid., 7.

6. Ibid., 13.

7. Ibid., 33.

8. *McConnell v. Marshall*, 467 S.W.2d 318 (Ky. 1971).

9. Lowell H. Harrison and James C. Klotter, *A New History of Kentucky* (Lexington: The University Press of Kentucky, 1997), 413.

10. Edward Bennett, "'Mitch' McConnell Cut Political Teeth While in College," *Louisville Times*, April 18, 1973, sec. B.

11. Ibid.

12. Edward Bennett, "Two Local GOP Leaders Call on Nixon to 'Clean House'," *Louisville Times*, April 24, 1973.

13. Mitch McConnell, "Election Ordinance Is, in Part, Reaction to Past Excesses," Louisville *Courier-Journal*, December 10, 1973.

14. Bill Billiter, "Mitch McConnell Resigns as GOP Chair," Louisville *Courier-Journal*, July 17, 1974, sec. B.

15. Ibid.

Chapter 4: "Horse Sense"

1. Senator Mitch McConnell, in discussion with the author, May 27, 2006.
2. Bob Johnson, "Money, Manure, and Madison Avenue," *Louisville Today,* February 1978.
3. Ibid.
4. Ibid.
5. Joe Schiff, in discussion with the author, March 2, 2006.
6. Mike Shea, in discussion with the author, March 11, 2005.
7. David McGinty, "The Making of Mitch," *Louisville Times Magazine,* January 24, 1978.
8. In 2005, McConnell would serve on the Executive Committee of a Louisville Arena Task Force that would make recommendations leading to the actual construction of an arena as he had proposed more than a quarter century earlier.
9. Schiff, in discussion with the author, March 2, 2006.
10. Johnson, "Money, Manure, and Madison Avenue."
11. Ibid.
12. Ibid.
13. Ibid.
14. Todd Hollenbach, in discussion with the author, February 8, 2005.
15. Ibid.; Shea, in discussion with the author, March 11, 2005.
16. *Board of Education of Jefferson County, Kentucky v. Newburg Area Council, Inc., cert. denied,* 429 U.S. 1074, *petition for rehearing denied,* 430 U.S. 941 (1977).
17. Hollenbach, in discussion with the author, February 8, 2005.
18. Johnson, "Money, Manure, and Madison Avenue."
19. McGinty, "The Making of Mitch."
20. Schiff, in discussion with the author, March 2, 2006.
21. Linda Raymond, "McConnell Shines as a Source of Hope for Kentucky GOP," *Louisville Times,* May 11, 1978.
22. Mike Brown, "Democrats Suggest McConnell is Inconsistent on Public Relations Stand," Louisville *Courier-Journal,* July 20, 1978.
23. *Baker v. County of Jefferson,* No. C 80–0039-L(A) (W. D. KY, 1980).
24. *Brown v. Hartlage,* 456 U.S. 45 (1982).
25. Editorial, "McConnell's Budget Seeks Modest Goals," *Louisville Times,* May 29, 1980.
26. Ibid.
27. Senator Mitch McConnell, in discussion with the author, January 15, 2007.

Chapter 5: From One Campaign to Another

1. Senator Mitch McConnell, in discussion with the author, January 20, 2007.
2. Michael Wines and Patrick Howington, "Despite His Pledge, McConnell has Kept Courthouse Politics," *Louisville Times,* May 20, 1981.
3. Elinor J. Brecher and Kay Stewart, "Victory Played Hide-and-Seek with Malone and McConnell," Louisville *Courier-Journal,* November 4, 1981.
4. Joe Schiff, in discussion with the author, March 2, 2006.
5. Mike Shea, in discussion with the author, March 11, 2005.
6. Brendan McKenna, "Major for the Majority," *Louisville Magazine,* January 2009.
7. McConnell never wavered in his belief that merger was the single most important thing that could be done to improve local government in Louisville and Jefferson County. He criticized later mayors and county judges for not risking their political capital to pursue it. McConnell consistently counseled putting the issue on the ballot in a presidential election year, believing that it would benefit from higher turnout. It took seventeen years for local leaders to heed his advice, however. In 2000, Mayor Dave Armstrong, a Democrat, and county judge Rebecca Jackson, a Republican, followed the Sloane-McConnell example of bipartisan cooperation, and a merged Louisville metro government finally passed.

Chapter 6: Hound Dogs

1. Walter D. Huddleston, interview by Terry L. Birdwhistell, October 29, 2002, transcript, Louie B. Nunn Center for Oral History, University of Kentucky Libraries, Lexington, Kentucky.
2. Bob Johnson, "McConnell Opens Senate Campaign," Louisville *Courier-Journal,* January 18, 1984.
3. Ibid.
4. Janet Mullins Grissom, in discussion with the author, February 21, 2005.
5. Huddleston, interview by Birdwhistell, October 29, 2002.
6. Terry Carmack, in discussion with the author, February 14, 2005.
7. Mike Shea, in discussion with the author, March 11, 2005.
8. Carmack, in discussion with the author, February 14, 2005.
9. Robert T. Garrett, "Fiery Ford Tops Huddleston-McConnell Bout at Fancy Farm," Louisville *Courier-Journal,* August 5, 1984.
10. Mullins Grissom, in discussion with the author, February 21, 2005.
11. Ibid.
12. Ibid.
13. Huddleston, interview by Birdwhistell, October 29, 2002.
14. Senator Mitch McConnell, in discussion with the author, February 4, 2007.

15. Carmack, in discussion with the author, February 14, 2005.

16. Shea, in discussion with the author, March 11, 2005.

17. Mullins Grissom, in discussion with the author, February 21, 2005.

18. Shea, in discussion with the author, March 11, 2005.

19. Bob Johnson, "McConnell Claims Win in Tight Race," Louisville *Courier-Journal,* November 7, 1984.

20. Andrew Wolfson, "Republican Rooters Let McConnell Crow a Little," Louisville *Courier-Journal,* November 7, 1984.

21. Mullins Grissom, in discussion with the author, February 21, 2005.

22. Wolfson, "Republican Rooters Let McConnell Crow a Little."

23. Johnson, "McConnell Claims Win in Tight Race."

24. Ibid.

25. Joe Schiff, in discussion with the author, March 2, 2006.

26. Huddleston, interview by Birdwhistell, October 29, 2002.

27. Johnson, "McConnell Claims Win in Tight Race."

28. Huddleston, interview by Birdwhistell, October 29, 2002.

29. Al Cross, in discussion with the author, June 1, 2006.

30. Mullins Grissom, in discussion with the author, February 21, 2005.

Chapter 7: Rookie

1. James R. Carroll, "McConnell Reflects on Career," Louisville *Courier-Journal,* January 11, 2009.

2. George Lardner Jr., "The Man Who Makes Money Talk," *Washington Post,* September 7, 1997.

3. Janet Mullins Grissom, in discussion with the author, February 21, 2005.

4. Ibid.

5. Mullins Grissom, in discussion with the author, February 21, 2005.

6. Senator Mitch McConnell, in discussion with the author, February 4, 2007.

7. See, e.g., George F. Will, *Restoration: Congress, Term Limits, and the Recovery of Deliberative Democracy* (New York: Free Press, 1992).

8. Thomas B. Edsall, "Congress' Free Rides," *Washington Post,* June 14, 1987.

9. Tax Reform Act of 1986. Pub.L. 99–514, 100 Stat. 2085, enacted October 22, 1986.

10. Joseph C. Wakefield, "The Tax Reform Act of 1986," *Survey of Current Business,* March 1, 1987.

Chapter 8: In the Minority

1. The 1987 highway bill contained 157 earmarks, or money set aside for particular projects important to members of Congress. Reagan ridiculed it by saying, "I haven't seen this much lard since I handed out blue ribbons at the Iowa State Fair." By contrast, after issuing a veto threat in 2005, President George W. Bush signed a $286 billion highway bill containing more than 6,000 earmarks. See "Pet Projects Make Roads Bill a Real Lulu," USATODAY.com, August 9, 2005, available at http://www.usatoday.com/news/opinion/editorials/2005–08–09-our-view_x.htm (accessed June 7, 2006); "Drunk with Power, Spending Out of Control," FOXNews.com, August 25, 2005, available at http://www.foxnews.com/story/0,2933,166682,00.html (accessed June 7, 2006). McConnell voted for both highway bills.
2. Linda Greenhouse, "Senate Rejects Reagan Plea and Votes 67–33 to Override His Veto of Highway Funds," *New York Times,* April 3, 1987.
3. See, e.g., John Cheves, "Price Tag Politics," *Lexington Herald-Leader,* Oct. 15, 2006.
4. Scott Harshbarger and Edwin Davis, "Federal Campaign Finance Reform: The Long and Winding Road," *National Civic Review 90:2,* Chapter 2, available at http://www.ncl.org/publications/ncr/90–2/chapter2.html (accessed June 6, 2006).
5. Thomas B. Edsall, "Congress' Free Rides," *Washington Post,* June 14, 1987.
6. Senator Mitch McConnell, in discussion with the author, July 2004.

Chapter 9: Fighting for Reelection

1. George H. W. Bush, "Remarks at a Fundraising Reception for Senator Mitch McConnell in Lexington, Kentucky," George Bush Presidential Library and Museum, available at http://bushlibrary.tamu.edu/research/papers/1989/89051303.html (accessed June 13, 2006).
2. Editorial, "Raking It In," Louisville *Courier-Journal,* May 16, 1989.
3. *Texas v. Johnson,* 491 U.S. 397 (1989).
4. Al Cross, "McConnell, Sloane Hurl Political Darts at Fancy Farm," Louisville *Courier-Journal,* August 6, 1989.
5. Associated Press, "'Goofy' Anti-Drug Proposal Splits Hopkins, McConnell," Louisville *Courier-Journal,* August 6, 1989.
6. The Dirksen Congressional Center, "Congressional Pay Raises," Congresslink, available at http://www.congresslink.org/print_basics_pay.htm (accessed June 19, 2006).
7. Kirk Victor, "In the Wings," *National Journal,* June 3, 2006.
8. Harvey Sloane, in discussion with the author, March 25, 2005.
9. Steven Law, in discussion with the author, March 7, 2005.
10. Senator Mitch McConnell, in discussion with the author, February 25, 2007.

11. Sloane, in discussion with the author, March 25, 2005.

12. Ibid.

13. Robert T. Garrett, "Sloane Needs to Shift Gears, Can't Seem to Find Clutch," Louisville *Courier-Journal*, October 7, 1990.

14. Mike Brown, "Low Profile but High Ambitions," Louisville *Courier-Journal*, October 28, 1990.

15. Hunter Bates, in discussion with the author, March 17, 2005.

16. Law, in discussion with the author, March 7, 2005.

17. McConnell, in discussion with the author, February 25, 2007.

18. Sloane, in discussion with the author, March 25, 2005.

19. George Lardner Jr., "The Man Who Makes Money Talk," *Washington Post*, September 7, 1997.

Chapter 10: New Term and New Wife

1. Gary L. Gregg II, in discussion with the author, July 1, 2005.

Chapter 11: Resistance and Revolution

1. Al Cross, "Kentucky Derby: How a GOP Darkhorse Won a Late Stretch Run and Left Surprised Democrats in the Dust," *Campaigns & Elections*, July 1994.

2. Ibid.

3. Newt Gingrich, *To Renew America* (New York: Harper Collins, 1995), 114.

4. Cross, "Kentucky Derby."

5. Ibid.

6. Senator Mitch McConnell, in discussion with the author, February 25, 2007.

7. Fred Barnes, "Master of the Senate," *Weekly Standard*, February 19, 2007.

8. Rich Lowry, "Louisville Slugger," *National Review*, September 29, 1997.

9. David Mudd, "Mitch and the Machine," *Louisville Magazine*, April 1995.

10. Al Cross, "A Wave by Any Other Name Still Swamps Democrats," Louisville *Courier-Journal*, November 13, 1994.

11. Mudd, "Mitch and the Machine."

12. Ibid.

13. Ibid.

Chapter 12: The Packwood Case

1. Michael Wines, "The Packwood Case: Man in the News: Kentucky Blend of Understatement and Ambition—Addison Mitchell McConnell," *New York Times*, September 7, 1995.

2. Katharine Q. Seelye, "The Packwood Case: The Overview: Packwood Says He Is Quitting as Ethics Panel Gives Evidence," *New York Times,* September 8, 1995.

3. "Key Events in the Packwood Case," *Washington Post,* September 8, 1995.

4. Michael Wines, "Packwood Loses Court Battle on Diaries," *New York Times,* March 3, 1994.

5. Senate Select Committee on Ethics, *Report on Resolution for Disciplinary Action,* 104th Cong., 1st sess., 1995, S. Rep. 104–137.

6. Seelye, "The Packwood Case: The Overview."

7. Jill Abramson and Allison Mitchell, "Senate Inquiry in Keating Case Tested McCain," *New York Times,* November 21, 1999.

8. Seelye, "The Packwood Case: The Overview."

9. Wines, "The Packwood Case: Man in the News."

Chapter 13: Third Term's a Charm

1. Billy Piper, in discussion with the author, February 21, 2005.

2. Steve Beshear, in discussion with the author, June 9, 2006.

3. David Mudd, "Mitch and the Machine," *Louisville Magazine,* April 1995.

4. Al Cross, in discussion with the author, June 1, 2006.

5. Piper, in discussion with the author, February 21, 2005.

6. Carla Anne Robbins, "Kentucky Senator, Handed Keys to Foreign Aid, to Be Most Potent Foe of Clinton's Russia Policy," *Wall Street Journal,* December 13, 1994.

7. Michael Wines, "The Packwood Case: Man in the News: Kentucky Blend of Understatement and Ambition—Addison Mitchell McConnell," *New York Times,* September 7, 1995.

8. George Lardner Jr., "The Man Who Makes Money Talk," *Washington Post,* September 7, 1997.

9. Beshear, in discussion with the author, June 9, 2006.

10. Al Cross, "Candidates Tangle at Fancy Farm Free-for-All," Louisville *Courier-Journal,* August 4, 1996.

11. Robert T. Garrett, "A Blizzard of Snow Jobs Obscures Gender Gap," Louisville *Courier-Journal,* October 6, 1996.

12. Beshear, in discussion with the author, June 9, 2006; Peter H. Stone, "Right on the Money," *National Journal,* February 15, 1997.

Chapter 14: Going National

1. Melvin I. Urofsky, *Money and Free Speech: Campaign Finance Reform and the Courts* (Lawrence: University Press of Kansas, 2005), 94.

2. Senate Committee on Governmental Affairs, *Investigation of Illegal or Improper*

Activities in Connection with 1996 Federal Election Campaigns, 105th Cong., 2nd sess., 1998, S. Rep. 105–167.

3. Peter H. Stone, "Right on the Money," *National Journal,* February 15, 1997.

4. 424 US 1 (1976).

5. Mitch McConnell, "The Money Gag," *National Review,* June 30, 1997.

6. Rich Lowry, "Louisville Slugger," *National Review,* September 29, 1997.

7. Urofsky, *Money and Free Speech,* 94.

8. George Lardner Jr., "The Man Who Makes Money Talk," *Washington Post,* September 7, 1997.

9. Amy Keller, "McConnell, Before a 'Final Funeral Service' for Reform, Announces New Weapon: Political Speech Think Tank," *Roll Call,* October 13, 1997.

10. Paul West, "McConnell Leads Efforts to Block Funding Reforms," *Baltimore Sun,* as reprinted in the *Paducah Sun,* February 19, 1997.

11. "Decision Makers: The Washington 100," *National Journal,* June 14, 1997.

12. McConnell, "The Money Gag."

13. Paul A. Gigot, "Forget About Bipartisanship, Thank God," *Wall Street Journal,* August 15, 1997.

14. Lardner, "The Man Who Makes Money Talk."

15. "Mitch McConnell, Money-Man," *The Economist,* September 13, 1997.

16. Lowry, "Louisville Slugger."

17. Robert T. Garrett, "McConnell Arrives as Washington Hotshot," Louisville *Courier-Journal,* September 21, 1997.

Chapter 15: Campaign Kingpin

1. Peter H. Stone, "Right on the Money," *National Journal,* February 15, 1997.

2. Ed G. Lane, "One-on-One," *Lane Report,* August 1998, available at http://www.lanereport.com/lanereport/departments/oneonone/oneonone898.html (accessed July 19, 2006).

3. Ibid.

4. Ibid.

5. "Bunning Ekes Out win Against Baesler," CNN.com, November 3, 1998, available at http://www.cnn.com/ALLPOLITICS/stories/1998/11/03/election/Senate/kentucky (accessed July 20, 2006).

6. Helen Dewar, "Senate Races Energize Democrats," *Washington Post,* Nov. 5, 1998.

Chapter 16: New Beginnings at Millennium's End

1. A few months later, McConnell would introduce, and the Senate would pass by unanimous consent, a resolution providing that "the desk located within the Sen-

ate Chamber and used by Senator Henry Clay shall, at the request of the senior Senator from the State of Kentucky, be assigned to that Senator for use in carrying out his or her senatorial duties during that Senator's term of office."

2. James Carroll, "The President on Trial," Louisville *Courier-Journal,* Feb. 8, 1999.

3. Mitch McConnell, "Independence for Kosovo," *Washington Post,* January 22, 1999.

4. See *Final Report of the Independent Counsel In Re: Janet G. Mullins,* November 30, 1995. Independent Counsel Joseph E. diGenova's investigation began in December 1992 and ended in November 1995. DiGenova found no evidence warranting the criminal prosecution of Mullins or anyone else for their conduct in connection with the passport files search, the disclosure of information from the files, or State's investigation of the search. In announcing his conclusions, diGenova blamed the duration and extent of his investigation on an "incompetent" initial inquiry by the State Department's inspector general and said, "Today, a Kafkaesque journey for a group of innocent Americans comes to an end."

5. Elizabeth Drew, *Citizen McCain* (New York: Simon & Schuster, 2002); John David Dyche, "The Gospel According to John (McCain)," Louisville *Courier-Journal,* July 28, 2002.

6. Mitch McConnell, "Why That McConnell Fellow Is So Adamant," *Washington Post,* June 28, 1999.

7. Marc Fisher, "The Senator on the Eve of Obstruction," *Washington Post,* October 12, 1999; Robin Toner, "The 'Designated Spear Catcher' on Campaign Finance," *New York Times,* October 18, 1999.

8. Joby Warrick, "In Harm's Way, and in the Dark," *Washington Post,* Aug. 8, 1999.

9. David Hawpe, "Congress' Odd Couple: McConnell, Kennedy Are Legislative 'Drivers,'" Louisville *Courier-Journal,* November 7, 1999.

10. Al Cross, "Nineties Proved Pivotal Decade for Politics in Kentucky," Louisville *Courier-Journal,* December 26, 1999.

11. Carroll, "The President on Trial."

12. *Bush v. Gore,* 531 U.S. 98 (2000).

Chapter 17: Everything Changes

1. Gary L. Gregg II, ed., *Securing Democracy: Why We Have an Electoral College* (Wilmington, Delaware: ISI Books, 2001).

2. Mitch McConnell, "In Defense of Soft Money," *New York Times,* April 1, 2001.

3. Senator Mitch McConnell, Statement on the Senate Floor, April 2, 2001, available at http://www.c-spanarchives.org/congress/?q=node/77531&id=8233895 (accessed January 24, 2009).

4. Philip Shenon, "Two Senators, Galaxies Apart on the Issue of Money," *New York*

Times, April 3, 2001.

5. Paul A. Gigot, "Farewell," *Wall Street Journal,* August 24, 2001.

6. Fred Barnes, "Jesse Helms's America: The Senate's No. 1 Conservative Announces His Retirement," *Weekly Standard,* September 3, 2001.

7. Mitch McConnell, "The State of the Judicial Confirmation Process," Lecture, Heritage Foundation, Washington, DC, April 30, 2002.

8. Steven J. Law, letter to the editor, *New Republic,* May 28, 2001.

9. Mitch McConnell., "The Chinese Connection: McConnell Criticizes Stories Concerning Links to China," Louisville *Courier-Journal,* April 22, 2001.

10. Senator Mitch McConnell, in discussion with the author, April 1, 2007.

Chapter 18: Record-Breaking Republican

1. Senator Phil Gramm, Statement on the Senate Floor, March 20, 2002, available at http://bulk.resource.org/gpo.gov/record/2002/2002_S02103.pdf (accessed January 24, 2009).

2. Senator Mitch McConnell, Statement on the Senate Floor, March 20, 2002, available at http://www.c-spanarchives.org/congress/?q=node/77531&id=8159190 (accessed January 24, 2009).

3. Senator John McCain, Statement on the Senate Floor, March 20, 2002, available at http://www.law.stanford.edu/publications/projects/campaignfinance/collection/mccain.3.20.pdf (accessed January 24, 2009).

4. Senator Mitch McConnell, in discussion with the author, April 1, 2007.

5. Ibid.

6. "The official name of the party whip in the U. S. is *assistant floor leader....* The word comes from 'whipper-in,' a man assigned to keep the hounds from straying in a fox hunt, and was turned into a political word in England in the eighteenth century. Benjamin Disraeli said the Government Chief Whip's office required 'consummate knowledge of human nature, the most amiable flexibility, and complete self-control.'" William Safire, *Safire's Political Dictionary* (New York: Random House, 1978), 788.

7. James R. Carroll, "McConnell to Be Senate's Majority Whip," Louisville *Courier-Journal,* November 8, 2002.

8. Michael Barone with Richard E. Cohen and Grant Ujifusa, *The Almanac of American Politics* (Washington, DC: National Journal, 2005), 704, 945.

Chapter 19: Surgery and Successes

1. Al Cross, "McConnell Proud of Role in Fletcher's Campaign," Louisville *Courier-Journal,* July 20, 2003.

2. *Heleringer v. Brown,* 193 S.W.3d 397 (2003).

3. Cross, "McConnell Proud of Role in Fletcher's Campaign."

4. *McConnell v. Federal Election Commission,* 251 F.Supp.2d 176 (D.D.C. 2003).

5. Melvin I. Urofsky, *Money and Free Speech* (Lawrence: University Press of Kansas, 2005), 194.

6. *McConnell v. Federal Election Commission,* 540 U.S. 93 (2003).

7. Carl Hulse and Glen Justice, "Losing Crusade May Still Pay Dividends for a Senator," *New York Times,* December 27, 2003.

8. Ibid.

Chapter 20: Buyout, Bunning, and Bush

1. Senator Mitch McConnell, Statement on the Senate Floor, April 8, 2004, 108th Cong., 2nd sess. *Congressional Record* 150, no. 49, daily ed. (April 8, 2004): S 3963–64.

2. "Kentucky: Tobacco Farmers Prepare for New Era without Tobacco Program," Associated Press, October 8, 2004, available at http://act.tobaccochina.net/englishnew/content.aspx?id=13132 (accessed January 24, 2009).

3. Mitch McConnell, "Lawmaker Unfairly Attacks Work on Tobacco Buyout," *Lexington Herald-Leader,* February 21, 2005.

4. "Santorum Will Seek Whip Slot," *Roll Call,* September 29, 2004.

5. "Senate Race Goes to Bunning Barely, Mongiardo's Manager Explains It," *Kentucky Gazette,* November 10, 2004.

6. Senator Mitch McConnell, in discussion with the author, April 1, 2007.

Chapter 21: An In-Between Year

1. Howard Fineman, "Eyes on a New Prize," *Newsweek,* December 27, 2004/January 3, 2005.

2. Senator Mitch McConnell, "Floor Speech by Senator Mitch McConnell on the Nomination of Harriet Miers to the Supreme Court," news release, October 4, 2005.

3. Kirk Victor, "In the Wings," *National Journal,* June 3, 2006.

4. Ibid.

5. Mitch McConnell, "Newspaper Column by Senator Mitch McConnell on Independence Day," States News Service, July 4, 2005.

6. Brief of United States Senator Mitch McConnell as *Amicus Curiae* in Support of Appellant in *Wisconsin Right to Life, Inc. v. Federal Election Commission,* Supreme Court of the U.S., No. 04–1581 (November 14, 2005).

7. Mitch McConnell and John McCain, "Lady Liberty," *Wall Street Journal,* June 15, 2005.

8. James Carroll, "Delegation Defends Delivering the 'Pork,'" Louisville *Courier-Journal*, November 27, 2005.

9. "Congressional Insiders Poll," *National Journal*, May 2005.

10. Erin P. Billings, "Congress' Top Partisan Fighters," *Roll Call*, May 31, 2005.

11. Jonathan Allen, "McConnell Gets Ready to Step into Frist's Shoes," *The Hill*, October 18, 2005.

12. Ryan Alessi, "McConnell Already Filling '08 War Chest," *Lexington Herald-Leader*, November 21, 2005.

Chapter 22: Republican Leader

1. Marisa Newhall, "Alfalfa Club Hears Bush Speak as President for the Last Time," *Washington Post*, January 27, 2008.

2. *Randall v. Sorrell*, 126 S.Ct. 2479 (U.S. 2006).

3. David Rogers, "Republicans Juggle Defense and Domestic Funds," *Wall Street Journal*, July 19, 2006.

4. Kirk Victor, "In the Wings," *National Journal*, June 3, 2006.

5. Bruce Schreiner, "McConnell Makes Goals with Downsized Role," Associated Press, December 3, 2006.

6. Mitch McConnell, "Amendment More Harmful Than Burning American Flag," *Kentucky Gazette*, June 28, 2006.

7. "Ratings of Congress," American Conservative Union, available at http://www.acuratings.org/2006all.htm#KY (accessed November 11, 2007).

8. "Senate Conservative Scores," *National Journal*, available at http://nationaljournal.com/voteratings/sen/cons.htm (accessed November 11, 1007).

9. "2006 ADA Voting Records," Americans for Democratic Action, available at http://www.adaction.org/2006Senatevr.htm (accessed November 11, 2007).

10. "Congressional Voting Record," AFL-CIO, available at http://www.aflcio.org/issues/legislativealert/votes/member.cfm?state=KY&pg=1 (accessed November 11, 2007).

11. Bruce Schriener, "McConnell Offers Assessment of Iraq War," Associated Press, August 14, 2006.

12. *Hamdan v. Rumsfeld*, 548 U.S. 557, 126 S.Ct. 2749, 165 L.Ed.2d (2006).

13. Victor, "In the Wings."

14. Ibid.

15. "Lott Prepares for a Possible Return to Senate Leadership Role," Bloomberg, May 24, 2006.

16. "Congrats, McConnell," *Lexington Herald-Leader*, November 17, 2006.

17. Charles Babington, "Elections May Bring New Accord in Senate," *Washington Post*, October 29, 2006.

18. John Cheves, "Price Tag Politics" and "Good Medicine for Drug Firms," *Lexington Herald-Leader,* October 15, 2006.

19. John Cheves, "Two for the Money" and "Wedded to Free Trade in China," *Lexington Herald-Leader,* October 20, 2006.

20. John Cheves, "A Lucrative Connection" and "Bates Ride from Driver to Gatekeeper," *Lexington Herald-Leader,* October 22, 2006.

21. David Espo, "In Wake of Losses, Republicans Turn Anger on Campaign Committee," Associated Press, December 23, 2006.

22. Senator Mitch McConnell, interview by Hugh Hewitt, *The Hugh Hewitt Show,* November 15, 2006.

23. Victor, "In the Wings."

24. Eric Pianin, "McConnell Pledges Cooperation," *Washington Post,* Nov. 29, 2006.

25. David S. Broder, "McConnell: What Kind of Leader?" Louisville *Courier-Journal,* December 3, 2006.

26. Carl Hulse, "Senate GOP Leader Adapts to an Unexpected Role," *New York Times,* November 30, 2006.

27. John Stanton and Erin P. Billings, "McConnell Bides His Time," *Roll Call,* June 14, 2006.

28. Dan Balz, "McCain Tests New Road to Nomination," *Washington Post,* March 12, 2006.

Chapter 23: The Defensive Coordinator

1. Senator Mitch McConnell, "Alfalfa Club Farewell Address," remarks, Alfalfa Club dinner, Washington, DC, January 27, 2007.

2. James R. Carroll, "Old Senate Chamber Fosters Spirit of Compromise," Louisville *Courier-Journal,* January 7, 2007.

3. Senator Mitch McConnell, "Gen. Petraeus Is an Outstanding Choice," news release, January 26, 2007.

4. Robert D. Novak, "Who Won in the Senate?" RealClearPolitics, February 8, 2007, available at http://www.realclearpolitics.com/articles/2007/02/who_won_in_the_Senate.html (accessed February 8, 2007).

5. Senator Mitch McConnell, interview by Bob Schieffer, *Face the Nation,* CBS, January 28, 2007.

6. Ryan Alessi, "Democrat Owen Sharply Critical of Sen. McConnell," *Lexington Herald-Leader,* January 31, 2007.

7. Fred Barnes, "Master of the Senate," *Weekly Standard,* February 19, 2007.

8. Novak, "Who Won in the Senate?"

9. Mark Halperin, Teddy Davis, Tahman Bradley, Matt Stuart, and Emily O'Donnell with Matthew Zavala, Paul Fidalgo, and Michelle Dubert, "Seek and

Ye Shall Find," The Note, February 26, 2007, available at http://abcnews.go.com/Politics/pring?id=156238&cacheKill=325701 (accessed February 26, 2007).

10. William Kristol, "Why Republicans Are Smiling," *Time*, March 1, 2007.

11. Barnes, "Master of the Senate."

12. Senator Mitch McConnell, remarks to winter meeting of Republican National Committee, January 19, 2007.

13. Michael A. Fletcher, "Bush Helps GOP Senators Raise $2.1 Million," *Washington Post*, March 3, 2007.

14. "Cash Over Conscience," Louisville *Courier-Journal*, March 2, 2007.

15. Senator Mitch McConnell, letter to the editor, Louisville *Courier-Journal*, March 5, 2007.

16. "Tell Mitch McConnell: Stop Blocking Change in Iraq," Americans United for Change, March 27, 2007, available at http://www.americansunitedforchange.org/blog/entries/tell_mitch_mcconnell_stop_blocking_change_in_iraq/ (accessed December 25, 2007).

17. "McConnell Responds to Ad Campaign Target [*sic*] His Iraq Stance," April 1, 2007, available at http://www.kentucky.com/471/v-print/story/31816.html (accessed April 3, 2007).

18. Al Cross, "In Final Days, Not Much Hope Remains for Fletcher," Louisville *Courier-Journal*, November 4, 2007.

19. Anne Flaherty, "Bush Signs Iraq Spending Bill," Associated Press, May 25, 2007.

20. Senator Mitch McConnell, in discussion with the author, January 21, 2008.

21. Michael Sandler and Jonathan Allen, "Senate Gives Up on Immigration Bill," CQ Today, June 7, 2007 available at http://public.cq.com/docs/cqt/news110–000002527366.html (accessed December 30, 2007).

22. David Stout and Robert Pear, "Immigration Bill Clears Test Vote in Senate," *New York Times*, June 26, 2007.

23. Erin P. Billings, "A Wary Mitch McConnell on the Spot Again," *Roll Call*, September 6, 2007, as reprinted in Louisville *Courier-Journal*, September 9, 2007.

24. Robert D. Novak, "McConnell's Immigration Failure," *Washington Post*, July 2, 2007.

25. Senator Mitch McConnell, "People's Will Was Heard," news release, June 28, 2007.

26. *Federal Election Commission v. Wisconsin Right to Life, Inc.*, 551 U.S. 127 S.Ct. 2652, 168 L. Ed. 2d 329 (2007).

27. Senator Mitch McConnell, "McConnell: Court Decision 'Victory for the First Amendment and Political Debate,'" news release, June 25, 2007.

28. James R. Carroll, "Democrats' Ad Targets McConnell," Louisville *Courier-Journal*, July 11, 2007.

29. Shailagh Murray and Paul Kane, "Democrats Won't Force War Vote," *Washington Post,* July 19, 2007.

30. James R. Carroll, "Comity Dissolves," *The Arena,* July 19, 2007, available at http://www.courier-journal.com/blogs/politics/blog.html (accessed July 19, 2007).

31. Fred Barnes, "McConnell Holds the Line, at Least Until September," *Weekly Standard,* July 18, 2007.

32. Carl Hulse, "Breakdown in Relations in Senate Hobbles Its Ability to Get Things Done," *New York Times,* July 20, 2007.

33. Chris Cillizza, "A Real Challenge for McConnell?" The Fix, July 24, 2007, available at http://blog.washingtonpost.com/thefix;2007/07/a_real_challenge_for_mcconnell.html (accessed July 25, 2007).

34. Stephen George, "What, Me Worry? Inside the Growing Movement to Oust Sen. Mitch McConnell," *LEO,* September 5, 2007.

35. David Hawpe, "McConnell as the New Clements, Not the New Barkley," Louisville *Courier-Journal,* November 14, 2007.

36. Carl Hulse, "Rising Pressure from GOP Led Senator to Quit," *New York Times,* September 2, 2007.

37. Sam Youngman, "Facing Anger, McConnell Gets Ready for Trail," *New York Times,* November 9, 2007.

38. "Senate Party Leader Critic of Myanmar," Associated Press, October 10, 2007.

39. Mitch McConnell, "Democrats' Bill Squanders CHIP Funds," *Lexington Herald-Leader,* August 13, 2007.

40. Andrew Taylor, "House Approves $70 Billion More for War," Associated Press, December 19, 2007.

41. "The GOP and Earmarks," *Wall Street Journal,* December 24, 2007.

42. Robert D. Novak, "GOP Senators Opt for Pork," *Washington Post,* December 10, 2007.

43. Senator Mitch McConnell, in discussion with the author, January 21, 2008.

44. Mark Hebert, "Poll Shows Big Turnaround for McConnell," WHAS11.com Political Blog, December 22, 2007, http://www.beloblog.com/WHAS_Blogs/PoliticalBlogger/2007/12/poll-shows-big-turnaround-for.html (accessed Dec. 22, 2007).

45. Senator Mitch McConnell, "Lessons of the First Session of the 110th," news release, December 19, 2007.

46. Jim VandeHei and Jon F. Harris, "McConnell Plays Rough—at a Cost," Politico.com, December 11, 2007, available at http://www.politico.com/news/stories/1207/7334.html (accessed December 12, 2007); David M. Herszenhorn, "Muscle Flexing in Senate: GOP Defends Strategy," *New York Times,* December 12, 2007.

Chapter 24: The Most Consequential Republican

1. George F. Will, "Kentuckian in the Breach," *Washington Post,* November 13, 2008.
2. Senator Mitch McConnell, in discussion with the author, November 6, 2008.
3. Ibid.
4. McConnell Senate Committee 2008, "McConnell's Record-Breaking Fundraising Continues," news release, January 3, 2008.
5. Office of the U.S. Senate Republican Leader, "McConnell: We Must Work Together Toward Common Goals," news release, January 22, 2008.
6. Halimah Abdullah, "McConnell: Versed in the Ways of Power," *Lexington Herald-Leader,* October 21, 2008.
7. "Election 2008: Kentucky Senate," *Rasmussen Reports,* May 27, 2008.
8. McConnell Senate Committee 2008, "McConnell Poll Shows Double Digit Lead," news release, May 29, 2008.
9. Larry Kudlow, "A Command Performance by McConnell," *Money Politics,* June 5, 2008, available at http://www.cnbc.com/id/24990709/ (accessed November 26, 2008).
10. Manu Raju, "Senate Fight Night," TheHill.com, June 5, 2008.
11. Joseph Gerth, "Lunsford His Own Biggest Donor," Louisville *Courier-Journal,* July 15, 2008.
12. Mitch McConnell, "Democrats Should Let Us Drill," *Wall Street Journal,* July 18, 2008.
13. *Davis v. Federal Election Comm'n,* 554 U.S. 128 S.Ct. 2759, 171 L. Ed. 2d 737 (2008).
14. Joseph Gerth, "Lunsford, McConnell Lambaste and Skewer," Louisville *Courier-Journal,* August 3, 2008.
15. Joseph Gerth, "Lunsford Campaign Team Ss Revamped," Louisville *Courier-Journal,* August 6, 2008.
16. Bruce Schreiner, "McConnell: McCain Should Run Against Congress," Associated Press, September 17, 2008.
17. Ryan Alessi, "Lunsford Ad Implies McConnell Is Corrupt," *Lexington Herald-Leader,* September 17, 2008.
18. Ryan Alessi, "McConnell Asks about Policy, Lunsford Hits on Process," *Lexington Herald-Leader,* September 14, 2008.
19. Bruce Schreiner, "McConnell, Lunsford Spar in Hard Hitting Debate," Associated Press, September 17, 2008.
20. Office of the U.S. Senate Republican Leader, "McConnell: Main Street Needs to Be Insulated from Wall Street," news release, September 24, 2008.

21. Joseph Gerth, "Senate Hopefuls in Dead Heat," Louisville *Courier-Journal,* September 28, 2008.

22. Abdullah, "McConnell: Versed in the Ways of Power."

23. Office of the U.S. Senate Republican Leader, "McConnell: Senate Will Act to Protect Main Street," news release, October 1, 2008.

24. Will, "Kentuckian in the Breach."

25. Ryan Alessi, "Kentucky's Senate Race Second Only to Presidential Contest," *Lexington Herald-Leader,* October 31, 2008.

26. Joseph Gerth, "McConnell $2 Million in Debt," Louisville *Courier-Journal,* December 7, 2008.

27. Ryan Alessi, "McConnell Raises Record Funds," *Lexington Herald-Leader,* October 16, 2008.

28. John Cheves, "Firm of 'Vulture Investor' Is No. 2 Donor to McConnell," *Lexington Herald-Leader,* October 16, 2008.

29. Ryan Alessi and Jack Brammer, "McConnell's Military Record Attacked," *Lexington Herald-Leader,* October 22, 2008.

30. John Cheves, "McConnell Discharged Honorably," *Lexington Herald-Leader,* October 23, 2008.

31. Ryan Alessi, "McConnell Leads Lunsford by 4 Points," *Lexington Herald-Leader,* October 23, 2008; Joseph Gerth, "Bluegrass Poll: McConnell Leads by Five Points," Louisville *Courier-Journal,* October 30, 2008.

32. Martin Kady II, "McConnell: The Most Powerful Republican," Politico.com, November 5, 2008 available at http://dyn.politico.com/printstory.cfm?uuid=6C79CB07–18FE-70B2-A8F9F829ABBAB196 (accessed November 5, 2008).

33. Senator Mitch McConnell, in discussion with the author, November 9, 2008.

34. Ryan Alessi and Halimah Abdullah, "McConnell Must Strike Fine Balance as GOP Leader," *Lexington-Herald Leader,* November 6, 2008.

35. Manu Raju, "McConnell: GOP Becoming 'Regional Party,'" Politico.com, January 29, 2009 (accessed February 16, 2009).

36. "Republicans Seeking Relevance," *The Economist,* Lexington, January 31, 2009.

Author's Note

A FEW WORDS ABOUT methodology and sources are appropriate. The general outline of this book is based on a series of personal and private oral history interviews Senator McConnell has given over the years to a distinguished Kentucky historian, John Kleber. The senator allowed me to listen to, and later participate in, these sessions on an off-the-record basis. He retained the right to review and approve the use of any quotations from these interviews. Almost all otherwise unattributed quotations from McConnell in the book come from this source.

At the author's request, Senator McConnell also agreed to review drafts of portions of the manuscript to ensure factual accuracy and to provide the foundation for several on-the-record interviews he was kind enough to give. He cooperated in most other respects as well, but not in all.

Senator McConnell has never attempted to exercise any control over this book's content. He made comments from time to time, most of which were welcome, but in the course of so doing always acknowledged, "It's your book." And it is.

In the interests of full disclosure, however, it should be stated that the author likes Senator McConnell personally, is *generally* in sympathy with his politics, and believes that a book presented from such a perspective is altogether appropriate to provide some badly needed balance in light of the many volumes' worth of critical coverage and commentary that the senator has received from both local and national press over the course of decades.

I would be remiss if I did not thank the many McConnell associates, colleagues, friends, and staffers who cooperated with this project by giving interviews and providing information. My gratitude also goes out to the many editors, reporters, and scholars, especially in Kentucky, on whose work I relied in writing this book. Former foes and rivals of McConnell's—such as Todd Hollenbach, Harvey Sloane, Dee Huddleston, and Steve Beshear—deserve a special thanks for consenting to interviews or allowing use of their materials even though they knew the book might not necessarily be something they would want to read.

Thanks also to my editors as ISI Books—Jeremy Beer, Jed Donahue, and David Mills—whose courtesy, expertise, and patience I appreciate. I also thank my friends Ronnie Ellis and Howard Mann for reading the draft manuscript and offering constructive comments, and Andrew Wolfson for his help.

Finally, I must lovingly thank my family, to whom I dedicate this book. My parents, Bob and Boots Dyche, worked hard and sacrificed much to provide me with the foundation upon which to build a happy and productive life. My sister and brother, Paige and Robbie, have been blessings to me since my birth. My greatest and most heartfelt gratitude goes out to my wife, Laura, and my children, Katy, Aaron, and Mary. They have not only supported me in this longer-than-expected project, but have made my life fulfilling and fun.

Outsiders often ridicule Kentuckians as benighted provincials, and sometimes with reason. But Senator McConnell's career is a resounding refutation of such condescending attitudes. I hope that in some small way, this book is, too. Most of the mistakes herein are mine, of course, but I am not quite able or prepared to own up to absolutely all of them at this point.

John David Dyche
Louisville, Kentucky

Index

About the Author

John David Dyche, a graduate of Centre College and Harvard Law School, is a practicing lawyer in Louisville, Kentucky. He has written a regular political column for the Louisville *Courier-Journal*, provided political commentary for Kentucky Educational Television, and published articles in the *Weekly Standard*, among other periodicals. A native of London, Kentucky, he lives in Louisville with his family.